664

The Synod of Whitby meets to decide between the Celtic and Roman branches of Christianity

c.650

The Huari people of Peru create distinctive and artistically advanced textiles woven with cotton and feathers.

683

The great Maya ruler, Pacal, dies at the age of 80, having turned the small town of Palenque in the central American jungle into one of the Maya's mightiest cities.

650

668

In Korea, the Silla king, Munmu, defeats the neighbouring kingdoms of Paekche and Kuguryo and founds the all-Korean kingdom of Great Silla.

691

The Dome of the Rock is completed in Jerusalem. It was built by Caliph Abd-al-Malik of the Umayyad dynasty, who ruled the Muslim world from 685 to 705.

EUROPE

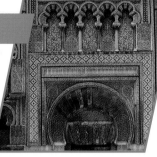

711
The Moors, under their commander in chief, Tariq, cross the Strait of Gibraltar and land in Spain.

732
At Tours, Charles Martel wins a decisive victory over the Moors, halting the Muslim advance into Europe.

756
The Frankish k Pepin, grants a has conquered Rome and Rave the Pope, creatin Church State.

AMERICA

c.750
The Tiahuanaco culture of the Andes reaches its peak.

700

AFRICA

ASIA

710
In Japan, Emperor Genmeia founds a new capital, Nara, closely modelled on the Chinese capital, Chang'an.

c.750
The displacement of Buddhism by Hinduism in India is virtually complete. The older religion absorbed elements of Buddhist teaching, and even found a place for the Buddha in the Hindu pantheon.

OCEANIA

s he
und
to

787

The Council of Nicaea ends the iconoclast controversy in the Christian Church by declaring the veneration of icons permissible.

800

Charlemagne, king of the Franks, is crowned Holy Roman Emperor by Pope Leo III in St Peter's Church in Rome, uniting Western Europe in an empire for the first time since the fall of the Romans.

800

789

The Idrisid kingdom is founded in Morocco by Idris I. Idris dies just two years later.

790

In Ghana, Kaya Maghan Cisse of the Soninke people founds the Cisse Tunkara dynasty. Over the following centuries, Ghana develops into a significant trading power.

800

The Aghlabid dynasty comes to power in Tunisia.

828

Idris II dies after a successful 37-year reign in Morocco. His tomb in Mulai becomes an important place of pilgrimage.

813

Al-Mamun wins the struggle for power in the Abbasid caliphate. During his rule (until 833) the Abbasid capital, Baghdad, becomes one of the cultural centres of the world, preserving the classical heritage of Greece and Rome.

830

The great Buddhist temple complex of Borobudur on Java, built by the Sailendra kings, is completed. A Hindu complex, at Prambanan, was completed by the rival Sanjaya kings in 856.

the
s wife

565

Justinian I dies and with him the Roman Empire ceases to exist. The Byzantine Empire begins.

596

Pope Gregory sends Benedictine monks to Britain to convert the pagan Anglo-Saxons. Some 30 years earlier, in 563, Columba had arrived from Ireland to found a Celtic Christian mission on Iona.

625

King Redwald of Eas Anglia is buried at Sutton Hoo in Suffolk. His grave, uncovered i the 20th century, is one of the greatest finds of Anglo-Saxon treasure.

c.600

In the Mexican lowlands, thriving Mayan cities such as Copán, Tikal, Yaxchitlán and Palenque compete with each other politically and culturally.

600

534

Gelimer, king of the Vandals, capitulates in the face of an army sent by Justinian I, emperor of the Eastern Roman Empire. This brings to an end the independent Germanic kingdom just a century after it was founded.

c.570

Muhammad is born in Mecca, a city which is already a well-known place of pilgrimage with its holy sanctuary of the Kaaba.

618

The Tang dynasty comes to power in China. The Tang emperors keep a splendid court and hold power until 907.

451

Theodoric I, king of the Visigoths, dies in battle against the Huns on the Catalaunian Plains.

c.486

Clovis I, the Merovingian king of France, is baptised. He obtains the support of the Church, which legitimises his conquests of non-Christian peoples.

521

Justinian ascend[s] imperial throne i[n] Byzantium with h[is] Theodora, a former actress, at his side as empress.

450

The Moche culture in the northern lowlands of Peru reaches its peak period. It will continue to thrive until the 7th century. The Moche people are skilled in agriculture and crafts.

c.500

The Totonac culture comes to prominence on Mexico's Gulf coast, centred on the temple city of El Tajin with its temples, palaces and ball-game courts.

c.510

Tiahuanaco, not far from Lake Titicaca in Bolivia, becomes the centre of a kingdom which, over the following centuries, will expand its influence as far as the Pacific coast.

500

493

The ancient kingdom of Ghana becomes a force in Africa. Fertile soils, gold mines and caravan trade routes make the country rich.

493

Buddhism reaches its peak in China. Splendid temple complexes are created, including the famous Longmen caves.

531

In Persia, Khosrow I ascends the throne. With him the Sassanian Empire attains its political and cultural peak.

823

Christians in northwest Spain claim the discovery of the tomb of St James the apostle at Compostela, providing a focus for resistance to Spain's Islamic rulers.

865

Two monks, Cyril and Methodios, translate the Bible and other liturgical texts into the Slavic language, inventing the Cyrillic alphabet in the process.

c.900

The Maya abandon their cities in the Mexican lowlands to settle on the Yucatan peninsula.

850

c.850

With the Idrisid dynasty in power in Morocco, the city of Fez becomes a flourishing centre of trade and of Islamic culture.

BETWEEN
CROSS AND CRESCENT

430 – 907

PUBLISHED BY THE READER'S DIGEST ASSOCIATION LIMITED
LONDON • NEW YORK • SYDNEY • MONTREAL

An architectural and religious icon The great church of Hagia Sophia in Constantinople was built by Emperor Justinian I between 532 and 537. For the next thousand years it was the heart of Christianity in the Byzantine Empire and to this day it remains the quintessential Byzantine building. In 1453 the city fell to the Ottoman conqueror, Sultan Mehmed, who was so impressed by the beauty of the church he had it converted into a mosque. The minarets were added during the 500 years that the building was used for Islamic worship. A final change came in 1935 when Hagia Sophia was turned into a museum by Turkey's new secular ruler, Mustafa Kemal Atatürk.

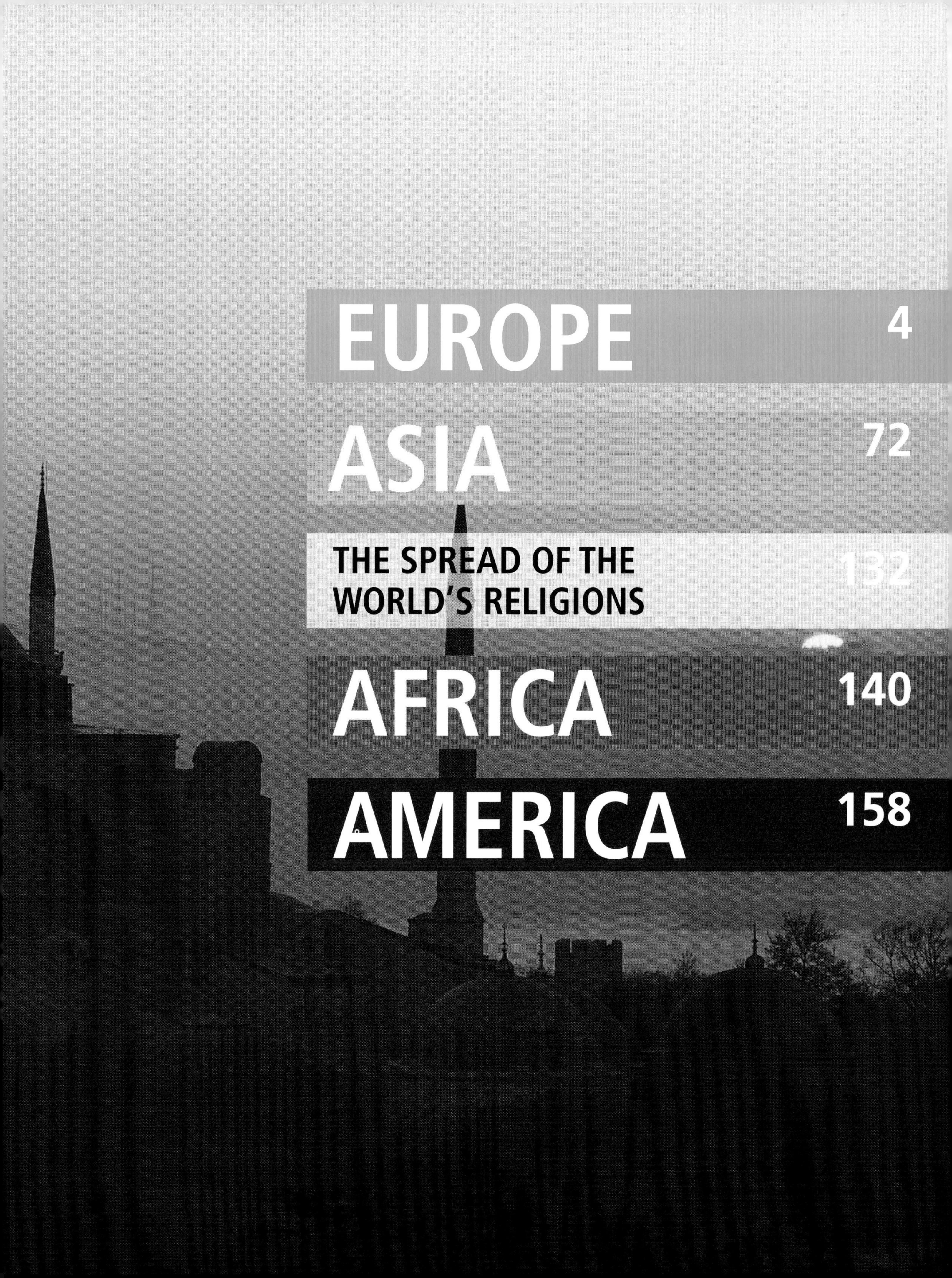

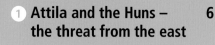

EUROPE

Attila the horseman
This French illustration of Attila on his horse was made in the mid 20th century. Horsemen were fundamental to the Huns' fighting methods. Many fought as mounted archers, but Attila's armies also included a core of armour-bearing horsemen.

Attila and the Huns – the threat from the East

The invasion of Europe by the Huns caused huge panic and triggered great waves of migration among the Germanic peoples. Even Roman emperors were at times obliged to buy off Attila with generous tribute payments.

To their many enemies, the Huns were the warriors from Hell. Greek and Roman authors painted the wild mounted bands in the blackest of colours, calling them barbarians and cannibals bred of witches and succubi (female demons), the very dregs of the human race. The nomads spent much of their time on horseback, seemingly welded to their scruffy little mounts – animals described as being as ugly as their owners.

The ancient chroniclers claimed that the Huns had no homes to go to and wore their fur clothes until they rotted off their bodies. Their food was said to consist of roots and raw meat, which they put under their saddles while riding, to tenderise it.

This picture was almost certainly a distortion fuelled by fear and loathing. The classical world had good reason to fear the Huns, whose various incursions, stretching over several decades, seemed to foretell the end of civilisation as the Romans knew it. Some of the assertions, however, were the result of simple misunderstandings – for instance, the story about tenderising raw meat. The Huns did indeed put meat under their saddles, but not to prepare it for eating; the practice was intended to help to heal their horses' saddle sores.

A few individuals managed to retain a level of objectivity, however. A Roman veterinarian called Vegetius wrote on military matters and kept a small herd of Hunnish horses to study. He described them as being very undemanding, extremely tough and hardworking.

Protective headgear
This banded helmet made from iron dates from the 5th or 6th century. Such helmets originated in the east, and in the period of the great migrations they were popular with both imperial troops and Germanic warriors.

A distant homeland
Like the later Turks and Mongols, the Huns originated on the steppes of central Asia and lived by breeding cattle. The reasons for their exodus to the west are

still obscure. They launched their first attack on the Alans, a people inhabiting the region of Sarmatia, east of the River Volga, and quickly overwhelmed them. Then, in about AD 375, they overran the kingdom of the Ostrogoths, north of the Black Sea. From there they swept across the River Danube into the Roman Empire, robbing, pillaging and burning settlements and towns. One group crossed the Caucasus Mountains and laid waste to Rome's eastern provinces in Asia Minor. This raid triggered the greatest movement of people known to history: the Germanic migrations that it set in motion were to change the map of Europe and put an end to the Western Roman Empire.

Under kings called Ruga and Octar, the Huns came to dominate a swathe of territory stretching as far as the floodplain of the River Tisza in Hungary. After about ten years two brothers, Attila and Bleda, jointly took power, but Attila soon asserted himself as the dominant partner. In 445 he had Bleda killed and ruled single-handed from that time on.

According to a description of the time, Attila was not particularly tall; he had a flat nose, deep-set eyes and a sparse beard. He could be terrible when angered, but at other times was considered a just ruler who was prepared to behave generously towards his enemies so long as they accepted his authority and dealt honestly with him. As a son of the steppes he believed in the predictions of the shamans, but contrary to the usual picture of him as a brutal, bloodthirsty barbarian,

The stuff of legend
Attila and the Huns made a profound impression on the Germanic tribes, and tales of their feats were incorporated into medieval epics like the tale of the Nibelungs. This image of Attila and his horsemen is from a 14th-century account by the Italian poet Nicola da Casola.

he also respected Roman culture and surrounded himself with Greek, Roman and Germanic writers and aides.

Wars and diplomacy

Wars with Rome were non-stop under Attila's rule, but sometimes the Huns fought alongside the Romans against peoples usually allied to the empire – for example, they aided the Roman commander Aëtius against the Visigoths and Burgundians in Gaul. Indeed, their battle with the Burgundians later inspired the great German medieval epic, the *Nibelungenlied* ('Song of the Nibelungs').

In about 440 the Huns once more invaded the eastern Roman provinces south of the Danube. In a peace treaty signed in 443 they were granted grazing lands along the river by Emperor Theodosius II, who also paid them six thousand pounds of gold (2700kg), along with the promise of further annual gold payments of over two thousand pounds (1000kg). Despite – or perhaps because of – these concessions, the Huns renewed their attacks over the following years.

In the hope of persuading Attila to call off the raids, the emperors in Rome and Byzantium sent a string of ambassadors to negotiate at his court. High-ranking dignitaries of the Byzantine court avoided these missions, fearing to confront a supposedly unpredictable and dangerous enemy. In fact, their concerns were unfounded: hospitality to strangers was considered a sacred duty among the Huns, who never harmed a hair of any diplomat's head. Fearing the worst, however, the noblemen regularly sent minor civil servants in their place, a ruse the Huns saw through immediately, and which caused great offence as it threw into question their own honour. Further gold and gifts were required to placate them.

A taste for precious things
Precious stones and glass once probably adorned this golden vessel from the early 5th century. Found in Hungary in the grave of a Hunnish nobleman, it is typical of the wealth that tribute payments brought to the nomad chiefs.

Attila at court

A Byzantine envoy named Priscus, who formed part of such a delegation in 449, left a colourful description of the Huns' court and customs. Attila's headquarters on the Tisza plain bore all the hallmarks of a steppe chieftain's camp. The ruler himself lived in a large wooden residence, made from planed planks, that stood on a small mound surrounded by a palisade and guard towers. At a respectful distance lay the wooden dwellings of the Hunnish nobles. There was only one building made of stone – a bath-house built for Attila by Roman prisoners.

The splendour of the court was best seen at the night-time banquets prepared in honour of the legation. Hunnish and Germanic nobles sat along the side walls

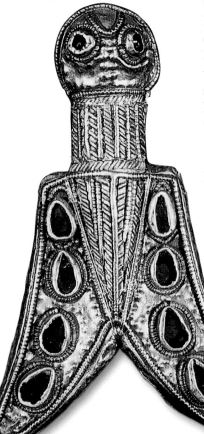

Mediterranean motif
Wealthy Huns fastened their robes with finely worked jewellery, like this cicada-shaped brooch found in Hungary.

of the Great Hall, dressed in precious robes and golden jewellery and carrying weapons decorated with gold. Attila reclined on a Roman couch. He started by drinking a toast to his guests, as was the custom with the Huns, then servants brought in tables laden with food. The guests drank from goblets of gold or silver and ate from silver platters, but Attila's own tableware was made of wood, and he was content with plain fare. The banquet continued late into the night by the light of flaming torches, as Priscus and his fellow-diners were regaled by two singers celebrating Attila and his heroic deeds.

Unexpected defeat

In 451 Attila prepared for a huge military campaign aimed at conquering Gaul. The Hunnish army, reinforced by Germanic warriors, crossed the River Rhine and seized the town of Metz – Roman Divodurum – and burned it down. Then they went on to lay siege to Orléans.

To defend the empire, the Roman commander Aëtius assembled an army of Romans, Visigoths, Burgundians and Franks. One of history's great battles then took place on the Catalaunian Plains (*Campi Catalaunii*), located between Châlons-sur-Marne and Troyes in north-eastern France. The Visigoths succeeded in taking a central hill, forcing the Huns into retreat. Instead of pressing home this advantage and destroying the enemy while he had the chance, however, Aëtius allowed them to get away, rather than be forced into a position of

Long-lasting reputation
This bronze plate, made in the 16th or 17th century, still refers to Attila as the 'Scourge of God'.

dependence on his Visigoth allies. It was Attila's first defeat, and it was a heavy one. Crestfallen, he retreated to Hungary.

The next year he returned with a new army, marching across the Alps into northern Italy. His warriors ravaged the countryside, seizing Aquileia, Pavia and Milan, where Attila took up residence in the imperial palace. There he received a legation sent by Pope Leo I, hoping to dissuade him from moving on Rome. Attila did withdraw from Italy, probably less out of any respect for the Papacy than because of the spread of disease among his troops and the shortage of food in the ravaged countryside. Also, he had heard that Byzantine forces had crossed the Danube into Hunnish territories.

Attila died in 453 soon after his return to Hungary, struck down on the night of his marriage to a Goth woman called Ildico. The cause of death was said to be a haemorrhage, but there were rumours that his new wife had murdered him.

A swift end

The first signs of the break-up of Attila's kingdom came soon after his death. Some of his subject Germanic tribes took up arms against Ellak, his son and heir, who died in battle against the rebels in 455. Ellak's successor Dengizik launched a fresh attack on the Eastern Roman Empire, but he too was defeated and killed in 469; his decapitated head was displayed on a pole in Constantinople. The unity of the Huns had been broken, and the surviving bands went back to settle in southern Russia, to the north and east of the Black Sea.

Toulouse to Toledo – the kingdom of the Visigoths

Despite almost constant warfare, a late classical civilisation flourished in the kingdom that the Visigoths had won for themselves in Gaul and Spain. Germanic and Roman elements blended to form a culture that was unique.

In the year 410, an event took place that had once seemed unthinkable: a foreign army conquered and plundered Rome. It shook the already weakened Western Roman Empire to its foundations. The last time that the imperial capital had suffered such an indignity had been in 390 BC, eight centuries earlier, when Gauls had sacked the city. To make matters even worse, Galla Placidia, Emperor Honorius's own sister, was captured and held prisoner by the invaders.

The attackers were the Visigoths. Under their great military leader Alaric, they had been ravaging Greece and Dalmatia for the previous 15 years, destroying and burning whole regions. From Rome they went on to southern Italy, intending to cross over to Sicily, but Alaric died on the way. Under his successor Athaulf, the Visigoths turned instead to southern Gaul in search of a new home.

Partners with Rome

In 418 Honorius forged a treaty with a new Visigoth leader, Wallia. This granted to the Visigoths the wealthy area between the Loire and Garonne rivers in southwestern Gaul for settlement. As official allies of Rome, the Visigoths were given substantial rights of ownership in return for a promise to support the imperial cause. They became masters of a large swathe of land, along with the slaves and dependent tenants who worked it. In return, they agreed to provide Rome with support against enemies who were pressing into the imperial lands – mainly the Suebi, Alans and Vandals who had swept into the Iberian peninsula in AD 409.

The alliance with Rome weakened under Wallia's successor Theodoric I, who used his long tenure of power from 418 to 451 to create a largely independent Visigoth kingdom. Even so, he was prepared to support the Romans against the Huns when they invaded Gaul in 451. It was largely thanks to Visigoth help that Rome and her allies won the decisive Battle of the Catalaunian Plains. Theodoric himself, however, died in the battle.

His successor, Theodoric II, continued to fulfil his duty as an ally of Rome. In 452, he intervened in Spain to push the Suebi back to the northern region of Galicia. The Visigoths stayed on in the Iberian peninsula, and under Theodoric's successor, Euric, pursued an aggressive policy of expansion that brought much of Spain under their control in addition to their territories in

The Visigoths were skilled metalworkers. This golden votive crown created in the 7th century shows both Roman and Byzantine influence.

Gaul, a move that the enfeebled Romans were unable to oppose. In 475, Emperor Julius Nepos officially acknowledged the independence of the Visigoth kingdom.

The second half of the 5th century saw the high point of this realm, sometimes known as the Tolosan kingdom after its

Eagle clasps The Visigoths made great use of fibulas – clasps, often decorated with animal motifs – to hold together their garments. These 6th-century cloisonné eagles, with garnets and rock crystal as inlays in gilded bronze, are typical of the age.

capital of Tolosa (now Toulouse). For a time, the Visigoth rulers were the most powerful kings in Europe, with control over lands that stretched from the English Channel to the Straits of Gibraltar. But in this troubled era of the great Germanic migrations, insecurity was never far away.

Many cities in Gaul, including Tolosa, survived as bastions of late Roman culture inside a ring of fortifications. Remnants of the classical lifestyle flourished in the tiled houses and palaces of the local Gallo-Roman aristocracy and of the civil

servants and administrators employed in the service of the king. Tolosa had up to 15,000 inhabitants and was considered an important craft centre, with a particular reputation for its goldwork.

A divided society

The Visigoths, like nearly all other Germanic peoples, were forbidden by ancient law from marrying the indigenous inhabitants of the lands they conquered. A major reason for this segregation was religion: the Visigoths were converts to the Arian branch of Christianity, while the Romans of Gaul and Spain were firmly in the Catholic camp. The Arians – followers of the doctrine of Arius of Alexandria – believed that Christ had been created by God and was therefore inferior to him. This view clashed with Catholic orthodoxy, which held that God the Father and God the Son were one, sharing the same essence.

Despite doctrinal differences, the old Gallo-Roman aristocracy, which had traditionally supplied civil servants to administer the empire, remained influential under Visigoth rule. In fact, the new rulers had an even greater need for administrators and scribes, as they themselves lacked the necessary knowledge and skills. They also continued to employ artists and craftsmen from the indigenous population.

In theory, only Visigoths were called on to serve in the army, but in practice the native land-owning aristocracy were expected to supply and lead contingents to fight alongside them. The Visigoth fleet was commanded by officers of Roman descent, as the Goths themselves had no experience whatsoever of naval matters.

Two peoples, two systems of law

Several million Romano-Gauls and Hispano-Romans continued to live in the Visigoth kingdom, alongside a Visigoth immigrant population estimated at a mere

200,000. To help the two populations to co-exist peacefully, there were two entirely separate sets of laws, one applying to the Germanic peoples and the other to their Roman subjects; other laws regulated relations between the communities. The indigenous people were given substantial protection under the system. Arbitrary confiscation of land was stopped, and those Visigoths who had seized estates had to pay the former owners in cash. Gradually, a culture evolved that mixed Germanic and Roman elements, shaping society not only in the Visigoth kingdom but also influencing other Germanic states in what had once been Roman imperial territory.

At the head of the Visigoth state was the king, ruling from the royal palace in Tolosa. He held court in some splendour, receiving Roman legations and ambassadors from foreign courts in an audience hall fitted out with colourful Roman and Byzantine fabrics and furniture. Around him was a retinue of his closest followers, their wealth manifest in their fur-trimmed clothing, their richly decorated belt decorations and the golden fibulas (clasps) that fastened their robes. The king's weapons-bearers were among the most trusted; equipped with shields, lances, and long swords, they stood ready to intervene if danger threatened.

The trek to the south

For all its magnificence, Visigoth rule in Gaul did not last long. Early in the 6th century the kingdom came under attack from the ambitious Frankish king, Clovis. As a renowned opponent of Arianism, Clovis could count on the support of the Catholic church and its bishops. In 507 a decisive battle took place at Vouillé near Poitiers in which the Visigoth king, Alaric II, was killed, possibly by Clovis himself. The Franks destroyed the Visigoth army and incorporated all of their Gallic lands into their own kingdom, with the exception of a strip along France's south

coast. About 100,000 refugees – men, women and children – fled across the Pyrenees in exhausting forced marches to find a new home in the remaining Visigoth territories in Spain.

The next few decades were a time of great confusion in which members of various noble houses fought for power and the Visigoth throne. Theodoric the Great, the Ostrogoth ruler of Italy, even exerted nominal control at times as Great King of the Goths. One contender for power went so far as to seek support from the Eastern Roman Empire: the emperor sent Byzantine troops who conquered the coastal area of southern Spain between Cádiz, Cordoba and Cartagena.

A new power beyond the Pyrenees

Order was finally restored by Leovigild, a strong king who conquered the Suebi and began to win back the areas occupied by the Byzantines. He established his capital at Toledo, situated on a rocky hill above the River Tagus, and reigned from 568 to 586. Leovigild's reign was marked by the introduction of Byzantine ceremonial to

The sacrifice of Isaac
Classical motifs were often combined with biblical illustrations in Visigothic stone carvings, as in this finely carved column capital. The hand of God can be seen emerging from the heavens (left) to prevent Abraham sacrificing his son; the goat that takes Isaac's place is shown on the right.

A counterbalancing force
Ecclesiastical councils, like this one shown in a 10th-century book illustration, played an important role in the state after the Visigoth conversion to Catholicism. The Church acted as a check on the autocratic power of the ruler, seeking to mediate between the king, the aristocracy and the people.

the Visigoth court; for instance, a new and detailed etiquette fixed the order of rank in which courtiers offered greetings and obeisance before the king. Such rituals helped to unify the kingdom, which increasingly began to resemble a Roman state and found growing support within the Hispano-Roman population.

This trend accelerated under Reccared, Leovigild's son. On acceding to power in 586, Reccared not only continued his father's policies but removed the principal remaining obstacle to assimilation by converting to the Catholic faith. By doing so he forged a strong link between the crown and the bishops, who had always had great influence on the indigenous population. The increasing importance of the Catholic faith was visible in the small but impressive churches built in Spain at this time. The relief carvings decorating the buildings united Christian themes with late classical motifs.

The drive to bring kingdom and peoples together, expressed in Reccared's conversion, was also mirrored in new legal codes based on Roman law and applying equally to all. The days when Visigoths

could easily be distinguished from the native Hispano-Romans by their clothing and language were rapidly passing. By the end of the 6th century the Visigothic language had given way to Latin and the prohibition on mixed marriage had been lifted. Even so, the complete assimilation of immigrant and native populations, as achieved in some other Germanic kingdoms, did not happen in Spain.

Trade and influence from the East

In addition to churches, Spain's Visigoth rulers built fortresses protected by mighty towers in the late Romano-Byzantine style. Leovigild erected the defensive bastion of Reccopolis in honour of his son. Sited on a hill north of Toledo, it sheltered behind huge walls studded with square towers. Inside the fortifications lay a palace and a church, as well as residential quarters built on a grid plan after the Roman model.

While the aristocracy of Visigothic Spain combined native and immigrant elements, the rest of the population was predominantly Hispano-Roman. The economy was primarily agricultural, but some towns survived in which crafts flourished, as did trade with the rest of the Mediterranean world. Byzantine ships docked at Spanish ports bringing textiles, silk, vessels of gold and silver, and ecclesiastical accoutrements such as incense burners and lamps.

Oriental merchants set up trading posts at Merida, Tortosa and Tarragona, importing a steady stream of goods from North Africa and from the eastern Mediterranean. They also established harbours in the Balearic Islands for ships heading for Spain. The Visigoth link with the Eastern Empire was also visible in their art, in which Germanic and Roman stylistic elements gradually gave way to Byzantine motifs.

An elected monarchy

The Visigoth kingdom saw its final peak in the reign of King Svinthila (621–631), who drove the Byzantines from their last strongholds on the south coast, winning control of virtually the entire Iberian peninsula. But in the second half of the 7th century, the power of the Visigoth kings visibly diminished, and their method of settling the succession was largely to blame. The kings had attempted to replace the practice of electing monarchs with a straightforward hereditary system, but this was vigorously resisted by the aristocracy and church hierarchy. The result was disunity, coups and rebellions.

By the late 7th century, conflicts over the succession had led to economic crises, famines and epidemics, leaving the kingdom easy prey for the Arabs who had swept to power in North Africa in the previous 50 years. In 711, the relatives of an unsuccessful candidate for the Visigoth throne appealed to the Muslim governor

TIME WITNESS

A day in the life of Theoderic I

Sidonius Apollinaris, a Gallo-Roman poet who became Bishop of Augustonometum (modern Clermont-Ferrand), left this account of the daily life of Theoderic I, king of the Visigoths from 418 to 451:

'He prays with great reverence before daybreak... The rest of the morning is taken up with concerns involving the administration of the kingdom... In the second hour he rises from the throne, spending his free time inspecting his treasures and visiting his stables... After the midday meal he has a very short nap, which he sometime omits entirely... At the ninth hour he again takes up government business...'

of Tangiers for help. Landing at Gibraltar with a relatively small force, he defeated King Roderic and his Visigoth army. Roderic himself fell in the battle, leaving a leaderless kingdom to face the Arab invaders. Many retreated to the rugged lands of north-western Spain, which the Arabs never succeeded in conquering. Here, they created the independent Christian kingdom of Asturias, which would be the starting-point of the eventual reconquest of the entire peninsula.

The power of faith
This 10th-century Visigothic manuscript image, now in Verona, illustrates the mutual dependence of the religious and secular authorities. As the highest ecclesiastical dignitary of the realm, the Bishop of Toledo was responsible for anointing and crowning the Visigoth king, and the ruler in turn appointed the bishops. But both ultimately derived their power from God.

Learned messengers of God

Benedict of Nursia and his countless fellow monks are considered the fathers of the Christian faith in the West. From the monasteries came a wave of missionaries who set out to spread the word of God.

How can one find God? For over a quarter of a century Benedict of Nursia had pondered this question. As a young man, in about the year 500, he had decided to give up his studies in Rome in order to lead a life that was pleasing to God, far from all secular temptations. But even a regime of strict asceticism, both alone and in the company of similarly inclined individuals, had not really brought him any closer to his Creator. As he grew older, Benedict became convinced that a life devoted to God's service could best be realised in a community that was governed by firm rules. At about the age of 50 he made a final attempt to put these ideals into practice. He moved with his most loyal followers to Monte Cassino, midway between Rome and Naples. There he founded a monastery in which he and his companions, through contemplation and prayer, could find the path to God.

The move worked, and Benedict used the experience to compile his Rule – a set of regulations governing monastic life.

A site rich in history
It was in the monastery of Monte Cassino, founded in 529, that the Benedictine Order and the whole Western monastic tradition had their origins. Today, the restored monastery (above) still stands on the hill overlooking the town of Cassino.

Its guiding maxim was *Ora et labora*: 'Pray and work.' Following this principle, the days at Monte Cassino were carefully divided into separate periods for prayer, study and manual labour.

In addition to fulfilling religious duties, every monk had to be physically active for between three and eight hours each day, either in the fields, monastery workshops, the kitchen or household duties. Quite apart from providing the monks with exercise and a break from contemplation, this gave the monastery the labour force it needed to run smoothly and to be self-sufficient – the only way in which it could avoid external interference.

Work, poverty and prayer

Each monastic community was headed by an abbot; at Monte Cassino, this was Benedict himself. The Rule specified that the abbot be elected by his brothers and seek their advice on important questions, but he alone made final decisions and his authority was absolute. Would-be monks were taken in on probation; if they chose to stay at the end of the year, they made an unbreakable vow of obedience.

Benedict is thought to have died sometime between 555 and 560. Although the Lombards destroyed Monte Cassino soon after, his Rule survived and set a pattern for the future development of European monasticism.

Benedict of Nursia, founder of the Benedictine Order, is considered the father of Western monasticism. In 1964 Pope Paul VI proclaimed him the patron saint of Europe.

Benedict's ideal

Benedict could never have guessed that the meditative seclusion of his order would become the foundation of a new Christian culture. For him all that mattered was a life dedicated to God. He sought only to remain 'knowingly unknowing', and to throw off all worldly encumbrances that might prove a hindrance in the search for God.

Yet the world was also calling out for a more active, proselytising brand of Christianity. This need seemed to be felt particularly strongly on Europe's outer periphery, in Ireland, where the persistent resistance of pagan Druids forced the monks to look for new ways to win people over to Christianity. Ireland had never been conquered by the Romans and had only come into contact with

An evangelist at work
In this margin illumination from the Lindisfarne Gospels, St Matthew is shown writing the scripture with a guardian angel – his symbol – watching over him.

Christianity relatively late, in the 5th century. The Irish conversion is traditionally ascribed to St Patrick, a missionary probably born in south Wales, who was originally taken to Ireland by pirate raiders. Early Irish monks lived in solitary cells, practised great asceticism, and gathered only for prayer. In their discipline they sought to emulate the Desert Fathers – hermits of the Egyptian wilderness – and to outdo them in piety and charitable works.

A second generation of Irish monks began to move away from this hermit-like tradition. They realised that Christianity could only triumph if its flagbearers ceased to restrict themselves to prayer and contemplation alone. They had to overcome the appeal of the indigenous Celtic culture, and to do this they had to

An eminent biographer
Half a century after Benedict's death, Pope Gregory the Great – himself a former Benedictine monk – compiled a biography of his pious hero. The illustration below shows a scene from the saint's life at Monte Cassino, where the book is still kept.

compete with the Druids, a powerful and learned class of priests who held a leading position in the existing social hierarchy. It may have been through emulation of the Druids that many of the monasteries founded in Ireland and on the nearby Scottish coast developed into centres of art and scholarship. At the same time, the Celtic heritage inevitably left its mark on the new faith, providing it with a special character of its own.

A Celtic missionary force

In time, Ireland's Celtic-influenced monasteries became sources of missionary activity whose graduates sought to spread the Christian message not just to their own people but to those of neighbouring lands. Like their model the patriarch Abraham, who had gone to serve God in foreign parts, these monks, too, wandered through the world as pilgrims.

One crucial figure was St Columba, who in 563 set out to evangelise the Picts of Scotland. Columba founded a monastery on the tiny island of Iona, off the coast of Mull, and from there monks fanned out across northern Britain. In 635 one of these, St Aidan, created another missionary centre on Lindisfarne, off England's northeast coast, as a base for spreading the word to the kingdom of Northumbria. Iona and Lindisfarne, together with their numerous offshoot foundations, played a vital role in implanting the Celtic form of Christianity across northern England and Scotland as far as the Outer Hebrides.

Illuminated masterpieces

The Celtic monastic communities quickly became renowned for scholarship in Latin – the language of the liturgy and holy writ – philosophy and poetry. To pass on the cultural heritage, monks copied out old handwritten manuscripts, often embellishing or 'illuminating' them with exquisite illustrations and border decorations. They worked in specially equipped writing chambers called *scriptoria*.

Two famous gospels from the great age of Celtic monasticism show the Celtic style at its peak. The Lindisfarne Gospels were prepared between 715 and 721 in the monastery St Aidan had founded 80 years earlier off the Northumbrian coast. The book was probably the work of Eadfrith, then Bishop of Lindisfarne, who copied out the gospel texts in Latin on 259 parchment sheets, and then used his talents as an illuminator to decorate the margins with curving initials, complicated knot patterns, and colourful depictions of animals. An unknown but equally gifted artist created the Book of Kells, probably begun in the monastery of Iona and later taken to the monastery of Kells in Ireland for safe-keeping. Its 680 pages contain some of the most beautiful miniature illustrations ever seen.

Spreading the word

From their bases in Northumbria and Scotland, the Celtic monks next set out to carry the Christian message to Europe. One major target was the Merovingian kingdom of France, which had been nominally Christian since the conversion of King Clovis around the year 500. The roots of the new faith did not, however, run deep: kings and nobles accepted baptism less as a matter of conviction than as a way of legitimising their power.

St Columban, an Irish monk from Leinster, is generally considered to be the chief revitaliser of the Frankish church. He founded three monasteries in the Vosges Mountains region of eastern France, including the famous Luxeuil, and made them bases for missionary work. In later years he was forced out of France for his attacks on the luxury lifestyle of the Merovingian court. He

Celtic influence This 10th-century sandstone Celtic cross stands outside a ruined monastery in County Offaly in Eire (below). The monastery of Iona (background) was the first monastic community founded by Celtic monks outside Ireland.

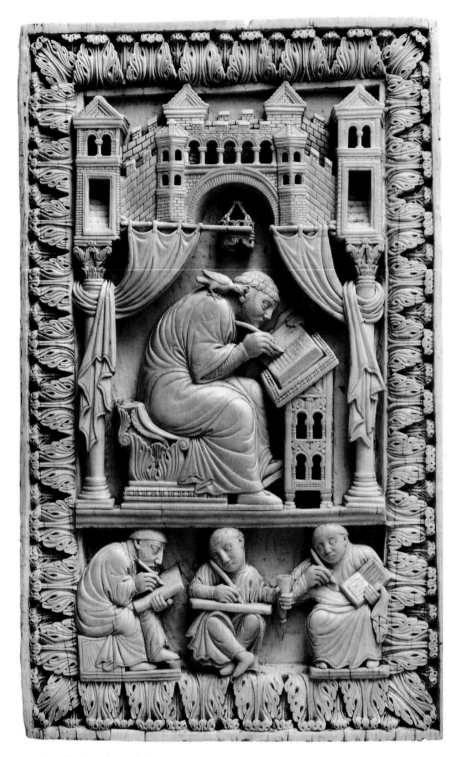

Celtic monk, St Gall, who founded a hermitage on the site in 612. For the most part, though, their unremitting asceticism fell on barren soil, and in the long run they failed to leave much of a mark on the continent.

Competition from Rome

In Britain the monks had to compete with the Roman Catholic Church. The southern parts of the island had been superficially Christianised under Roman rule, but had largely relapsed into paganism following the departure of the legions and the arrival of the Anglo-Saxons. While St Columba and other Celts sought to convert the island from the north, Pope Gregory the Great, a former Benedictine monk, launched a missionary drive of his own in the south. In 596 Gregory sent Augustine, the prior of a Benedictine monastery in Rome, across the Channel with 40 companions to win back Britain for the Catholic Church. Augustine succeeded in establishing a foothold in Kent and converted the local king. He set up his base at Canterbury, which has been ever since the seat of England's principal archbishopric.

Two separate and rival Christian traditions were now struggling for the soul

Working for the glory of God
Shown in an ivory carving from the Swiss monastery of St Gall (or St Gallen) a monk bends over a manuscript in his *scriptorium*. Monasteries also housed craft workshops producing not just exquisite ivory pieces, but also sophisticated metalwork like this golden reliquary (right) now in the treasury of Monza cathedral.

moved first to Switzerland to preach to the Alemanni, and then into the Lombard kingdom in northern Italy, where he died in 615 in the last of his monastic foundations, the monastery of Bobbio.

The Celtic monks had some undoubted successes; the great monastery of St Gallen in Switzerland traces its roots back to a

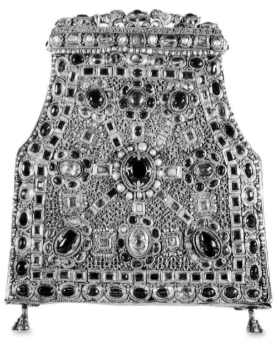

of Britain. The two groups disagreed over such matters as papal supremacy and the organisation of dioceses, as well as some doctrinal questions such as the date of Easter, which was changed by papal decree in 485. Matters came to a head in 664, when the Christian king of Northumbria summoned a synod, or meeting of church leaders, at Whitby on the Yorkshire coast to decide whether to accept Celtic or Roman usage. After a great deal of debate, the decision went in favour of Rome.

The only Celtic tradition to survive into later times was, in fact, private confession. In the Roman Church in classical times, confession had been a public affair, but the practice was already being questioned long before the Synod of Whitby. As early as the 5th century, St Augustine of Hippo, one of the revered figures of the early church, had become convinced that sinning done in private should only be confessed in private, and the Papacy eventually determined to abandon the practice of public confession.

The apostle of the Germans

In the wake of the Synod of Whitby, the Catholic missionary drive swept triumphantly through Britain and across the pagan areas of continental Europe. The Anglo-Saxon convert Willibrord evangelised the Low Countries, and his compatriot Boniface, often called the 'Apostle of the Germans', extended his work eastwards, carrying the message to the central German regions of Thuringia and Hesse and south into Bavaria.

Boniface was a great champion of the papal cause and founded numerous monasteries, among them such notable centres as Fritzlar and Fulda. He was supported in all his activities by Charles Martel. Although nominally Martel held only the office of mayor of the palace, he was in fact the real power behind the throne in the Frankish kingdom.

Martel's main considerations were political: converting his subjects to Christianity seemed to him the best way

The 'Donation of Constantine'

In 756 Pepin repaid the Papacy for its help in legitimising his usurpation of the Frankish throne. Rome had been under threat from the Lombards for some time, and deprived of any hope of assistance from the emperor of the Eastern Empire because of the theological differences that divided the Byzantine and Roman churches, Pope Stephen II looked instead to the new Frankish king. After duly driving back the Lombards, Pepin handed over the territories he had conquered around Rome and Ravenna to 'Saint Peter in the hands of the Pope'.

Yet despite its debt to the Franks for this 'Donation of Pepin', the Papacy continued formally to acknowledge the authority of the Eastern emperor as titular head of the empire and hence as ultimate ruler of Rome. This anomaly left the pope's own legal and political position in doubt, and it provided the background to the most famous forgery of the Middle Ages – the so-called

'Donation of Constantine'. This document purported to show that as early as the 4th century AD, Constantine the Great, the first Christian Roman emperor, had handed the city of Rome and 'all the provinces of Italy and the West' over to the Papacy in thanks for the pope's help in miraculously curing him of leprosy.

The origin of the document is still unclear, but it seems to have been created around 765, either in Rome itself or else somewhere in the Frankish lands. Its authenticity was accepted throughout the Middle Ages, when it was repeatedly used as the basis for the Church's claims to temporal power.

A gift of the imagination
This mosaic in the Church of the Quattro Santi Coronati in Rome shows Emperor Constantine making his supposed donation of Rome's Western Empire to Pope Sylvester I.

of binding the people to the king, whose rule, of course, was in harmony with God's will. But the Church, too, had a vested interest in securing its position within the Frankish realm – so much so that it was prepared to support and justify deposing the last Merovingian king, Childeric III, in favour of Charles Martel's son Pepin.

Boniface was permitted to anoint Pepin on the express instructions of Pope Zacharias, and the last Merovingian mayor of the palace was thereby, in 751, raised to be the first ruler of the Carolingian dynasty. The unstoppable advance of the Frankish kingdom was, therefore, intimately linked with the triumphal progress of Christianity across Europe.

England under the Anglo-Saxons

Soon after the last Roman legions were withdrawn, the Anglo-Saxons invaded Britain. These Germanic tribes quickly came to dominate England, leaving just Scotland, Wales and the far west in native British hands.

A Pictish standing stone
The Picts were an indigenous people inhabiting much of Scotland. They left many inscribed stones, most dating from the 6th to the 8th centuries, bearing realistic or symbolic designs.

Looking back from the last decades of the 5th century, the remnants of the Romano-British population of England and Wales would probably have admitted that life had been good in the province of Britannia under Roman rule. For more than three centuries they had grown used to peace and the rule of law. They had enjoyed the fruits of Roman civilisation in towns, equipped with temples, baths and amphitheatres, that were linked by a network of well-built roads. Many had attained a degree of affluence as merchants or the proprietors of landed estates.

But then, within a very short time, everything was wiped away. The Romans abandoned Britain because the troops were needed to defend Rome itself. The last legions left in about AD 400, and soon the political order and the administrative system imported by the Romans collapsed, along with the cultural achievements linked with Roman rule. Roads deteriorated, towns were abandoned, and the Christian religion, a recent import, almost disappeared. What followed was a time of chaos and confusion – the 'Dark Ages' – in which local warlords seized and held power by force. In the north, the Pictish people of Scotland broke through Hadrian's Wall, which had been erected three centuries earlier to keep them out. Unwittingly, these Pictish raiders set in motion the final demise of Roman Britain.

The arrival of the Anglo-Saxons

According to the earliest surviving written histories, one of the local rulers, Vortigern, sent for the help of Germanic mercenaries, promising them land in return for their services. His appeal, traditionally dated to AD 449, is now thought to have gone out in about 430.

Vortigern's cry for help was answered by three Germanic peoples – the Jutes, Angles and Saxons, whose homelands lay in northern Germany and the Jutland peninsula. Some of their compatriots had already settled peacefully as farmers or traders in southern England after the withdrawal of the Romans. Now, large numbers followed them. The Angles and Jutes emigrated in such numbers across the North Sea that all trace of them was lost on the Continent.

The incomers were experienced seafarers. Travelling in ships powered by oars, each about 25m (80ft) long and holding about 40 people, they could have made the crossing in about 10 days. What happened after their arrival in Britain

The ruins of the abbey at Whitby – it was here that the famous church council, the Synod of Whitby, was held in 664 to determine the future shape of Christianity in Britain.

Buried treasure This decorative Anglo-Saxon helmet, made of iron and gilt bronze, was found at the Sutton Hoo ship burial.

Fearsome weapon
Anglo-Saxon warriors carried battle axes like this one found at Littlebourne in Kent. Sometimes, on a signal from a commander, they hurled them in unison at their enemy.

remains unclear. Perhaps there was a dispute with Vortigern over payment once the Picts had been pushed back north. At some point, however, Hengist and Horsa, the two leaders of the Anglo-Saxon forces, turned on their erstwhile employer. The war that followed involved almost the whole southern part of mainland Britain.

The seven kingdoms of England

At first the Germanic warriors had the best of the fighting, firmly establishing their presence in the south and east. Then the Romano-Britons rallied, rising up against the newcomers and vanquishing them, sometime near the end of the 5th century, at the Battle of Mons Badonicus (Mount Badon – so far an unidentified site). Violent confrontations alternated with phases of peaceful coexistence until about 550, when the Anglo-Saxons launched a new offensive and the Romano-Britons, weakened by internal disputes, were unable to drive out the immigrants. By the time the fighting stopped, the Jutes were settled in the southeast and along the south coast of England, the Angles in central areas and the northeast, and the Saxons in the southwest and west. By the start of the 7th

century, the newcomers controlled large parts of the island and had a firm hold over the Romano-British population.

In spite of their common background, the settlers engaged in bloodthirsty power struggles with one another. Gildas, a 6th-century monk who left the earliest surviving history of the times, described the new rulers of the island as 'savages with the terrible name of Saxons' who 'were hated by man and God alike', and who brought death and destruction to the indigenous people.

Over time, however, a hybrid Germanic-British population evolved. Against the usual run of events in the age of the great migrations, the Britons absorbed both the language and many customs of their conquerors. Even today the English names for days of the week are based on pagan Germanic gods: Wednesday and Thursday, for example, recall Wotan and Thor. Those who resisted were either forced to flee to the last remaining Celtic enclaves in Wales, Cornwall and Scotland or crossed the Channel to Gaul, where they settled on the Armorican peninsula, still called Britanny after these immigrants.

By the end of the 7th century, seven kingdoms had emerged in what is now England: East Anglia, Kent, Essex, Sussex, Wessex, Northumbria and Mercia.

Mission to the English

In this time of troubles Christianity, which had enjoyed an initial delicate flowering in Roman Britain, was almost swept away. Pope Gregory the Great determined to win back the lost ground. In 596 he sent a group of Benedictine monks to England with the task of bringing the Roman Catholic faith to the pagan Anglo-Saxons.

For all the effort that Augustine and his brother monks put into the task of conversion, their success was initially limited. Their greatest achievement lay in persuading Ethelbert, the king of Kent, to accept baptism, along with the leading nobles of his kingdom. It took time for the Christian message to spread beyond the boundaries of Kent, but it gradually took root in the neighbouring kingdoms of Essex and East Anglia. There were setbacks along the way: King Redwald of East Anglia, an early convert, later relapsed into paganism, preferring the prospect of eternal life in Valhalla to that offered by the Christian heaven.

The last pagan burials

The burial sites of Anglo-Saxon kings show how strongly the Germanic peoples remained attached to their old faith. The grave of Redwald, who died in 625, was found on the Sutton Hoo estate in Suffolk in 1939. In accordance with the customs of Germanic peoples living along the North Sea coast, the king was interred in one of the wooden ships in which his ancestors had arrived in Britain. He made his journey into the afterlife accompanied by a gilded helmet, sword scabbards inlaid with garnets, and exquisite gold brooches, fibulas and other jewellery, the earliest surviving examples of Anglo-Saxon art.

Another royal grave, found recently at Southend-on-Sea in Essex, demonstrates mixed Christian and pagan burial customs. The dead man is thought to have been King Saebert of Essex, who was baptised in 604 and remained a Christian until his death in 616. His grave enclosed two small gold crosses, as well as the remains of a reliquary, but other objects found there hardly suggest a Christian view of the afterlife: they included a gaming board, a lyre, drinking horns and cutlery. Grave furnishings of this sort were typical of a period in which elements of the old and new faiths mingled in the hearts and minds of believers.

Celtic or Roman leanings?

The Benedictine missionaries kept up their efforts, achieving a major success in 627 with the conversion of King Edwin of Northumbria. The Papacy planned an ecclesiastical organisation based on the Roman model: a network of bishops would oversee dioceses under the general supervision of the Archbishop of Canterbury, where Augustine had established Britain's first see. But the Roman Church was not the sole representative of Christianity in Britain. It faced competition from the Celtic Church, brought by missionaries from Ireland, which did not accept the primacy of Rome and followed a different tradition; bishops, for example, were peripatetic, and did not have fixed sees.

This state of affairs was quite untenable and in 664 King Oswy of Northumbria summoned a synod, a gathering of church leaders, to meet at Whitby to choose between the two traditions. The Roman side won and in the wake of their triumph Theodore of Tarsus, appointed Archbishop of Canterbury in 669, was able to set up a stable church organisation. He created new dioceses to match the Anglo-Saxon ethnic divisions and brought all the monastic foundations under papal control. From that time on, Anglo-Saxon England was fully integrated into the Catholic Church, maintaining a close connection to Rome.

Emergence of an overlord

Meanwhile, the seven kingdoms into which Anglo-Saxon England was divided came together in a loose federation in which the most powerful ruler was recognised as an overlord bearing the title *bretwalda* – 'far-ruling one'. The first *bretwaldas* came from the kingdoms along the south coast, but later Northumbria, Mercia

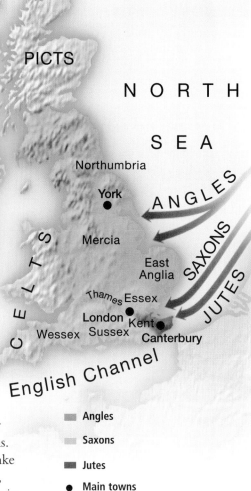

Angles
Saxons
Jutes
● Main towns

Costume jewellery This disc-shaped Anglo-Saxon brooch from the early 7th century is decorated with semi-precious stones. It was found at Wingham in Kent.

and Wessex in turn all claimed supremacy. Northumbria predominated for much of the 7th century, while Mercia took the lead in the 8th.

The height of Mercian power came in the long reign of King Offa, from 757 to 796, which brought internal stability accompanied by a considerable economic upswing. At the time of Offa's accession the people of England lived almost exclusively from agriculture. Ancient forests and marshes still covered large swathes of the land, and trades and crafts were restricted to a few larger settlements, such as London, York and Oxford that aspired to the condition of towns. Most people, however, lived in the countryside. The men were liable to be called up for military service, if required, but in times of peace they and their families cultivated wheat, rye and barley, and reared goats, pigs, cattle and, above all, sheep, prized for their wool.

Offa's reign saw a renewal of trade with the Continent, the chief exports being woven and embroidered goods. An obstacle to commerce had been the lack of an accepted medium of exchange – the barter system in use was cumbersome and inefficient. Offa solved the problem by minting the first Anglo-Saxon silver coins.

The golden age of Mercia

Offa's reputation spread widely enough for him to be treated as an equal by the Emperor Charlemagne, who corresponded with him and even sought one of his daughters in marriage for his son. However, Offa overplayed his hand by insisting that his own son should marry a

Two mighty kings
King Offa of Mercia (above) and Alfred the Great (background) were among the most important rulers in Britain in the early Middle Ages.

daughter of the Frankish emperor. Charlemagne's refusal led to a three-year period when Continental ports were closed to English traders.

Offa's greatest legacy was a defensive wall that he had built along Mercia's western border, separating his realm from Celtic Wales. Offa's Dyke, as it became known, stood 8m (25ft) high and extended for almost 200km (120 miles). Yet as a bastion to protect Anglo-Saxon England it had limited value, for the real threat came not from the Celts but from an entirely different source: Viking raiders from Denmark attacking across the North Sea.

New invaders from over the sea

Offa died in 796, by which time Viking raids were sending shock waves across England. The first was recorded in 787: three enemy ships reportedly struck the south coast, and a royal official was killed. Then in 793 Norsemen attacked and burned the monastery of Lindisfarne, one of England's greatest cultural centres, on the Northumbrian coast.

The raiders returned in increasing numbers in later decades, presenting such a threat that by the middle of the 9th century the demise of Anglo-Saxon England seemed imminent. In 839 a Danish fleet of more than 350 ships anchored in the Thames while their crews plundered London and Canterbury. A great Danish army arrived on the east coast in 865, prepared to overwinter in England. In 867, Northumbria succumbed to the enemy, and two years later East Anglia also was forced to submit. At first the Vikings had been content to raid and return home, but now the warriors chose instead to settle, bringing their wives and children with them and making homes in the lands they conquered.

In 871 the Danes came into conflict with the kingdom of Wessex which, after Offa's death, had taken precedence among the seven Anglo-Saxon kingdoms. The invaders, who by that time had conquered and settled much of the east coast, were at a disadvantage in the struggle as they could not reach Wessex via the Thames, their main artery inland, and had to fight entirely on land. Ethelred, the ruler of Wessex, offered fierce resistance until he was struck down in battle. His army fled, leaving Ethelred's younger brother Alfred, just 22 years old, to make peace on any terms he could to save his kingdom.

A great king

The Danes moved on to impose their rule over Mercia and Essex. By the time they turned their attention back to Wessex, Alfred was ready for them. After a first defeat, he won a decisive victory at Edington in 878. The battle marked a turning point in England's history, for without it the later unification of the Anglo-Saxon kingdoms would not have been possible. The defeated Danes withdrew to the east, to an area that was known as the Danelaw.

Alfred meanwhile went on to capture London and to win all the areas of England not under Danish control. He built a small fleet to counter the Danes at sea – the beginnings of the British navy – and constructed fortified towns to serve as bastions against future attack. He created a unified legal code, set up a welfare system for the poor, and fostered intellectual life, personally translating important Latin texts into Old English and encouraging the compilation of the Anglo-Saxon Chronicle, a year-by-year record of events.

When Norse raiders, supported by their countrymen in the Danelaw, launched a fresh attack on Wessex in 892, Alfred's defensive measures proved their worth. Thanks in part to the new fleet he had built, the invaders were repelled.

Alfred himself died in 899 at the age of 52. He had united Anglo-Saxon England and provided a foundation for the later reconquest of the Danelaw lands by his successors. Although Alfred was never king of all England, his achievements made him the true founder of the unified Anglo-Saxon kingdom of the 10th and 11th centuries.

A typical farmhouse The art of building in stone almost died out in Britain after Roman rule came to an end. Most people lived in rectangular wooden houses with wattle-and-daub walls and thatched roofs.

Merovingian France

After the fall of the Western Empire, the Germanic Franks won for themselves the rich lands of Gaul. They integrated the Roman culture they found there with their own traditions and so laid the foundations of the Christian west.

Symbol of nobility
This gravestone from the Rhineland shows an image of Wotan, carrying a sword and combing his hair. For the Merovingians, long hair was the mark of an aristocrat.

The entire city was watching, it seemed, when Clovis, third king of the Frankish Merovingian dynasty (named after his grandfather Merovich), made his way at the head of his retinue into the diocesan church of Rheims. Bishop Remigius was waiting for him in the baptistry. There the king recited the Creed, publicly acknowledging that he had renounced paganism in favour of Christianity. Then he took off his clothes, climbed into the bath-sized font, and submerged himself three times. As he did so, the bishop urged: 'Bend your head, proud Sicambrian! Burn the things you once worshipped! Worship now the things you burned!' Then he anointed the Frankish ruler as king, and went on to baptize 3000 of his followers. So, in about 498, Clovis and the Franks joined the new faith, an event with far-reaching consequences for the future of France and Europe.

Clovis's conversion was a milestone on the path to a Christian Europe. During his 29-year reign, from 482 to 511, Clovis built a powerful kingdom stretching from the North Sea to the Pyrenees and from France's Atlantic coast to the River Rhine. By adopting the Christian faith of his Gallo-Roman subjects, he formed a spiritual bond between his own Germanic followers and the indigenous people of what had been one of the most prosperous regions of the Roman Empire. The successful merging of the two cultures explains why the Frankish kingdom that Clovis founded lasted so much longer than most of the Germanic realms of the time, becoming the foundation of the future kingdom of France. With Clovis, the classical era came to an end and medieval Europe was born.

The rise of the Franks – the name means 'free and courageous' – to the status of a great power took place in close allegiance with Rome. In its decline, the Western Empire had been barely able to withstand the onslaught of foreign peoples at its borders. Allies were found in the Germanic tribes that had settled along the middle and lower courses of the Rhine, and were united in a loose federation.

Clovis the conqueror

Childeric I, the heir of Merovich and father of Clovis, had been among these allies – the *foederati* or 'federates'. As an ally of Aegidius, the Roman military commander of Gaul, during the war against the invading Visigoths, Childeric earned the trust of the people in lands that are now Belgium and the Netherlands. He passed this loyalty on to his son Clovis, who was about 16 years old when he came into his father's legacy in 482. Clovis was too ambitious to remain content with the small territory he had inherited, which was centred in Belgium with its capital at Tournai. He turned on Syagrius, the last imperial representative in Gaul, and defeated him at Soissons in about 486.

The victory won Clovis a reputation as a warrior – and all the Roman territory between the Seine and Loire rivers in France. In the following decade he expanded his kingdom at the expense of the Alemanni in Alsace and the Visigoths,

Family outing This 14th-century manuscript illumination shows the Merovingian King Chilperic I of Neustria riding out with his wife Fredegunda. After Chilperic's murder in 584, Fredegunda became regent for the minor Clothar II.

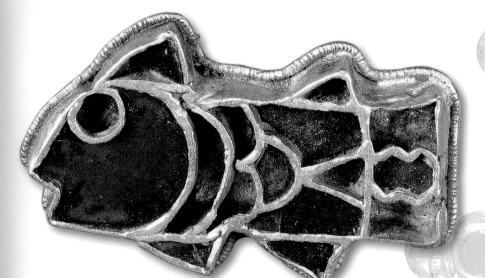

Frankish fibulas
This brooch in the shape of a fish, and the gilded-silver fibulas in the background, are fine examples of Merovingian jewellery.

Longstanding place of faith
The crypt of the Church of St Paul at Jouars near Paris is one of the few structures to have survived from the Merovingian period.

who ruled the largest realm in Europe, covering much of France and Spain. By his victory at Vouillé in 507, Clovis forced the Visigoths over the Pyrenees, extending his own lands to the Spanish border.

Having won a great kingdom, Clovis unified it by melding the culture of his Germanic followers with that of the Gallo-Roman world. The Franks inherited the administrative structures of the late classical period, replacing the old Roman town governors with bishops. They settled in northeastern France around Paris, Soissons and Rheims, without driving out the Gallo-Roman landowners.

Clovis's decision to convert to the Christian faith helped to integrate the two cultures. Following the example of his wife, the Burgundian princess Clotilda, he accepted the Roman form of Christianity rather than the Arianism that was followed by the Visigoths and other Germanic peoples. The choice was significant, as it enabled Clovis to be seen as a champion of Roman orthodoxy: the Arian belief that Jesus Christ was subordinate to, rather than consubstantial with, God had been condemned as heretical by councils of the Roman Church.

A politic move

Conversion to Christianity provided Clovis with obvious immediate political advantages: he gained official recognition from the Eastern Roman emperor in Constantinople who, in 508, accorded Clovis the title of honorary consul; he was able to justify his military campaigns against his Germanic neighbours as crusades for the true faith; and he won over the local Gallo-Roman aristocracy, from whose ranks he recruited most of his bishops.

After Clovis's death in 511 his four sons divided up his

kingdom. Despite the bitter and bloody competition provoked by this partition, the Merovingian domain flourished. In 531 the German region of Thuringia was conquered, and in 534 Clovis's heirs took the mighty kingdom of Burgundy, sharing its lands. Two years later they secured part of Provence, thus gaining access to the Mediterranean, then they conquered Bavaria and raided northern Italy. Clovis's grandson, Theudebert I, even considered seizing Constantinople.

Family conflict

But from the second half of the 6th century, conflict within the royal family began to overshadow external triumphs. Three large kingdoms were formed whose leaders, although closely related, were fierce rivals. The western kingdom of Neustria, with its capital at Soissons, was the wealthiest, with Paris, Tours and Rouen situated within its bounds. Austrasia, ruled from Rheims, comprised what is now the Champagne region and the territories between the rivers Rhine and Maas, and had a mainly Germanic population. Burgundy, whose ruler had his main residence in Orléans, stretched southward into the Romanised areas of the Loire and Rhône valleys.

In the pervading atmosphere of rivalry, a feud between queens Brunhilda of Austrasia and Fredegunda of Neustria escalated into a tragic saga. Fredegunda incited her husband, Chilperic I, to kill his second wife, the Visigoth princess Galswinth, who was a sister of Brunhilda. In revenge, Brunhilda urged her own husband, Sigibert I, to invade Neustria. The blood feud that ensued raged through three generations and cost the lives of ten kings: child murder, torture and executions were the order of the day, and the feud only came to an end in 613 with the murder of Brunhilda, who was tied to a horse and dragged to her death. The saga was immortalised in the great medieval epic the *Nibelungenlied* – the 'Song of the Nibelungs'.

The baptism of Clovis

The baptism of Clovis quickly became embroidered with legends and tales of miracles. One account held that the king had made a vow while fighting the Alemanni at Tolbiac in 496, swearing to be baptised if God granted him victory. However, this story is so reminiscent of the story of the Roman Emperor Constantine's conversion in 312 at the Battle of the Milvian Bridge that historians have tended to regard it with a degree of suspicion.

In fact, personal conviction seems to have been less important than politics in Clovis's conversion. There was a Germanic tradition by which rulers enjoyed a special relationship with the gods, acting as intermediaries between the divine powers and their subjects. Clovis may well have had something similar in mind when he accepted Christianity. By doing so he was not only gaining the support of the Church but was also helping to legitimise Merovingian rule in the eyes of his Christian Gallo-Roman subjects.

There were advantages for the Church, too. According to tradition, Clovis was baptised at Rheims, and the bishops of that city thereafter claimed the right to crown all French kings. Supposedly, the oil that was used to anoint Clovis was brought straight down from Heaven by a dove.

Defining moment This illumination from a 14th-century manuscript shows King Clovis being baptised. Gregory of Tours, who wrote a chronicle of the Franks at the end of the 6th century, celebrated Clovis as a new Constantine after his baptism.

The pagan hangover

Such bloody clashes only served to highlight the internal contradictions of the Merovingian kingdoms. Despite the royal house's conversion to Christianity, many pagan traditions survived, including polygamy: kings and leading noblemen regularly took several wives, and women from the lowest strata of society could aspire to become queens. As all the royal children had claims to inherit, a miasma of intrigue hung over the royal courts. Contenders for power murdered or locked up their rivals in monasteries where their hair was shorn, removing the luxuriant locks that were Merovingian society's most visible symbol of power and dignity.

The readiness of the Franks to resort to violence suggests how little they were truly touched by Christian ideals. Only in the towns and cities, where the bishops combined civic and spiritual duties, was Merovingian society really able to unite the classical Roman ideals of education with the values of the Chuch. The bishops

ensured that schools were founded to educate the next generations of clerics, and also took steps to look after the poor: the first almshouses in Europe were created during the Merovingian period.

The church's contribution

The bishops were also responsible for prodding and persuading the Merovingian elite into financing the building of churches and monasteries. The first big stone structures went up in the main religious centres, usually around the graves of saints and martyrs; ruins of buildings from the classical age often served as foundations. Only the most important churches at the time had glass windows, as the art of glass manufacture had been all but lost. Ecclesiastical foundations were often endowed by their patrons with huge estates and dazzling goldware. Such luxury drew scorn from visiting Irish missionaries including Columban, who outspokenly criticised the extravagant lifestyle of the Merovingian kings.

A portable throne This folding Merovingian chair, known as Dagobert's throne, dates from the 6th century. The back and arm rests were added later.

The rise of the palace mayors

Meanwhile, Merovingian political power was dying at its core. The aristocrats were benefiting from the constant rivalries that dogged the royal courts. It was the Austrasian nobility, under Bishop Arnulf of Metz and Pepin the Elder, progenitor of the Carolingian dynasty, who finally toppled the all-too-powerful Brunhilda. They then offered the Austrasian throne to the Neustrian king, Clothar II, who rewarded them by issuing an edict confirming and enhancing the rights of the nobility. Although the Merovingian realm had been briefly reunited, Clothar's act, announced at a council held in Paris in 614, effectively broke the power of the Merovingian crown.

Over the next century and a half the office of mayor of the palace became central to the running of the Merovingian state. The mayor was responsible for running the royal household and the state finances. In time the position became hereditary and the aristocrats who held the office used it as a launchpad to power. Gradually they took over the functions of the nominal rulers, who were reduced to the shadowy status of *rois fainéants* – 'do-nothing kings'.

The Austrasian Pepinids proved the most assertive of the new mayoral dynasties, and in time they won control of the entire Frankish kingdom. Charles Martel – a nickname meaning 'hammer', reflecting his military prowess – fought successfully against the Thuringians and the Alamans, but he won his greatest victory in 732 when he halted the Arab advance from Spain. This decisive battle, fought near Tours, saved the Christian cause in Europe.

After this triumph Charles assumed power in his own name, and when the nominal Merovingian ruler died in 737, he was not replaced. On Charles's own death in 741, however, his sons Carloman and Pepin bowed to tradition by placing the last scion of the Merovingian house, Childeric III, on the throne as a puppet king. Six years later, Carloman voluntarily ceded power to his brother, whereupon Pepin, as sole ruler, decided to do away with the Merovingian line once and for all. Having secured the support of the Church, he stripped Childeric of his remaining powers and, in 751, Pepin had himself crowned king of the Franks. With this act, the great Carolingian dynasty made its appearance on the stage of world history.

Theodoric the Great and the Ostrogoths in Italy

The Ostrogoth king, Theodoric, led his people to Italy and took over the entire country. His capital, Ravenna, developed into a flourishing centre of late classical culture and learning.

Monumental tomb Theodoric's mausoleum in Ravenna may have been modelled on the tomb of Constantine in Constantinople. In the 9th century Theodoric's body was discovered to be missing; who took it is still a mystery.

In the autumn of 488, Theodoric, king of the Ostrogoths in the Balkan peninsula, called on his people to set out on a great journey to Italy. Once again, much of the Ostrogoth population was on the move to find a new home. The great column of migrants included about 20,000 warriors and their families – some 100,000 people in all.

The Byzantine Emperor Zeno had initiated the exodus as an astute political manoeuvre. Following the withdrawal of the Huns, the Ostrogoths had settled in the Balkans from where they launched raids into Byzantine imperial territory. Eventually, the Eastern emperors granted them Byzantine land to settle on in what is now Bulgaria, but they

military commander and patrician on Theodoric, giving him instructions to depose Odoacer and to rule Italy in his place as the emperor's representative.

Gothic art of warfare

The Ostrogoths had to fight their way to Italy. Near the present-day town of Vukovar in Croatia, the Gepids, another Germanic people, blocked their path. Theodoric's warriors brushed them aside, only to find themselves under attack from nomadic Sarmatians. In spite of such problems, Theodoric reached the River Isonzo at the head of the Adriatic in 489 – where Odoacer was waiting for him with his army. The invaders had the better of the ensuing battle, and so were able to push on into Italy itself.

In his youth, Theodoric had been held as a hostage at the Byzantine court and there had learned the art of warfare. He was a brave man who personally led his army of foot soldiers and armoured horsemen in many battles. The Ostrogoth cavalry drew their strength from close contact with the nomadic Alans and Huns on the steppes of southern Russia, where they had learned the tactics of mounted warfare. Their principal strategy involved launching surprise attacks on the flanks and rear of enemy infantry; if these were unsuccessful, they quickly withdrew behind their own lines.

Odoacer's downfall

The Ostrogoths defeated Odoacer's forces twice more in the following months, and by 490 they had managed to pin down

Two churches for one saint
The columned basilica of San Appolinare Nuovo (above) was built by Theodoric in his new capital of Ravenna. It has three naves and the tendril-like decorations adorning the arches are typical of late-classical architecture; the mosaics show a strong Byzantine influence. The Basilica of San Appolinare in Classe (background) stands in the port area of Ravenna; its construction started in 535, nine years after Theodoric's death.

remained apprehensive of their restive allies, fearing they would start plundering their territories anew. Zeno had good reason to deflect their attentions from his own heartland towards Italy.

At the time, Italy was under the rule of the Germanic commander Odoacer, who had deposed the last Western Roman emperor in 476. Officially he ruled as the representative of the Eastern Roman emperor, who still claimed overlordship over Italy and all the old imperial lands. In reality, however, Odoacer acted as an independent ruler. Seeking to rid himself of two barbarian leaders with one blow, Zeno was happy to bestow the titles of their opponent in his capital of Ravenna on the Adriatic. The city itself, however, was well-nigh impregnable, and Odoacer held out for almost three years. Eventually the local bishop negotiated a settlement under which the two opponents agreed to rule Italy jointly.

Theodoric pretended to accept the deal and was admitted to Ravenna. Ten days later, Odoacer lay dead. At an evening banquet, two conspirators grabbed hold of him while Theodoric cut him down with his sword. Odoacer's wife and brother were also murdered: his wife, Sunigilda, was starved to death, and his brother Hunulf, who had sought sanctuary in a church, was shot by archers.

Theodoric now ruled all of Italy and Sicily. Official recognition from Byzantium was slow in coming, however; it was not until 497 that Anastasius I, Zeno's successor, officially proclaimed him king.

Coins for power-sharers Although the Byzantine Emperor Anastasius, seen here, held the right to mint currency for the Ostrogoth kingdom, Theodoric's monogram appears on the reverse side of the coin.

The hub of the kingdom

With peace restored to Italy at last, the economy started to recover. Theodoric launched an active building programme, equipping cities, including Rome and Ravenna, with fresh defences, aqueducts, palaces and churches. He commissioned his own tomb in Ravenna, too – a monumental structure made of huge blocks of stone, crowned by a dome-shaped block measuring 11m (36ft) across and weighing 300 tonnes. The capstone may have been intended to resemble the domes of Byzantine churches – or perhaps even the burial mounds in which earlier Germanic rulers were laid to rest.

Ravenna stood out among the Italian cities of the day. The Roman legacy lived on in its late-classical stone buildings, roofed with fired tiles. Theodoric and his successors enlarged the city considerably. An impressive system of walls surrounded several of the city's quarters, with the suburbs extending out beyond them. Its port was one of the chief trading centres of the late classical world. Ships from all over the Mediterranean docked there, and it also provided a terminus for trade routes across the Alps.

A centre of culture

Theodoric held court in splendour in his Adriatic capital, turning Ravenna into one of the most important centres of late classical philosophy and learning. Although long considered illiterate by historians, as he used a specially made template to set his signature to documents, Theodoric had, in fact, learned to read and write in his youth at the Byzantine court, and he took care to install a large library in his palace. He also liked to surround himself with scholars, among them Symmachus, Boethius and Cassiodorus, whose works included a history of the Goths.

Two peoples, two administrations

The Ostrogoths' arrival in Italy seems not to have greatly disrupted existing patterns of property ownership. The newcomers settled mainly in the north, although garrisons were posted in all of the larger towns throughout the peninsula. Theodoric provided his troops with accommodation and with an income. drawn from taxes, to keep their families. The nobility invested their earnings in land, and soon had large estates at their disposal, as did the king himself.

Theodoric was the supreme judge in criminal cases and had the exclusive right to grant pardons. However, his power in Italy was limited, in theory at least, by the

---

EVERYDAY LIFE

The spectre of hunger

Through his sound economic policies, Theodoric the Great provided stability in Italy throughout his 33-year reign, enabling the mass of the population to enjoy the benefits of a reliable food supply. All that changed, however, during the 20-year war with the Byzantines that followed his death.

The situation soon became critical as the war progressed. The large estates were no longer properly maintained and many tenant farmers and slaves were forced to flee the land. Vast stretches of once productive countryside were laid waste, and the devastating loss of harvests led to famine across the country.

Some profiteers, including a Gothic merchant known as Bessass, managed to turn the situation to their own financial advantage. By selling food at vastly inflated prices, they amassed enormous fortunes.

A woman in power This ivory carving shows Amalasuntha, Theodoric's daughter, bearing the insignia of royal power. When the teenage son for whom she acted as regent died, her opponents had her drowned in her bath.

overlordship of the Eastern Roman emperor, which prevented him from promulgating laws in his own name. In practice, Theodoric got around this by issuing edicts that had the force of law. He appointed Gothic officials to oversee Roman administration, which was otherwise left to function as before. Theodoric also kept an eye on the Church, even though the Ostrogoths subscribed to the Arian version of Christianity rather than the Catholic faith of their Italian subjects.

Respecting tradition

Theodoric modelled his rule on the Byzantine court, even though he never laid claim to an imperial title itself. The appointment of consuls and senators to govern the Roman population of his kingdom remained the prerogative of the emperor in Byzantium, but Theodoric put forward nominees for the posts. Theodoric's public appearances were in the great tradition of the Western Roman Empire. His triumphal arrival in Rome, in the year 500, was accompanied by gifts of grain for the citizens and games in the Colosseum.

The new ruler was also careful to pay due respect to the Senate and to the Papacy, and to offer generous gifts to influential individuals. Representations of Theodoric show him in imperial guise and wearing late-classical scaled armour, although he always retained his own Gothic hairstyle and beard.

Clouds of suspicion

Theodoric secured his kingdom externally with the aid of treaties and diplomatic marriages. He was also prepared to use force to win back areas west of the Alps and south of the Tyrol for Italy. In the north, his power extended far into the foothills of the Alps; at times he even exercised authority over the kingdom of the Visigoths in southern Gaul and Spain. He also cultivated close contacts with other Germanic peoples, including the Franks, Burgundians, Thuringians and Vandals.

The last years of Theodoric's reign were clouded by mistrust and suspicion. In 523, he got wind of secret correspondence between a Roman senator named Albinus and the Byzantine court on the subject of his succession. He instantly suspected a plot, and his relations with the Roman population and Byzantium soured.

Fearing the worst, Theodoric accused Albinus of treason and had him executed, together with the scholar Boethius, author of *The Consolation of Philosophy*, and the senator Symmachus, Boethius's father-in-law. When the Byzantine court took his behaviour as evidence of anti-Catholic persecution, Theodoric sent Pope John I to Constantinople to put his case. Deeming that the pope had spent longer than strictly necessary in Byzantium, however, Theodoric had him thrown into prison on his return, where he died in 526. Theodoric himself fell victim to dysentery in the same year.

The Byzantine backlash

The kingdom that Theodoric had created did not long survive his death. His daughter Amalasuntha assumed power as regent for her son, Athalaric, who was still a minor. When the youngster also died soon after, her position became untenable. She tried to bolster it by appointing her cousin Theodahad as co-regent, but he had barely accepted the honour when he had her murdered. Amalasuntha's death provided Byzantium's new and ambitious

emperor, Justinian I, with the grounds he needed for declaring war. He launched attacks on Italy, simultaneously, from the north and the south. While the Gothic forces managed to block the northern incursion, they failed to prevent the Byzantine commander Belisarius from effecting a landing on the south coast from his base in Sicily. The Byzantine troops then marched on Rome and occupied the city.

Meanwhile, the Goths had deposed Theodahad and elected Witigis, a capable leader, in his place. In 537 he laid siege to Rome. In spite of famine and disease, the Byzantine forces managed to ward off the besiegers with much bloodshed. Breaking out, Belisarius penetrated deep into Ostrogoth territory in northern Italy, with the aid of fresh cavalry forces sent as reinforcements. To complicate matters further, Frankish forces invaded Italy from the north in 539, confronting both the Goths and the imperial army. However, they were soon forced back through a shortage of supplies.

The bitter end

Witigis was eventually trapped by the imperial army in Ravenna, and was forced to enter into peace negotiations with Belisarius. Faced with a hopeless situation, the Ostrogoths finally surrendered the city and Witigis was taken prisoner.

The battle for Italy was not over, however, as numerous pockets of resistance held out in cities such as Pavia and Verona. Justinian exacerbated the situation by seeking to recoup the expense of his expedition through taxes that the exhausted population could not afford. Soon imperial troops were deserting

because they had not been paid. From 541 on, the Goths, under a new king, Totila, managed to win back large parts of the country.

The war dragged on amid immense human suffering for more than ten years. In 552 the Byzantines launched a fresh offensive, sending a new army under a commander called Narses overland to Italy via Dalmatia. The decisive battle was fought at Tadinae in present-day Umbria. Totila ordered his cavalry to charge the Byzantines head-on, but the attack collapsed under a hail of arrows, fired by a force of 8000 imperial bowmen. The Goths were defeated, losing their king and 6000 warriors.

The new king, Teja, doggedly continued the struggle, but by now the fate of the Goths was sealed. In October 552, the last battle of the war was fought at *Mons Lactarius*, 'Milk Hill', near Salerno. Teja himself was killed and his army was destroyed. The Ostrogoths' attempt to take over the mantle of the Western Roman emperor in Italy had come to nothing.

Rare representations
Church mosaics provide most of the few remaining images from the Ostrogoth period. They supply valuable information on clothing styles (top) and the appearance of towns (above), particularly the non-religious structures which for the most part have not survived.

Justinian I and the Roman Empire revived

Beloved imperial beauty
This mosaic shows the Empress Theodora, adored wife of Justinian, adorned with magnificent jewellery and a saint's halo.

Justinian I was the last emperor to attempt to restore the old Roman Empire in all its glory. He brought in financial and legal reforms, built Constantinople's great church of Hagia Sophia – and risked everything for the love of an actress.

In 559, Justinian I formally celebrated victory over the Kotrigur Huns, a people from the steppes, with a triumphal procession into Constantinople accompanied by the city prefect and the senators. His path led past the Church of the Holy Apostles, where he unexpectedly dismounted. He entered the church, said a prayer, then lit some candles and placed them in front of the grave of his wife, Theodora, who had died 16 years earlier.

Justinian had risked his throne and even his life for Theodora, and had found in her a wise counsellor who had been his strongest support until her death. Her memory was so sacred to him that he never married again, even though they had had no children. Contemporary observers described Theodora as beautiful: small, graceful and with a determined gaze. She can still be seen with her court, frozen in time, in the mosaics of the church of San Vitale in Ravenna. She is wearing the purple mantle reserved for empresses, a halo circling her head. She wears a crown of pearls, and her shoulders are adorned with a gold chain and jewelled collar befitting her imperial power.

According to the Greek author Procopius, her consort Justinian was of medium build and had a round, healthy face. His sparse, curly hair was already greying by the time he came to power. He, too, stands stiffly under his halo in the Ravenna mosaics, wearing the imperial mantle and a crown of pearls.

A scandalous marriage

The marriage of Justinian and Theodora scandalised Constantinople society, from high-ranking senators to the prurient masses. It was widely known that the empress's origins lay in the city's underworld. Her mother had performed on the stage as a dancer while her father kept wild animals for the Hippodrome, Constantinople's main stadium.

Theodora followed in her mother's footsteps, becoming an actress. In addition to pantomimes and comedy acts, a favourite entertainment of the time was the *mimus* (mime), a louche genre in which plots involving marital mix-ups and adultery were acted out through gesture and body language, with much erotic innuendo. Women actors were restricted to playing in the *mimus*, where they were expected to display a great deal of bare leg and much else. At a time when well-brought-up women never left the house without their head and arms covered, showing off any part of the body was considered shocking. The Church regularly inveighed against the depravity of the *mimus* shows, even though priests were sometimes accused of attending

This colourful mosaic of Emperor Justinian is in the basilica of San Apollinare Nuovo in Ravenna.

Church and state on display
Besides the church of Hagia Sophia in Constantinople (background), Justinian adorned other churches, including the basilica of San Vitale in Ravenna. The mosaics decorating the apses (top) present a colourful picture of the Eastern Roman court, showing priests, advisors and soldiers clustered around the emperor himself.

them. Many of the actresses also engaged in prostitution or lived as kept women, supported by their wealthy lovers.

From actress to empress

Actresses at the time were securely contracted to their employers and could only buy their release with large sums of money. The man who provided the cash to free Theodora was Hekebolos of Tyre, a high government functionary. He took her to Alexandria in Egypt, where he held office, but the two soon quarreled. With poverty staring her in the face, Theodora, who by now had at least one illegitimate child, somehow managed to make her way back to Constantinople. There she assumed the life of a penitent, earning her living by spinning wool.

In 520 she attracted the attention of Justinian, and one of the great love stories in history began. The two could hardly have been more different. She spoke Greek, he spoke Latin; eastern culture had shaped her life, western culture his; she came from the city, he had grown up in rural Illyria (now in Serbia); she was making amends for her former sins, he possessed power and high office. But both had great intelligence, energy and ambition. She gave up her life as a penitent for him, and he risked his future for her.

Normally in such circumstances, Justinian could have been expected to make Theodora his mistress in a private arrangement; even the Church reluctantly accepted that wealthy young men made such arrangements before marriage. But Justinian refused this solution. Nothing less than marriage would do.

Perhaps Justinian's attitude reflected his own unusual background. Born the son of a Slavonic peasant in about 482, he was not an obvious candidate for emperor. His uncle, however, rose to become Emperor Justin I. Justinian was educated in Constantinople and in 521 Justin had him proclaimed consul. In 525, Justinian and Theodora finally married, and two years later, on April 1, 527, Justinian succeeded to the throne following Justin's death. The new emperor was 45 at the time and Theodora, his empress, was about 28.

A God-given mission

Justinian started his reign with two goals: to restore the Roman Empire of old, and to unify Christian belief across the empire. He followed the classical tradition, in which the emperor ruled by God's will with a duty to ensure order, prosperity and the rule of law across his dominions. Justinian stated his aims clearly in the introduction to one of the legal codes for which he became famous: 'Appointed by God, controlling the empire given to us by the Most High, we bring wars to a successful conclusion, celebrate peace, and safeguard the existence of the state.' He gathered an exceptional team of aides to help him, including the generals Belisarius and Narses, the administrator John of Cappadocia, and Tribonian, the most famous legal expert of his day.

The Nika riots

To finance the incessant wars needed to achieve his goals, as well as his expensive building projects, Justinian was forced to increase taxes. He turned to John of Cappadocia as Praetorian Prefect, who showed considerable ingenuity in finding new sources of revenue. John Lydus, the author of a work on the Byzantine bureaucracy, listed 27 different taxes, including one on unused plots of land and another on air. The effect of these often exorbitant charges so impoverished many people that they had to move out of Constantinople, bringing the city to the verge of collapse.

The tensions stirred by high taxation finally exploded in January 532 in the Nika riots, so called from the cries of *Nika!* ('Victory!') chanted by spectators in the Hippodrome, which was where the trouble began. Groups of fans followed either the Blue or Green teams in the chariot races, quite as passionately as supporters of football teams today. Bloody feuding between the two factions led to widespread street disorders that culminated in a conspiracy to depose the emperor. After

days of hesitation during which fires spread across much of the city, Justinian eventually ordered his soldiers, led by Belisarius and Narses, to storm the packed stadium. More than 30,000 people were killed in the ensuing bloodbath, after which, according to the chronicler Theophanes, 'There was great fear, and peace returned to the city, so that there were no more chariot races for a long time.' Thoroughly demoralised, the city's masses were cowed into silence.

The cathedral of Hagia Sophia

Constantinople's great church was badly damaged in the fires during the unrest, so Justinian commissioned the architects Anthemius of Tralles and Isidorus of Miletus to rebuild it. In less than six years they erected one of the largest domed structures of antiquity. A monumental

BACKGROUND

The hippodrome factions

Constantinople's Hippodrome was the greatest place of entertainment in the Eastern Empire. The spectators split into two main factions: the Greens and the Blues. These groups had semi-official status, receiving financial backing from the imperial treasury and administrative support from civil servants. In return, they provided a vocal outlet for public opinion: supporters would chant their views at the emperor as he and his entourage sat in the royal box watching races, giving the games an important political function. By Justinian's time, however, the rivalry between the two groups was getting out of hand; support for different contenders in the arena all too easily spilled over into hooligan behaviour and violence.

The principal attraction of the Hippodrome was chariot racing. The sport demanded great technical skill on the part of the charioteers, and the most successful racers became celebrities who could earn huge sums of money. The state commemorated their feats by issuing medals that not only perpetuated the names of the charioteers themselves but often also honoured those of the best-known horses.

A savage spectacle This ivory diptych shows wild animals fighting before the royal box in Constantinople's Hippodrome.

A venerable settlement
The monastery of St Catherine is a prime example of the early Christian architecture of Justinian's day. It is located on the Sinai Peninsula, near the site where Moses was said to have received the Ten Commandments.

Constantinople, and followers of different views held them so passionately that they rarely hesitated to condemn or persecute those who did not share their beliefs.

The Monophysite party was particularly strong. Their argument with orthodox dogma concerned the nature of Christ's divinity. In 451 the Council of Chalcedon had upheld the doctrine of Christ's dual nature, human and divine. The Monophysites, however, insisted that he was all divine – a doctrine that, in extreme form, denied that he had endured suffering on the Cross, only having seemed to do so. Justinian initially persecuted the Monophysites, but Theodora took up their cause, and under her influence he moderated his position, trying to find a compromise. But he risked alienating both sides, and a schism duly opened up between the Churches in Rome and Constantinople that would simmer on for the rest of the century.

A stylish court

Justinian's official residence in Constantinople occupied an entire quarter of the city, west of the Bosphorus. It housed residential and governmental quarters for the emperor and his entourage, as well as barracks, churches, audience and assembly halls, gardens, workshops and separate housing for the domestic slaves. The Hippodrome also lay within its walls. Only fragments of the complex have survived, most notably the famous 6th and 7th-century floor mosaics that are now in Istanbul's Sultan Ahmet Mosque.

In its day, the palace was a showcase for the splendour of the late-classical empire. Walls and floors were marble or covered with brilliantly coloured mosaics depicting the emperor's glory. Gold and silver were used in abundance. Such fairytale wealth was intended to impress visitors to the palace. Any commoner who had business with the emperor passed through a darkened hall before entering the dazzling splendour of the throne room. There, as choirs and organ music sounded, the

cupola 56m (180ft) high and 31m (100ft) wide rose above the gigantic central nave and the internal decoration of the church matched the splendour of the exterior.

In his role as Christian emperor by the grace of God, Justinian felt duty bound to build churches and found monasteries. For the same reason, he was also quick to intervene in matters affecting Christian doctrine. In 529 he closed down the celebrated Academy in Athens because pagan philosophers were teaching the doctrines of Neoplatonism. This effectively quenched the spirit of intellectual enquiry and many philosophers fled to the lands of Persia's Sassanian kings, who welcomed them with open arms.

Doctrinal divisions

Justinian also became embroiled in the bitter theological disputes that continued to rack the Christian Church. Sects such as Arianism and Monophysitism challenged the orthodoxy preached by the pope in Rome and the Patriarch in

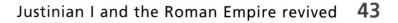

emperor sat enthroned under a canopy symbolising the heavens. Special servants, the *silentarii*, enforced absolute silence on all those waiting to approach the emperor. More privileged visitors were presented to the emperor or empress in a smaller chamber furnished with equal magnificence. After waiting in an antechamber, they were finally admitted to a public audience at which their royal hosts were surrounded by advisors and servants.

Codifying the law

Justinian I ruled from this residence with such tireless energy that he was called 'the emperor who never slept'. One of his greatest reforms involved the legal system. At his accession, Roman law was in confusion. Made up as it was of separate imperial decrees stretching back over centuries, legal judgments pronounced by successive emperors and jurists' opinions, it had become full of contradictions and was difficult even for lawyers to interpret.

On February 13, 528, Justinian I ordered a ten-strong commission of lawyers to edit this jumble, preserving only those laws that could still be applied and amending them where necessary to meet changed circumstances. By April 529 the reformed Codex Justinianus had been approved and was put into practice. A further commission, chaired by Tribonian, thematically catalogued the work of the Roman jurists, taking just three years to complete a task expected to require ten. In December 533 the results of their work, the Digest, was made available in 50 books, and judges were able to consult it in making legal decisions.

Much of Justinian's attention during his reign focused on foreign policy as he sought to maintain and expand the boundaries of his realm. The result was an almost continuous state of war on the empire's borders. The eastern frontier was constantly under threat from Persia's Sassanid rulers, while a variety of different peoples were pressing in from the Balkans in the north.

Extending the frontiers

Justinian was particularly concerned with winning back the Roman Empire's former lands in the west, where Germanic peoples had established themselves: Ostrogoths in Italy, Visigoths in Spain, Franks in Gaul, Vandals in North Africa. In a campaign against the Vandal kingdom in 533–534, some of the empire's richest agricultural lands were retrieved, along with some territory in southern Spain. Then in 535 Justinian launched a campaign against the Ostrogoths in Italy; it took 19 years of hard fighting that largely exhausted the country in the process, but Italy was once more part of the empire, with Ravenna as the capital of its western portion. The emperor finally bought peace with the Sassanids in 561, securing his borders at the cost of a heavy annual tribute for the next 50 years.

Justinian died in 565 after a 38-year reign. He had briefly restored something of the splendour of the old Roman Empire, but his tenure of power had proved a watershed. No future emperor would be so ambitious or so foolhardy. After his death the Roman Empire finally metamorphosed into the still glorious but less far-reaching Byzantine Empire.

Byzantine finery Studded with precious stones, this golden bracelet and brooch in the form of a Greek cross (below and background) were both created in the 6th century by Byzantine craftsmen.

The Lombards in Italy

Under the Lombards, Italy finally broke free of the Eastern Roman Empire. In two centuries of Lombardic influence, the late classical era gave way to the early Middle Ages.

Symbol of faith This gold cross studded with precious gems is from the crown of Agilulf, king of the Lombards from 590 to 616. In the later years of Lombard rule, it became common practice for nobles to be buried with valuable crucifixes as a mark of their dedication to the Christian faith.

In the spring of 568, Alboin, king of the Lombards, gathered his people for a great migration. For months he had been preparing for the long journey to a new home. Horse-drawn carts, heavily laden with all the necessary food and equipment, lurched into action. The gigantic cavalcade was divided up into groups of inter-related families that sometimes moved independently of one another; larger groups were usually under the command of a duke, smaller ones under a count. Armed horsemen and foot soldiers protected both the people and their herds of cattle following behind. For safety each evening, the wagons drew up in a defensive circle. A spectator observing the column would have recognised a nation on the move: about 200,000 people set out on the journey, and their ranks were further swelled along the way by some 40,000 Saxons, as well as stragglers from other peoples.

The Lombards themselves are thought to have come originally from southern Sweden. They settled the lower course of the River Elbe in Germany in the 1st century AD, and in the 5th pushed farther south into the region along the middle course of the Danube. By the early 6th century they dominated extensive regions of Moravia, lower Austria and western Hungary. Here Alboin formed an alliance with the Avars, nomadic migrants from the steppes, to destroy the kingdom of the Gepids, which extended across Hungary and Transylvania. However, not trusting his unpredictable partners, he decided not to stay to enjoy the fruits of victory; instead, he lead his people on to Italy.

An easy victory in Italy

As luck would have it, the Lombards entered northern Italy almost unopposed. They had chosen their time well; they arrived in 568, just three years after the death of the Byzantine emperor Justinian, whose long wars against the Ostrogoths had left the country exhausted. Punitive taxes and lethal epidemics had sapped both local morale and manpower, and the defensive outposts protecting the Alpine frontier were no longer garrisoned. Italy was ripe for the taking.

Most of the northern cities surrendered without a fight, among them Milan, which Alboin occupied in 569. Only Pavia held out, enduring a three-year siege. By the time it finally fell, the Lombards had taken control of much of the peninsula. In the south they founded the duchies of Spoleto and Benevento, which in later years would function almost as independent kingdoms. The bulk of the migrants, however, settled north of the River Po, in the region that is known to this day as Lombardy.

The Byzantine Empire, which had struggled so hard to master Italy, was left with only scattered possessions. Its main surviving stronghold was a corridor of land linking Rome on the west coast to Ravenna and its surrounding territory on the east. In addition, thanks to their sea power, the Byzantines were able to hold onto Liguria – the coastal strip along the Mediterranean between Rimini and Ancona – and small areas around Venice and Naples, along with the toe and heel of the Italian peninsula.

A murderous marriage

King Alboin did not enjoy his triumph for long. Like many of his compatriots he was a heavy drinker, and intoxicated one night he made a fatal error. He forced his wife Rosamund, daughter of the Gepid king who had been killed in the Lombards' victory, to drink from a goblet made from her father's skull. Deeply offended and humiliated, Rosamund plotted her revenge with Helmichis, the king's shield-bearer and her lover. The two managed to induce a young warrior named Peredeo to carry out the deed, which was done one afternoon when Alboin retired for a nap in his palace in Verona; Rosamund had strapped his sword to the bedhead so that he could not draw it to defend himself. The assassins had, however, misjudged the reaction their act would provoke. Alboin was greatly mourned, and Rosamund and Helmichis had to take refuge in Byzantine Ravenna. They died there soon after, killed, it was said, by one another's hand.

A decade of lawlessness

After Alboin's death in 572 the Lombards chose a general, Clepho, as their king, but he too was soon assassinated and nominal power passed to Clepho's son, Authari. As Authari was still a minor, in reality power was shared by the 30 strongest dukes, who split Italy among them. They ruled brutally from behind the walls of fortified cities and strategic castles. The Roman population, having endured decades of warfare, now lost most of their remaining rights and property. Estates were

Treasures for a queen
This magnificent golden goblet was buried with Queen Theodelinda, wife of King Agilulf (and also of his predecessor, King Authari). Born a Bavarian princess and brought up as a Catholic, Queen Theodelinda received a Christian burial in a church that she herself had founded in Monza in northern Italy. Even so, she was laid to rest in a style reminiscent of pagan Germanic tradition, dressed in her finery and surrounded by valuable grave goods. Both Theodelinda's goblet and crown (background), as well as Agilulf's crucifix (far left), are now in the treasury of the cathedral of Monza.

A fertile valley Most of the Lombards who made the trek across the Alps settled in the fertile Po Valley, which stretches across northern Italy. Today, much of the delta region of the River Po is given over to paddy fields for growing rice (background).

confiscated and the owners killed or driven off the land. Much Church property was also seized at this time. The Lombards paid lip-service to Arian Christianity, but their conversion was superficial at best, and many were still pagan at heart. They felt few qualms about plundering Church possessions; priests were frequently murdered, sometimes for refusing to acknowledge Germanic gods. In this state of lawlessness even the Lombard dukes realised that they needed to unite behind a ruler – a conviction that strengthened as the danger of intervention from Byzantium grew. In 584 Authari, who had by now reached an age to rule, took the reins of power and started bringing order back to the country.

BACKGROUND

Rothari's Edict

Until the mid 7th century, the laws of the Lombards were transmitted by word of mouth. King Rothari had them collected and written down for the first time in his Edict of 643. The introduction to the document made his intentions clear – and also that the document as it stood was not necessarily the final word on the law:

'We have collected...the ancient laws of our fathers, which had never been written down... We have had them written on parchment... We are well aware that we need to add to this edict, with God's help, everything about the ancient laws of the Lombards that we can recall through questioning one another or the old people...'

A royal legal hearing This illustration from an 11th-century manuscript shows King Rothari seated on a folding throne as he listens to his scholars expounding on their codification of legal measures in his pioneering Edict.

The Lombards adapt

The restoration of royal authority came none too soon. Lombard power was threatened in the late 580s, when the Byzantine emperor offered the Franks 50,000 gold pieces to attack the settlers. In 590 a huge Frankish army moved into northern Italy, but Authari used a combination of force and diplomacy to thwart the invaders. He married Theodelinda, daughter of the duke of Bavaria, who subsequently also wed his successor, Agilulf, when Authari died soon after the Franks withdrew. Theodolinda was a Catholic, and through her influence the Roman faith permeated through the upper ranks of Lombard society. Nobles began to found churches, choosing to be laid to rest in hallowed ground.

As the 7th century progressed, Lombard rule in Italy began to go through subtle changes. In the early years the Lombards had looked very different from the indigenous population. The men were hairy – the very word 'Lombard' is in fact a corruption of *Langobard*, or 'long beard' – and wore loose linen clothing and leather sandals, topped in cold weather by huge capes held together by decorated clasps. The women adorned themselves with long necklaces of coloured glass beads and with belt pendants decorated with little metal discs from which hung carved bone combs, iron scissors and small leather pouches. By the mid 600s, however, the Lombards were losing their distinctive appearance. After almost a century of occupation, they were finally starting to blend in with the locals.

In 636 King Rothari acceded to the throne. A strong king, he introduced measures to ensure peace among his subjects, whether Lombard or Roman. In 643 he issued a celebrated Edict: a document in Latin that codified Lombard law. He also strengthened the role of royal officials who answered directly to the king so they could serve as a counterbalance to the power of the dukes. In foreign policy, Rothari continued the struggle against the Byzantine enclaves, bringing Liguria under Lombard rule for the first time. He also campaigned on the Adriatic coast. Under Rothari's successors the differences between Arians and Catholics blurred as Lombards and Romans gradually merged into a single people.

In 662 Grimoald, the duke of Benevento, seized power. When a rival stirred up a rebellion, however, Grimoald had to call on the Avars for help, and once the rebellion was put down the Avars refused to leave. Grimoald eventually got rid of them by a ruse. He invited Avar ambassadors to inspect his troops, then marshalled his forces in such a way that the envoys unknowingly reviewed the same men several times over, on each occasion sporting different costumes and weapons. Awed by the multitudes under Grimoald's command, the Avars withdrew from Italy without further trouble.

The Byzantines, however, were a continuing threat. In 663, Emperor Constans II led a large army into Italy. Disembarking in the south, he marched on Rome and paid his respects to the Pope – but also ordered his soldiers to strip bronze statues and all other available metal objects from the city, intending to ship them back to Constantinople to melt down for armaments. Constans' visit – the first by any Eastern emperor since the barbarian takeover in the West – did nothing to improve relations with Rome, and only reinforced the gap that had opened up between Constantinople and the Italian territories over which it still nominally claimed overlordship.

Sudden downfall

The Lombard kingdom reached its greatest extent under Liutprand, who reigned from 712 to 744. He restored royal control over the southern duchies of Spoleto and Benevento, which had become semi-independent, and he renewed the assault on the Byzantine Rome–Ravenna corridor. Ravenna finally fell to King Aistulf in 751, putting an end once and for all to Byzantine rule in central and northern Italy. When Aistulf tried to gain control of Rome too, however, the Pope turned for help to the Franks, whose power was on the rise. Pepin, the Frankish king, marched into Italy, defeating Aistulf and forcing him to hand over the conquered Byzantine lands to the Papacy. They subsequently became the basis of the Papal States, which would play an important part in later Italian history.

Aistulf's defeat by the Franks marked the beginning of the end for the Lombard kingdom. When his successor Desiderius attempted to win back the lost territory in 773, the Pope called on the new Frankish leader, Charlemagne, to take action. Charlemagne launched a fresh invasion of northern Italy, capturing the Lombard capital of Pavia in 774. This defeat finally put an end to two centuries of Lombard rule in Italy.

Down to the very last drop
Drunkenness was a Lombard vice that led to the death of at least one king. The Lombard nobles never lost their taste for quaffing long draughts from drinking horns, often finely decorated ones, like this example in glass.

The Muslims in Spain

Muslim forces from North Africa conquered most of the Iberian peninsula. After a difficult start, they hosted a culture in which the arts and sciences flourished.

Spain was not invaded by the Muslims out of the blue – they were invited in by the heirs of the Visigothic ruler Witiza, who sought their aid when a rival claimant called Roderic seized the throne. Tariq ibn Zayad, the military governor of Tangiers, responded with a small force of about 7000 men. In 711 he crossed the narrow water separating North Africa from the southern tip of Spain, arriving near the promontory that has ever since borne his name – Gebal al Tariq, 'the rock of Tariq', anglicised as Gibraltar.

Tariq's small army fared better than he could reasonably have expected. Having defeated and killed Roderic in a battle near the River Guadalete, he found that resistance crumbled before him. When it became evident that large numbers of the Visigoths' subjects were welcoming him with open arms, he quickly lost interest in helping Witiza's heirs and instead claimed Spain for Islam.

Many of the inhabitants believed they would be better off under the Muslims. Taxes had become oppressive under the later Visigothic kings, and it soon became apparent that serfs who converted to Islam could advance their position under the new regime, rising from the status of bondsmen to freedmen in the service of the Moors. Muslim Spain also offered more religious tolerance than its predecessor, particularly for the Jews, who had endured harsh persecution. For all these reasons, the Muslim incursion quickly turned into a conquest.

In 712 Musa ibn Nusayr, the caliph of Damascus's representative in North Africa and Tariq's commander in chief, arrived in Spain with a second, larger army. In quick succession he captured the cities of Seville and Córdoba, and within two years the combined Muslim armies had occupied much of the Iberian peninsula. Resistance forces retreated to the mountains of Asturias in northwestern Spain, establishing an independent kingdom that, in time, provided the platform for a Christian fightback.

The conquerors' wise policies

Most of the indigenous population settled down happily enough under Muslim rule. The victors avoided triumphalism and treated their new subjects as partners. They reduced taxes and pursued a policy of religious tolerance that gave Christians freedom of worship and granted civil rights to Jews. Equality was not total as non-Muslims had to pay higher taxes, but this fiscal burden could be avoided by adopting Islam – which provided a powerful incentive to convert.

Spain's new masters proved less adept at dealing with one another. When Musa and Tariq were summoned from Spain to Damascus to report to the caliph on his new possession, a lengthy period of internal conflict set in. The Arab tribes that had taken part in the conquest were soon at loggerheads with one another, and also with the North African Berbers who had provided most of the troops.

The stag of Córdoba
This decorative stag is actually a water jug. Fashioned in the 9th century, it hints at the refined lifestyle that flourished at the court of Córdoba in the time of the caliphate.

Moorish design features such as horseshoe arches and patterned tiling feature prominently in the Puerta de San Esteban in Córdoba.

The Battle of Tours

Internal strife did not stop the newcomers from extending their conquests. From the 720s onward they launched raids across the Pyrenees into France that culminated in a full-scale invasion in the year 732. The Islamic forces had advanced three-quarters of the way to Paris before their progress was brought to a halt at the Battle of Tours, which ended in a decisive victory for the Frankish leader Charles Martel. The remnants of the Muslim army retreated to Spain, and no further attempts were made to extend Muslim control in western Europe.

An independent Muslim state

Continuing infighting among the Muslim leaders of Spain remained the greatest threat to their power – there were at least 20 governors in the first four decades of Islamic rule. When stability was eventually restored, it came from an unexpected quarter. In 750 a power struggle in the Near East ended in a massacre of the ruling Ummayad clan by the Abbasids of Persia, who took over the caliphate in their own name. The only Ummayad survivor was Abd ar-Rahman, who made his way to Spain and won the support of

tribes there that had long been loyal to the Umayyad cause. In 756 he established his own breakaway dynasty, claiming overlordship of the entire peninsula as the Emir of Córdoba. This broke the link with the caliphate in Baghdad, and Spain became an independent Islamic nation.

Abd ar-Rahman used all his fierce energy to reunite the kingdom, dealing ruthlessly with any sign of dissent. He fought off a Frankish invasion of northern Spain led by Charlemagne himself; the retreating Christians suffered an additional blow when Basque troops defeated their rearguard at Roncesvalles in the Pyrenees, an incident that provided the background for the great medieval epic poem *The Song of Roland*. The emir left his successors a newly united realm, although Merida, Saragossa and Toledo kept some of their independence. He also commissioned the Great Mosque of Córdoba, the Mezquita; work began in 785 and would continue for the next two centuries.

When Abd ar-Rahman died in 789, he left his son, Hisham I, a kingdom that was internally and externally secure and completely independent of Baghdad. This new unity was soon challenged and Hisham's successor, al-Hakam I, only managed to keep his rebellious nobles in check by savage repression, using Slav and Berber mercenaries to put down unrest.

The Arab legacy

Under Abd ar-Rahman II, who reigned from 822 to 852, Córdoba became the centre of a well-organised and powerful state distinguished by a cultural diversity that was unique for the age. Disturbances in the Abbasid realm caused many scholars to flee from Baghdad to Spain at this time, bringing with them a remarkable range of talents and implanting a distinctive culture that blended Oriental and Western traditions. The refugees brought fresh styles of poetry, music and

A flowering of the arts The hall of columns in Córdoba's Great Mosque (background) represents a high point of Islamic architecture. Under the emirate, Córdoba also became a renowned centre of ivory carving (below).

dance, introducing the guitar, tambourine and castanets to the peninsula; the art of flamenco, long associated with Andalusian gypsies, can be traced back to Arab roots.

Life in Muslim Spain was sophisticated and cosmopolitan. The Arabs brought with them unfamiliar fashions in clothes, food and drink. A flourishing Mediterranean trade provided a steady supply of luxury items, including costly fabrics and precious jewellery. Intellectual life blossomed as pioneering Arabic works on philosophy, medicine and astronomy reached the peninsula. A new form of architecture appeared, featuring glazed tiles and the horseshoe-shaped arches already familiar in the Near East. The Islamic passion for gardens also manifested itself, many of them with a water feature as their centrepiece. The Koran prohibited the pictorial representation of living beings, so the walls of the mosques and palaces that sprung up were decorated with stylised plant designs and geometric patterns.

A sign from God

The Christian Church was eclipsed for more than a century after the conquest. Then, sometime between 823 and 829, a hermit in the Christian enclave of Galicia in the far northwest had a vision that led him to the tomb of the Apostle James, whose body was said to have miraculously floated to Spain, accompanied by angels. Christians saw this as a sign from God. Over the grave they built a church that attracted a flood of pilgrims. They named the site Santiago de Compostela – 'Saint James of the Star Field'.

The discovery was a huge boost to Christian morale and 'Santiago' became the battle cry of Christian soldiers. The new mood of zealotry penetrated the Muslim lands also, leading a group of Christian extremists to revile publicly the Prophet Muhammad in the hope of attaining martyrdom. At first, Abd ar-Rahman II ignored them, but in the face of continued resistance he felt bound to react and 53 Christians were put to death.

Even so, the emir left a largely peaceful and united kingdom to his successors. Islamic Spain blossomed further under his namesake, Abd-ar-Rahman III, who in a long reign (912–961) was not merely able to deal as an equal with Byzantium and the other great powers of the day, but even assumed the mantle of the caliphs, claiming dominion over all Islam from his capital of Córdoba. Under his rule, Moorish culture on the Iberian peninsula reached its peak.

Religious fervour This sculpture of Saint James sits in a doorway of the cathedral of Santiago de Compostela in Galicia in north-western Spain. The discovery of the supposed tomb of the apostle stirred enthusiasm for the Christian fightback against the Moors. It also founded a new place of pilgrimage which helped to raise the money needed to fund the struggle.

Byzantium and the iconoclast controversy

The 8th and 9th centuries were a time of crisis for the Byzantine Empire, as it risked tearing itself apart in a long, drawn-out religious conflict over the worship of icons.

Warrior hordes From the mid 7th century on, the Byzantine Empire found itself under attack not just from the Arabs to the east but also from the west in the form of the Bulgars, horsemen from the steppes who had settled in the Balkans. This 9th-century manuscript illustration, now in Spain's national library in Madrid, shows Byzantine soldiers fleeing from the Bulgarians.

It was the year 717 and Constantinople, the Byzantine capital, was in danger. Arab armies had conquered almost two-thirds of the Byzantine Empire over the previous 80 years, and now they were on the city's doorstep. A force 80,000 strong had moved to the European shore of the Dardanelles strait and was taking up position to besiege the city from its landward side. At the same time a fleet of 1800 ships was approaching by sea.

Byzantium's emperor, Leo III, was new to the throne, but he kept admirably calm in this desperate situation. He had an advantage in the form of a mysterious chemical weapon. This was the substance known as 'Greek fire', which had already proved its effectiveness during a previous Arab siege of the city in 673. The exact ingredients of Greek fire was a closely guarded secret, but it probably involved a mixture of naphtha, saltpetre and sulphur. It could be hurled in pots or fired from tubes resembling primitive flame-throwers, and it was so combustible that it even burned in water.

In order to retain control of the sea approaches, Leo equipped every ship in his fleet with this fearsome weapon and sent fireboats into the enemy anchorages. Without seaborne support the Arab army was eventually forced to withdraw, having spent a miserable winter camped beneath the city walls. The Byzantine capital had survived its greatest challenge.

A deceptive peace

Leo's victory ensured the survival of his realm, which had come into being as the eastern half of the Roman Empire in the 4th century AD. Following the collapse of the western part of the empire in the following century, Byzantium had become the main secular bulwark of Christendom, with an uneasy relationship with the Pope in Rome who claimed to exercise spiritual authority over the Church. In the intervening centuries doctrinal questions had often racked the Byzantine state. Now a new religious conflict broke out that was to cause a split that lasted more than 100 years.

The early Church had been wary of religious images, fearing they resembled pagan idols. In the intervening centuries, however, believers had increasingly turned to icons – portraits of Jesus Christ, the Virgin Mary and the Christian saints – as a focus of their faith. The sacred images were everywhere in the Byzantine lands, decorating homes and shops as well as churches and monasteries. People said prayers in front of them, lighting candles and burning incense in their honour. On special occasions the holiest icons were even paraded through the streets to invoke divine protection for the whole community.

Saviour and destroyer This coin shows Emperor Leo III, who saved Constantinople from the Arabs in 717. Leo was also the emperor responsible for outlawing the veneration of religious icons, and thus starting what became known as the Iconoclastic Controversy.

Iconoclastic controversy

The veneration of icons reached such proportions that it started to alarm many observers, among them Leo III. Brooding on the many disasters that had afflicted Byzantium over the past decades, he could not help wondering if they were somehow related to the growing cult, the more so because the burgeoning Muslims, who had done

BACKGROUND

The Cyrillic alphabet

Signalling its renewed self-confidence, the Byzantine Empire undertook fresh missionary activity among its pagan neighbours in the mid 9th century. Two brothers, Cyril and Methodius, were dispatched in 862 to convert the pagan Slavs of Moravia (on the borders of today's Czech Republic and Slovakia). They were highly successful, not least because they learned the Slavs' own language to deliver their message, even conducting church services in Slavonic rather than in Latin.

Finding that the lack of a Slavic written script was holding back their work, the two created an entire alphabet, based on Greek characters, which they used to translate the Bible and liturgical texts. The Cyrillic script that they invented remains in use today, forming the basis for the modern Russian alphabet.

Inventor of an alphabet
St Cyril (right) and his brother Methodius were born to a family of civil servants in Thessalonica. The Cyrillic script that they devised (background) has been used ever since to write Russian and other Slav languages.

such damage to the empire, rejected holy pictures. The more he considered the matter, the more convinced he became that icon-worshippers were offending against the biblical injunction against making graven images. His conviction was strengthened by a terrible earthquake that shook Constantinople in 726, which he took as further evidence of God's wrath. To address what seemed to him the root cause of the empire's problems, he issued an edict ordering the removal and destruction of icons from all churches.

The move was approved by a council of eastern bishops, but was deeply unpopular with the common people, who were used to their holy images and considered them an essential part of their faith. When armed soldiers began to remove the mosaic of Christ above the main entrance to the imperial palace in Constantinople, a group of indignant women attacked them and one of the men was killed in the struggle. In the face of armed resistance, and to avoid the risk of civil war, Leo III softened the enforcement of the edict.

A widening gap from Rome

The dispute – which became known as the Iconoclastic (from the Greek term for a 'destroyer of images') Controversy – also had important international repercussions. Relations between the Byzantine Church and the Papacy had been strained for many years, and now Pope Gregory II in Rome cast his lot against iconoclasm, issuing two edicts condemning the movement. Even though Gregory continued to offer Leo political support, Leo was not happy. In retaliation he confiscated papal estates in southern Italy and Sicily and transferred jurisidiction over the local bishoprics to the Patriarch of Constantinople.

Emperor against people

Leo III died in 741 and was succeeded by his son Constantine V. Constantine proved to be a great military leader during his 34-year reign, winning decisive victories against the Bulgars on Byzantium's western frontier, as well as the Arabs to the east. But he also intensified his father's religious policies, bringing the quarrel over icons to a climax. Constantine not only had all icons removed from churches and monasteries but also took violent action against those who opposed his orders: one Patriarch of Constantinople who dared to speak out in favour of the images was beheaded. The monkish chroniclers who recorded Constantine's deeds nicknamed him 'Copronymos', meaning 'whose name is excrement', which gives some indication of the hatred

he aroused in religious quarters. On the other hand, his military victories seem to have made him popular with other sections of the population.

Constantine's successors were keen to avoid such violent confrontation and adopted a more conciliatory attitude toward the icon-lovers. The change of heart was formalised by a decree of the Council of Nicaea in 787, which officially restored the veneration of icons. Although the iconoclastic party was outraged by the decision, the issue temporarily lost some of its prominence.

The first empress

The change of heart was largely the work of a woman – Irene, the mother of Emperor Constantine VI. Constantine was just 10 years old when he came to the throne in 780 and Irene served as his regent, developing a taste for power that left her unwilling to let go of the reins of government when her son came of age in 786. Her influence roused resentment, and in 790 a palace rebellion led to her temporary banishment. Two years later she was back, restored to her old position by her son – an unwise move for in 797 she staged a coup, not just deposing her son but also having him blinded to remove any possibility that he might retaliate. She then took the throne in her own name, becoming the first woman ever to rule the Byzantine Empire. As a sop to convention, she adopted the masculine title of *basileus* ('emperor').

Although Irene managed to hold onto power in Constantinople for five years, the legitimacy of her rule was strongly

To the greater glory of God
The ending of the iconoclast controversy was marked by an upsurge in monasticism across the Byzantine Empire, and many splendidly furnished monasteries were founded at this time. This bas-relief decorates the altar at the Lavra Monastery on Mount Athos in Greece.

Lethal weapon This Byzantine miniature, painted on parchment in about the 11th century, shows 'Greek fire' being used against Arab forces. Before the invention of gunpowder, no other weapon of comparable effectiveness existed.

Enamel art This gold and enamel Byzantine bowl from the 8th or 9th century is decorated with an image of a gryphon – a mythical winged beast.

contested. In Rome, Pope Leo III refused point-blank to recognise her authority, treating the Byzantine throne as vacant during her tenure of office. This situation was the main cause of Leo's decision to bestow the title of Holy Roman Emperor on the Frankish ruler Charlemagne in the year 800, so flouting Byzantium's claims to be the Roman Empire's only legitimate successor. Irene was toppled by another coup in 802 and banished to the Greek island of Lesbos, where she died soon after.

An end to conflict

Irene's successors proved ineffective in countering a renewed threat from the Bulgars on Byzantium's Balkan frontier. This led to a revival of iconoclasm, which was associated with military success: under the iconoclast emperors, Byzantium had known nothing but victory. In 815 the order went out once again to remove the holy images. The controversy was not resolved until the death of Theophilus, the final iconoclast emperor, in 842. With the support of his widow, a new Patriarch of Constantinople, Methodius, officially restored the worship of icons the following year. Full of enthusiasm,

a great procession of the faithful carried some of the most venerated images to the Church of Hagia Sophia ('Holy Wisdom'), Constantinople's most sacred shrine. The anniversary has been celebrated ever since by the Eastern Church, on the first Sunday of Lent, as the Feast of Orthodoxy.

Byzantium's fortunes revived as the Arab world was rent by internal strife, weakening the argument of those who linked veneration of icons with military defeat. By 867, when a new Macedonian dynasty came to the throne, the empire was on the verge of renewed greatness.

The Macedonian renaissance

The return of the icons encouraged a remarkable upsurge in artistic activity. The holy pictures quickly regained their position in the hearts and minds of believers, enabling the illiterate as well as the learned to glimpse something of God's glory. Besides icons, Byzantine craftsmen created exquisite mosaics and miniature paintings, wood and ivory carvings, glass and enamelware, as well as bronze and ironwork. Silk textiles were used to make altar cloths and priests' vestments, but also found a place in wealthy people's homes as curtains and cushion covers.

Byzantine ceramic artists had learned the art of enamel from the Persians in the 5th century, and now put it to use creating portrait medallions, crucifixes, reliquaries, bowls, goblets and other objects. They used a cloisonné technique, laying coloured glass on a clay or metal base divided up by thin wires; during the firing, the molten glass fused with the base to create a pattern with a characteristic sheen. This upswing in the visual arts and crafts was accompanied by a reawakening of scholarship, in a period spoken of ever since as the 'Byzantine Renaissance'.

Charlemagne, the father of Europe

Charlemagne brought most of Western Christendom under his sway and won fame in his own time as *rex pater Europae* – 'king and father of Europe'.

On Christmas Day 800, Saint Peter's Basilica in Rome was bedecked in more than its usual splendour. Gregorian chants and clouds of incense hung in the air as Pope Leo III placed a magnificent golden crown on the head of the Frankish King Charles, whom history would remember as Charlemagne – Charles the Great. 'To the illustrious Charles, the great peace-bringing emperor of the Romans, crowned by God; life and victory!' Leo proclaimed, as cheers resounded through the church. Then the pope knelt to the new emperor.

Sanctioned by the Church

Rome was swept by excitement, for the crowning of Charlemagne was unarguably one of the crucial events in the history of the West. After 300 years, a Western Roman Emperor once more reigned. In future years, claimants to the title of Holy Roman Emperor would feel obliged to make the trip to Rome to receive the imperial crown from the hands of successive popes. The need for the popes to confer legitimacy on their claims would also be at the root of the Church–State tensions that divided Western Christendom for much of the Middle Ages.

King of Christendom
This magnificent bust of Emperor Charlemagne is in the cathedral at Aachen in Germany.

A peoples' king This 9th-century manuscript illustration (right) shows Charlemagne and his wife in typical Frankish dress. He preferred wearing everyday clothes that were little different from those worn by most of his subjects.

Charlemagne's throne
This throne made of antique marble slabs was Charlemagne's seat while attending Mass in the Palatine Chapel at Aachen. After his death the chapel became the seat of imperial coronations: a total of 35 rulers sat on the same throne to receive homage from their noble followers after being crowned.

The bond between Rome and the Carolingian court had been forged under Charles's father, Pepin, who had looked to the pope to legitimise his rule when, as mayor of the palace and de facto ruler of the Frankish lands, he decided to depose the last Merovingian king and take power in his own name. In 751 Pepin received the homage of the Frankish nobility and had himself anointed king in Soissons by the Frankish Archbishop Boniface and other prelates. Not content with this ceremony alone, however, he subsequently invited Pope Stephen II to Paris. In the monastery of Saint Denis, the pontiff anointed the king and his sons, Charles and Carloman, thereby prohibiting all Franks, 'under pain of excommunication, from ever daring to choose a king from a different noble house'.

Charles is king

In 768 the 21-year-old Charles came into his inheritance as joint king of the Franks, then in 771, on the death of his brother Carloman, he became sole ruler. Preserving the bond with Rome was one of the aims of his reign – he saw himself as Christendom's champion; other aims included a desire to rule Italy and generally extend the borders of his kingdom, particularly into pagan lands. Charles spent much of his life in the saddle, either administering his existing territories or seeking to add to them. He launched a fresh military campaign almost every summer, for warfare was a way of life for the Franks.

Building on his inheritance

The start of Charles's reign was taken up with suppressing uprisings in Aquitaine in southwestern France, which he brought back fully under Frankish control. In 773, however, his father's policies caught up with him, when a legation from Pope Hadrian I arrived at his court. Their mission was to remind Charles of his duty as protector of the Roman Church, which was now in need of help against the Lombards. Charles had personal reasons for mistrusting the Lombard king, Desiderius; Gerberga, the widow of his brother Carloman, had fled with her children to the Lombard court, asking Desiderius for support in promoting their claims to the Frankish throne. For nine months the Frankish army besieged the Lombard capital of Pavia, until hunger and disease forced the city to capitulate. Desiderius, Gerberga and her sons were all dispatched to monasteries, and Charles had himself crowned king of the Lombards in Desiderius's place. He returned home politically strengthened, bearing the title king of the Franks and Lombards, and enriched by the Lombard treasury. In 781 he travelled to Rome to have his son Pepin crowned as king of Italy, firmly integrating his new lands into his expanding realm.

Back home, however, bad news awaited: unrest in the Saxon lands was threatening Charles's northeastern border. The Saxons occupied what is now the German state of Lower Saxony to the south and west of Hamburg; they were pagans who, under their charismatic leader Widukind, refused to abandon their old beliefs.

A long and bitter war

Convinced that a Christian ruler had a duty to fight for the faith, Charles battled the Saxons for almost three decades. The war was brutal, particularly after the Saxons reneged on a peace deal signed in 777 in their capital of Paderborn. The Frankish king reacted with fury, razing to the ground the town of Eresburg, south of Paderborn, and destroying the Irminsul, a great cult statue to the god Wotan that was sacred to the Saxons. In response, the Saxons repeatedly raided Frankish territory, plundering villages and churches.

In 782 Charles committed the worst atrocity of his reign, executing 4500 Saxon rebels for treason. He passed a draconian law prohibiting pagan rituals on pain of death and compelling all his subjects to undergo baptism. Yet still resistance continued, even after Widukind himself surrendered in 785. Peace was not fully restored until 800, after which the now Christianised Saxons rapidly integrated into the Frankish realm; by the 10th century they were even providing its ruling dynasty.

In other endangered border areas, known as the Marches, Charles appointed lords with special powers, which included the right to call up troops without waiting for the king's consent. The Spanish March was created to provide a buffer against the Muslims, and the Breton March against the Celts of Brittany. The Sorbic March in the east kept the Wends and other Slavs at a distance; the Pannonian March protected the Danube Basin.

Danger in the east

Once Charles had the upper hand over the Saxons, he turned his attention to another pagan enclave: the territory of the Avars, a war-like, horseriding people on his eastern border. Originally from central Asia, the Avars had been settled on the Hungarian plain for two centuries. Their khanate was centred in a circular-shaped area known as the Avar Ring, situated between the Danube and Tisza rivers.

To protect his southern flank for the struggle against the Avars, Charles first turned his attention to the Duchy of Bavaria, which lay between his territories in southern Germany and Italy. Although Bavaria had long enjoyed power in its own right, it owed nominal allegiance to the Frankish emperor, and its ruler, Duke Tassilo III, was a cousin of Charles. To preserve his independence, however, Tassilo had pursued a devious policy, courting the Lombards while they still ruled Italy and even making pacts with the Avars when it suited him.

Claiming his theoretical overlordship, Charles now accused the duke of treason, seized his lands and condemned him to death. The sentence was later commuted to confinement for life in a monastery. Charles then expanded Tassilo's dukedom to include Carinthia, which had been settled by Slavs, and incorporated it into his lands under the supervision of a count who was a royal appointee.

Now ready, Charles turned back to his

main purpose. In 796 the Frankish army forced its way into the Ring and destroyed the Avars. It took 15 wagons, each drawn by four oxen, to carry the khans' huge treasure of gold and silver back to the Frankish court.

Charlemagne's empire

Charles's victories created a vast empire: by the end of his 47-year reign, it covered an area of about 1 million km² (385,000 square miles) and was home to 15 million people. He ruled from the River Tiber in Italy to the North Sea, from the Pyrenees to the River Elbe. With all this as his domain, Charles had good reason to feel that he deserved coronation as successor to the Western Roman emperors of old.

The kingdom Charles inherited (768)

Full extent of Charlemagne's empire

● Royal residences and important cities

Fit for a king This exquisitely decorated sword is thought to have belonged to Charlemagne. It long formed part of the coronation insignia of the French kings.

In order to control this enormous realm effectively, he divided it into about 300 separate counties, each under the control of a count. As the emperor's representative, a count was responsible for enforcing law and order in his domain and providing conscripts for the imperial armies.

The feudal system

Charlemagne retained supreme authority in all political and military matters by sending royal envoys – usually in pairs, one being a secular official and the other a Church dignitary – to inspect and report back on the regions and the counts' actions. However, he could not prevent the counts, usually the most powerful magnates in the regions, from passing on their office as an inheritance to their sons. He knew the risks that such hereditary local power bases presented to central authority, and he tried to counter the threat by binding the office-holders to him by personal obligation. In return for confirming their rights to the lands they held in his name, he demanded an oath of loyalty and a commitment to provide knights and men at arms to serve in the imperial armies. In exchange, the counts were guaranteed royal protection if they were attacked. They passed on the use of some of the lands to their followers for similar services in return. In this way a feudal pyramid was created, with the emperor at its peak. Charlemagne relied on the support of the nobility, as they provided him with the major portion of his troops. In principle, every free man had to make himself available for military service, but as campaigning usually happened in spring and summer when able-bodied men were needed to work the land, allowance had to be made for economic circumstances. In practice, smallholders were allowed to band together in groups of four, with just one of them offered for military service.

The birth of the knight

Only the wealthiest nobles could afford to equip heavily armoured knights, who by Charlemagne's day were becoming the shock troops of his army. Technological innovations – including the adoption of bridles, high-backed war saddles and, above all, stirrups – had combined to make heavily armoured horsemen wielding lances an almost unstoppable force. The mere sight of a charging knight was terrible for any foe to behold. This was how the Franks appeared to the Lombards, who were no mean warriors themselves: 'The walls trembled under the weight of all the iron, and

Holy writings Ivory panels decorate the cover of the Lorsch Gospels (left). The central image shows Christ dispensing blessings with the scriptures open in his hand. Dated to about 810, the Gospels are named for Lorsch Abbey in central Germany, which was closely associated with the Carolingian court.

Illustrating God's word The four evangelists were popular subjects for Carolingian book illustrators, giving artists the chance to portray the human figure in an innovative way. The illustrations below are from the Lorsch Gospels.

the courage of the young and the wise counsel of the old fell away alike at the sight of so much metal.'

Administering the realm

Because Charlemagne needed the nobility on the battlefield, he involved them as much as possible in political activity. At annual imperial assemblies, no laws were passed without their consent. So the nobles became the emperor's partners in the transformation of everyday life. Charlemagne brought in a new gold currency alongside the old silver one, and the Carolingian silver penny became a universal medium of exchange. Weights and measures were largely standardised across the empire. Steps were taken to encourage education and found new schools, and the emperor even kept an eye on the day-to-day management of the huge royal demesne (or estates).

Charlemagne naturally entrusted the key positions at court to his most loyal supporters. Many of his top officials held positions with apparently menial titles but enjoyed direct contact with the ruler. Besides advising on affairs of state, the seneschal and the cup-bearer were responsible for ensuring that the king's table was supplied with food and drink, while the marshal looked after the horses and the stables. The count palatine supervised the courts

Portable protection This gilded-bronze reliquary purse was designed for the traveller; its owner would have placed holy relics inside for spiritual protection on a journey. Metal purses were relatively common in Carolingian times, replacing earlier fabric models. This one shows Mary carrying Jesus, flanked by Saints Peter and Paul.

in the territories held by noblemen as proxies for the king. The chamberlain supervised the royal treasury, while the chancellor oversaw the emperor's correspondence and the copying of documents. Unlike many of Charlemagne's other office-holders, his chancellors had to be literate and fluent in Latin, the language of trade and administration; most were therefore drawn from the clergy, the best-educated section of the population.

A family man

Life at Charlemagne's court was relaxed and pleasant. The ruler was never happier than when with his courtiers, his children (legitimate and illegitimate) and his many wives and lovers. Charlemagne married four times, had numerous mistresses, and is known to have fathered at least 18 children – to whom he was a tender and loving parent, making sure they received a good education. He was especially devoted to his eight daughters, rarely taking a meal except in their presence, and he found it hard to deprive himself of their company by giving them away as brides. So they all remained single, occupying themselves in amorous adventures at court under his benevolent paternal eye.

Life at court

When there were no military campaigns afoot, the courtiers hunted each autumn and swam in summer. Charlemagne himself was an excellent swimmer, and often more than a hundred people at a time would join him in the pool.

The courtiers were entertained at lengthy banquets by musicians playing lyres and zithers, and jesters and travelling players amused them. After dinner, poets might declaim on the beauty of the women of the court or set complicated riddles for the company to solve.

The arrival of foreign envoys bearing exotic gifts always provided excitement. The Byzantine emperor, the caliph of Baghdad, Spain's emirs and the Anglo-Saxon and Scandinavian kings all sent presents to Charlemagne. The first pipe organ to arrive in the West came as a gift from Byzantium, while the caliph sent an elephant that lived in Aachen for eight years. An African ruler is said to have given Charlemagne a lion.

Courtiers on the move

In the early years, Charlemagne's court moved constantly from one palatinate to the next, travelling like an army on the march, with their possessions following after them in horse-drawn wagons. The provisions to feed them came from the demesne lands – well-administered royal estates that regularly produced a surplus. Charlemagne's favourite resting-places included Herstal in the Maas Valley, where the Carolingian dynasty had its roots.

In the last years of his life, Charlemagne spent increasing amounts of time at Aachen, whose hot springs afforded him some relief from the rheumatism that plagued him. He turned the old Roman baths into a magnificent residence, with a throne room 53m (172ft) long and 18m (59ft) wide. Paintings decorated the walls, and an archive and the state treasury were accommodated in a flanking tower.

A covered passageway connected the Great Hall to a building thought to have served as a court room and to the Palatine Chapel – its octagonal structure imitated from a church in Ravenna – which still forms the centrepiece of Aachen Cathedral to this day. The chapel was the masterwork of its architect, Odo of Metz, who succeeded in erecting the first domed building to be built in Western Europe since Roman times, its roof soaring to 31m (100ft) high. The interior decoration matched the magnificence of the exterior. Charlemagne imported marble columns from Ravenna and Rome and had balustrades cast from solid bronze.

Throughout his life, Charlemagne saw himself as a patron of the arts and science. The Carolingian age witnessed an extraordinary flowering of the arts, such as manuscript illumination, ivory carving, and metalwork in gold and bronze. The ruler surrounded himself with scholars, poets and philosophers, taking pleasure

The gatehouse at Lorsch
The gatehouse or guesthall of the Benedictine abbey at Lorsch is the only building, apart from churches and chapels, to have survived from Charlemagne's day. Its facade is richly decorated with rounded arches, fluted pilasters, columns and patterned stonework.

in exchanging ideas with them and seeking their advice on ways of raising educational standards in his realm. Foremost among the schoolmen was Alcuin, from York in England, who became head of the palatine school at Charlemagne's court. Alcuin wrote numerous works on education, theology and philosophy and produced a revised Latin translation of the Bible.

Manuscripts from the monasteries

The Carolingian renaissance of learning owed much to the work of monks, who produced hand-written copies of the Bible and other works. The monks sat in rows in the scriptoria, which were often very cold, taking dictation from a reader.

In the margins, they might occasionally record a complaint about the cold, bad light or parchment that was too fibrous. The parchment they used was made from calfskin or sheepskin. For very important texts it might be dyed purple, with gold leaf lettering. A skilled copyist could complete about 30 pages a day.

Church bibles were decorated with beautiful miniature illustrations, sometimes signed by the artists. Experts today can identify the provenance of many monastic manuscripts from the style of the illuminations. The individual sheets of parchment were eventually gathered into book-sized codices, which were then sometimes bound in splendid covers of ivory or gold.

Monastic renaissance Monks in Charlemagne's time copied the classical authors as well as religious texts, thus preserving ancient astronomical and mathematical works, and even comedies by the Roman dramatist Terence. This 11th-century illustration is based on a Carolingian edition of 'The Universe', and shows the twelve months of the year and signs of the zodiac.

Educating the clergy

Thanks to the monks' efforts, the word of God was proclaimed right across Charlemagne's empire in a dignified form and in standard, accurate translations. Their manuscripts did much to answer the emperor's complaint, made in 789, that 'Many who wish to pray to God do so in the wrong way, because the books are full of errors'.

The emperor also sought to address the problem of ignorance by improving the educational standards of the clergy, many of whom spoke bad Latin and often barely understood the words they read out during Mass. In an effort to raise standards, Charlemagne, supported by Alcuin, decreed that schools should be established in every bishop's see and monastery to provide the next generation of priests with a solid grounding in reading, arithmetic and Latin, as well as in plainsong and the chanting of psalms. The schools were restricted to future clerics who had been taken into the Church's care at an early age.

Charlemagne's death

Charlemagne died on January 28, 814, at Aachen and was laid to rest in the Palatine Chapel. His passing after a reign of 46 years caused widespread sorrow. A monk in the monastery of Bobbio in Italy wrote: 'From sunrise to the shores of the western sea, sadness dwells in every breast... Franks, Romans and all believers are filled with misery and despair.'

The mourning turned out to be well justified, for the best years of Carolingian rule ended with Charlemagne's demise. The empire he had created had been held together largely by the force of his own personality, and under his successors it soon fell apart. Charlemagne's only surviving son, Louis the Pious, was a competent administrator who did his best to preserve the unity of the empire, but he entirely failed to control the rivalries of his own sons. Having originally crowned his eldest son Lothar as co-emperor, he

then had to cope with the frustrated ambitions of the younger two, Pepin and Louis the German. The situation deteriorated further when a fourth son, Charles, was born in 823, nine years into his reign. Louis's attempts at a settlement failed, and civil war broke out among the rival claimants.

Fraternal quarrels

The problem of the succession remained unresolved at Louis's death in 840, when the empire was split up into three parts. Louis's heirs soon found themselves fighting to preserve their inheritance, for by now Slavs, Muslims, Vikings and Magyars from the steppes were all pressing hard on the frontiers of Western Europe.

Exhausted by their own internal disputes, the successor kings were incapable of repelling the onslaught. Power devolved from the royal courts into the hands of local lords who could provide the protection their people needed. These feudal warriors gradually abandoned the pretence of paying homage to the Carolingian kings, whose last ruler, Charles the Fat, was deposed in 887.

In the next century, the Capetian dynasty would come to power in the West Frankish kingdom, while powerful Saxon dukes founded the Ottonian dynasty in the East Frankish lands. The unity of Western Europe was permanently broken, and the foundations of the future states of France and Germany laid down.

Defender of the faith
This manuscript illumination shows Charlemagne's son and heir, Louis the Pious, in his role as defender of the Christian faith. The picture was inserted in a collection of poems about the Cross that belonged to a 9th-century archbishop of Mainz.

The Vikings – terror from the north

In the 9th century Viking raiders, striking from the sea, spread fear and devastation across Europe. But these wild warriors were also daring explorers and skilled craftsmen.

Sea dragon This richly carved dragon's head decorated the top of a post that formed part of the grave goods buried with the Oseberg ship (opposite).

On a summer's day in 793, without any warning, fate dealt a blow to the monastery of Lindisfarne, off England's Northumbrian coast. Ships with dragon-headed prows suddenly appeared on the horizon: they were heading straight for the island which was famed across Christian Europe as a centre of piety and scholarship. When the boats landed, heavily armed warriors swarmed ashore, cutting down anyone in their path. They plundered the abbey of its precious church treasures and set the buildings alight. Hauling their booty, they hurried back to their ships and disappeared as fast as they had arrived.

Who were these pirates and why did they act in such a way? Contemporary chroniclers agonised over these questions. At a time when Christianity seemed to have triumphed across Europe, most agreed that the pagan 'sea wolves' from the north who committed such desecrations could only be a punishment sent by God.

The wanton destruction and naked aggression displayed by the raiders lent an apocalyptic tone to the pages of the monks who reported the acts, as though these seafaring warriors might somehow be harbingers of the end of the world.

Coming from Scandinavia, the raiders became known as Norsemen, or 'northerners'; their descendants, the Normans, would also take their name from the word. In eastern Europe, the Slavs called them Rus, thought to derive from a Finnish term for a Swede. As for the term 'Viking' itself, it started life as a verb: the Norsemen 'went viking', meaning they went raiding.

The first onslaught

The attack on Lindisfarne has traditionally been considered the start of the Viking age, although an attack on England's south coast was actually recorded in 787. Abruptly and unexpectedly, seafarers from lands that would later be identified as Norway, Denmark and Sweden set out on large-scale campaigns of robbery and war that took them into the rest of Europe and beyond. Groups living in Norway attacked the northwest coast of England and Scotland, travelling around the Shetland Isles and on to Ireland; their successors would go as far as Iceland, Greenland and even the North American coast. The Danes created havoc in eastern England and along the coast of mainland

Europe, reaching as far south as the Aquitaine region of France. Vikings from Sweden turned to the east, invading the Slav lands of Russia.

The temptation of plunder

Long before the Vikings were ever heard of, border raids were nothing unusual for the North Germanic peoples. Danish warriors were reported to have attacked Frankish territory as early as the 6th century. Growing trade relations between northern and western Europe, seen in an upsurge in demand for furs, gave the Norsemen a clear idea of the wealth of the places where they did business. Young men short of land to farm at home must have been easily tempted to search for booty in foreign countries.

In the early 9th century the Viking raids were restricted mainly to the coastal regions of northern Britain, Ireland, the Low Countries and France. In particular, they targeted the wealthy monasteries: at least 45 were attacked in England and Ireland between 810 and 850. As the century progressed, the raiders started to strike inland. In 842 they plundered the trading centre of Hamwic, near present-day Southampton. In 851 a force of 350 ships fell on Canterbury and London.

The attacks always followed a similar pattern: a surprise assault from the sea, followed by plundering then a quick withdrawal. Because of their small numbers, the attackers took care to avoid lengthy battles or sieges, disappearing over the horizon before their victims had time to call for armed help. All they left behind were corpses and the burned-out shells of buildings.

Some settlements were singled out for repeated visits. In 834 Danish Vikings attacked the wealthy trading centre of Dorestad on the Friesian coast, killing or capturing

its inhabitants and burning down part of the town. They returned in each of the next three years, perhaps intending to eliminate a rival port or else simply because the town provided easy pickings.

Over the course of time the Norsemen learned to take advantage of internal conflicts in the countries they raided. In Ireland and in England they forged treaties with local rulers eager to call on their services as mercenaries against rival kings. Even Lothar I, son of Louis the Pious, called on Viking support in his struggle against his rival brothers to win the succession to Charlemagne's empire.

The disunity that racked the Frankish kingdom after Louis's death in 840 proved particularly favourable to the raiders, preventing the Franks from coordinating their defences. Boat-borne warriors took advantage of the situation to penetrate far inland, plundering riverside towns including Rouen in 841 and Nantes in 843. In 845 they besieged Paris itself, only agreeing to leave on receipt of a huge payment of 7000 pounds of silver (3200kg). Even the Mediterranean was not safe. From 844 attacks were recorded in Andalusia, and in 859 Viking ships penetrated the Frankish kingdom from the south via the River Rhône.

Striking inland

The Vikings owed their success largely to the way they seamlessly combined land and sea

The Oseberg ship
One of very few Viking longboats to survive intact from the 9th century, the Oseberg ship was excavated in Norway in 1904. It was used as a burial ship and was found to contain the bodies of two women, probably a queen and her attendant.

operations, which at the time was a revolutionary method of waging war. They exploited the versatility of their ships to sail up rivers, turning up unexpectedly in inland areas that had never considered themselves vulnerable to boatborne attack.

Equipment for battle

Once they had beached their boats, the raiders would steal horses grazing in riverbank meadows to journey inland. Sometimes they would camp out on river islands, where they were usually safe from attack as their opponents could rarely muster enough boats to take on the invaders. They used their mobility to avoid engaging enemy forces, and they also gave a wide berth to fortified towns.

In hand-to-hand combat the Vikings used very much the same arms as their Frankish and Anglo-Saxon opponents. Germanic legends emphasise the profound relationship Norse warriors had with their weapon of choice – the double-edged sword. They particularly coveted swords from the Rhineland which had damascened blades – blades inlaid with other metals, often gold or silver, in decorative wave designs. Less wealthy fighters made do with long-handled battle axes, formidable weapons wielded with both hands and that were effective against helmets and armour. Throwing spears, lances with long, elegantly shaped heads, and bows and arrows also formed part of the Viking armoury. A short knife or dagger with a wooden or bone handle and a blade sharpened on one side completed their arms, but this was more often used as a tool than a weapon.

All the warriors carried round, leather-covered wooden shields that were painted in bright colours, with an iron boss in the centre. Vikings who could afford it wore expensive chain mail for body protection. Their iron helmets had a short protective nose-piece and sometimes a spectacle-shaped eye protector, but contrary to popular belief they never had horns or wings; these latter attributes were first dreamed up by 19th-century illustrators.

From raiders to settlers

From the mid 9th century on, the Vikings adopted new tactics, invading target areas in force and sometimes staying to settle the lands they conquered. The early Viking raids were conducted by groups of only a few hundred men, but as time went by different units started banding together into large bodies with many hundreds of ships. The pattern was set in 865, when a Danish Great Army landed in England, breaking over the country like a wave. Another part of the new strategy was that the armies wintered in

Face of a warrior This bearded man's head decorated a wooden cart that formed part of the Oseberg ship burial found near Oslo Fjord. The ornamental axehead (bottom) was uncovered in the grave of a 10th-century Danish nobleman. Viking art favoured elaborate patterns, often inspired by animal and plant motifs.

TIME WITNESS

The Vikings are coming!

Writing in the 860s, the Frankish monk Ermentarius of Noirmoutier described the Viking terror:

'The number of ships increase, and the hordes of Norsemen know no bounds... Everywhere Christians fall victim to massacres, fire and pillage... The Norsemen mow down everything that gets in their way, and nobody can stop them... Tours and Orléans have been devastated... Rouen has been attacked, plundered and burnt... Every town is under siege.'

In the Anglo-Saxon Chronicle, the account of the Viking raid on Lindisfarne clearly linked the attack with supernatural forces:

'In the year 793, ominous signs and omens were seen over the land of Northumbria... There were whirlwinds and strange lights; fiery dragons flew through the air... Shortly afterwards, the pagans mercilessly devastated God's church in Lindisfarne, plundering and murdering.'

Memorial stone
A gravestone from the Baltic island of Gotland shows the war god Odin mounted on Sleipnir, his eight-legged horse. Below him, sword-bearing warriors line the deck of a longship on its way to battle.

the lands they attacked, a move that naturally led on to permanent settlement. The invaders built fortified sites that often formed the nuclei of future towns; most of Ireland's largest cities, including Dublin, trace their origins to Viking foundations. The Great Army that invaded England extended its power over much of the east of the country. From this area, which became known as the Danelaw, they went on to attack the independent Anglo-Saxon kingdoms in the south and west.

Scourge of the Frankish lands

The onslaught on the Frankish lands reached a peak in the decade from 879. In 881 a Viking army attacked the Rhineland, sacking the cities of Cologne, Bonn, Aachen and Trier, among others. Charles the Fat, Charlemagne's successor as Holy Roman Emperor, paid the Vikings to leave, adopting a tactic that individual towns had long employed to ward off the threat of attack. The Vikings themselves were happy to accept protection money as an additional source of income. Another source was securing ransoms in exchange for wealthy hostages: one French abbot was handed back for the enormous sum of 685 pounds of gold (310kg) plus 3250 of silver (1475kg).

The raids did not go unopposed, but the Viking warriors were both bold and resourceful. In 866, Count Robert of Anjou managed to intercept a group of raiders near Angers in northern France. The Norsemen took shelter inside a church and, convinced that he had them trapped, the count sent for siege equipment and rashly took off his helmet and chain mail while waiting for it to arrive. Seizing their opportunity, the Vikings staged a sudden sortie, killing him and dragging his body back into the church. Left leaderless, the Frankish troops were helpless and the Vikings were able to escape back to their ships.

In time, the Franks learned ways of countering the Viking threat. Towns and abbeys were fortified, and bridges were provided with defences designed to prevent the Viking boats passing beneath. The raiders started at last to take heavy losses. The Franks allegedly killed 5000 Norsemen on one raid into what is now Belgium, and the raiders also suffered badly while failing to take Paris in the course of a long siege in 886. According to contemporary reports, the Franks used catapults to hurl spears at the attackers with such force that they sometimes skewered several warriors at once.

River raiders in Russia

From early on, Swedish Vikings penetrated European Russia, using the great rivers to travel as far south and east as the Black and Caspian seas. The Slavs inhabiting these lands were poorer and less urbanised than the peoples of the west, and the

Swedes found no towns or monasteries in these lands to provide easy plunder. Instead they exploited the natural resources of the region, in particular furs, which brought large profits. These Rus, as the Swedish settlers were known, set up trading posts along the rivers, sometimes taking over existing Slavic settlements but often creating new ones that quickly developed into sizeable towns, among them Novgorod. From these fortified burgs the Rus not only traded with the neighbouring tribes but also forced them to pay for protection.

In 860 a Viking fleet attacked Byzantium itself, but failed to take the great city. The Byzantine emperor was so impressed by their fighting qualities, however, that he employed Rus warriors as elite troops in the imperial guard. Rus merchants also developed trading relationships with the city. Even more significantly, Vikings from Novgorod, led by a chieftain named Oleg, captured Kiev in about 880, turning it into the nucleus of the first Russian state.

Master shipwrights and versatile vessels

The whole Viking expansion was only made possible because of their technological advances in shipbuilding. Their shipwrights drew on a northern tradition of boat-building that stretched

Thor's hammer Many people in the Viking age wore good-luck amulets representing Mjöllnir, the magical hammer of the storm god Thor. This 11th-century example from Sweden is made of silver decorated with gold inlay.

far back into the Bronze Age. They worked primarily with hatchets and axes – they had no saws. Using timber from freshly felled oaks, split radially into thin wedges, they took care to work with the grain of the wood, so the planks would not warp or shrink as they dried out.

To build a new boat, they started by preparing the keel, which was cut from a single trunk; the prow and stern reared up fore and aft following its line. The sides of the vessel were then built upwards from the keel in a succession of overlapping planks ('clinkers') that were clamped together by thousands of iron nails, inserted through holes drilled with augers. Afterwards, the inner ribs were inserted, and a heavy beam known as the keelson was attached horizontally across the centre of the vessel to hold the mast. The result was a boat that was light and flexible, well equipped to riding rough ocean waves. In addition to warships, they also built boats for shorter journeys or fishing, as well as large-bellied coastal vessels called knarrs that had plenty of cargo space.

The combination of sail and oar was the secret of the longship's success. The use of sails seems not to have been prevalent in northern Europe until the 6th or 7th centuries.

Baptismal font Christianity came late to the Viking world, and even after its adoption in the late 10th and 11th centuries pagan art styles continued to exert an influence. This 13th-century Varangian font from the Kremlin in Moscow is decorated with chiselled out runes.

The Viking ships were high-masted, harnessing the power of the winds to propel them on long ocean voyages, while the oars allowed rowers to manoeuvre the boats in shallow waters or up rivers.

The longships were near-perfect warships for the time. They were relatively light in weight, so could easily be dragged up onto beaches, and in an emergency they could be put back into the water very quickly; they could even be carried for short distances overland, an important factor on the rivers of Russia where portages were sometimes required. Their shallow draught enabled them to venture into inshore waters, and the oars made them manoeuvrable and prevented them from ever being becalmed.

Typical longships were 20–30m (65–100ft) long and 3–5m (10–16ft) wide. They normally carried a crew of 30 to 60 men, although the largest ships could accommodate up to 100. No distinction was made between seamen and warriors, for Vikings naturally performed both functions. Their leaders, the jarls, were not usually drawn from the hereditary aristocracy; instead they were self-made men who owed their position to their success as military commanders and the booty they had amassed.

The end of the Viking age

By the start of the 10th century the Vikings in western Europe found themselves confronted by tougher and better organised resistance than any they had encountered before.

In England, Alfred the Great had succeeded, from 878 on, in uniting the surviving Anglo-Saxon kingdoms against the invaders, in the process laying the foundations for a unified English monarchy. In the West Frankish kingdom, Viking attacks declined after 911, when Charles the Simple settled the Danish chieftain Rollo and his warriors in the area around Rouen, thereby creating the duchy of Normandy.

Yet the Norse threat was still far from over. Under Cnut, in the early 11th century, England was even to become part of a short-lived North Sea empire that also encompassed Norway and Denmark. And when the Anglo-Saxon kingdom finally fell to invaders in 1066, it was to Rollo's descendants, the Normans, who by now were firmly Christian, but were still as fearsome warriors as their Viking ancestors had ever been.

Life on the land A reconstructed longhouse suggests the conditions in which prosperous farming families lived in the agricultural regions of southern Scandinavia in the Viking age. Most people lived off the land, sharing their dwelling with their cattle, who occupied a separate byre at one end.

ASIA

Buddhism in China

From the fall of the Han dynasty in AD 220 to the nation's reunification under the Sui in 589, China endured political division and strife. The people turned to Buddhism for security, and art and culture flourished in the monasteries.

Warfare, uprisings, epidemics and famine drastically reduced the population of China after the collapse of the Han dynasty. The statistics are unreliable, but what census figures there are suggest that in AD 156 China had just under 11 million households sheltering some 56 million people; by AD 280, fewer than 2.5 million households remained with a population of 16 million.

The plummeting population was disastrous for the national economy and security of the kingdom. Early in the 4th century, mounted nomads of Tibetan, Turkish, Mongolian and Hunnish tribes, later known as the Five Barbarians, overran northern China. In 316 the remnants of the Jin dynasty, which had briefly reunited the empire in the years after 280, broke down under the onslaught. The remnants of the imperial family fled south with their followers, where they set up the so-called Eastern Jin kingdom with its capital at Jiankang (present-day Nanjing). The north endured centuries of chaotic non-Chinese rule, marked by widespread oppression, until the Turkic Toba managed to reunite all the northern lands from a base in Shanxi province, establishing the Northern Wei dynasty in 439.

Underground art One of the world's finest assemblages of Buddhist art lies in the Mogao caves outside the oasis town of Dunhuang in northwestern China, where paintings cover 45,000m² (485,000sq ft) of the walls. Just as extraordinary as the realistic images of Buddhas and saints (above) is the vivid depiction of a hunt (background picture, overleaf).

Redistributing the land

The Northern Wei rulers decided that radical measures were necessary to restore the economic health of their kingdom, which was weakened by centuries of warfare and misrule. Adopting traditional Chinese administrative structures, they resettled many thousands of people in parts of the country that had become depopulated, following a policy known as 'equal distribution of land'.

From 485 on, the Northern Wei state allocated an agricultural smallholding to every adult citizen under pensionable age, along with an additional plot for cultivating mulberry trees which were used to breed silk worms. A family of six with four slaves and 20 cattle could acquire 25 hectares (60 acres) of land, and the property was theirs to pass on to the next generation. The Toba undertook the measure for several good reasons: to prevent famine, to stop people emigrating to the south, and to increase the number of citizens paying taxes. They had limited success, however, as the taxes imposed were so heavy that many small-scale farmers found it easier to work for the great feudal landowners, just as their forebears had done for 300 years past.

The reforms were at least enlightened in that they did not discriminate against the native Chinese as earlier foreign rulers had done. At the end of the 5th century, the Toba took this even further when they brought in a Sinicisation policy, forcing their own people to adopt Chinese ways.

The largest carved Buddha in the Yungang caves near Datong in Shanxi province stands 17m (55ft) tall; the smallest figure measures just 2cm (less than 1in).

BACKGROUND

Civil servant examinations

The Sui emperors needed able civil servants in order to centralise power, organise their vast building projects and coordinate their military expeditions. To find them, they relied – like their imperial successors right up to the 20th century – on an exam system originally developed under the Han. This demanded of candidates a thorough knowledge of the Confucian classics.

By memorising the great sage's thoughts on society and the state, and honing their literary abilities in an officially approved way, successful examinees could open up lucrative career prospects. Different grades were given complimentary titles: a 'flowering talent' could expect a responsible administrative post, while an 'advanced scholar' might be destined to compile texts.

The exam system was not in fact as meritocratic as it might seem at first sight. Only the children of wealthy parents could afford the long course of studies involved, so the families of craftsmen or merchants were largely excluded. And nepotism meant that sons of high-ranking officials were often simply given the job.

Buried in style Figures made of clay, like this ox-drawn cart from the 6th century (right), became popular as grave goods, replacing human sacrifices that had been banned in China under the Han.

Civil servants had to wear Chinese dress, Toba family names were replaced by Chinese ones, only the Chinese language was spoken at court, and mixed marriages were encouraged.

In these challenging times, Buddhism implanted itself deeply into the nation's consciousness, gaining increasing numbers of followers in both the northern and southern parts of the country. By the year 500 Buddhism was already a millennium old and it was not new to China. Word of the religion had first reached the northern cities via overland trade routes from India and Central Asia as early as the 1st century AD, but it had made little impact outside the foreign merchant community. Among native Chinese, the Buddha's ideas appealed first to scholars intrigued by the very foreignness of some of his notions. The Buddhist concern with reincarnation, for instance, contrasted markedly with Confucian concerns with correct behaviour in this world, and the monastic ideal of celibacy contradicted the Chinese love of the family and children.

Buddhism and its opponents

From the start, Buddhism had much more in common with Daoism, China's other traditional faith. Like Daoists, Buddhists placed the search for immortality and for harmony with nature at the centre of life. The religion's foreign origin was not a problem at the court of the Toba emperors, who were not ethnic Chinese, and as the new faith established itself, upper-class families started using Buddhist monks as counsellors.

There was opposition to the new faith from Confucianists and committed Daoists, who both saw the Buddhists as rivals. Under their influence, in 446 one Northern Wei ruler banned Buddhism, ordering monks to be put to death. Luckily for them, he died just eight years later and the new ruler, Wecheng, made Buddhism the state religion, encouraging its spread with gifts of land and money. He appointed a monk named Tanyao as supreme administrator of all the Buddhist monasteries in the Northern Wei lands. Tanyao was responsible for guaranteeing the loyalty of his fellow monks.

Buddhist monasteries now spread rapidly throughout China, providing oases of peace and security in a troubled world. They became centres of the arts and sciences, notably mathematics, astronomy and medicine, which benefited from the introduction of Indian ideas. Monastic schools translated Indian texts into Chinese, breathing new life into literature. The monasteries also prospered economically, profiting from the security of their walled compounds to provide banking and money-lending services as well as organising auctions and lotteries.

Buddhism's influence on the arts can still be seen in the sandstone grottoes at Yungang, near the original Northern Wei capital in Shanxi province. Starting in 489, a workforce 10,000 strong carved ornate sanctuaries into the cliff face. Pilgrims came in their thousands to admire the 100,000 statues and reliefs that decorated the 50 or more shrines, most of them showing scenes from the life of the Buddha and Buddhist saints.

A centre of faith

In 493, the Northern Wei moved their capital south to Luoyang near the Huang He (Yellow River), where the original Wei dynasty had reigned some two centuries earlier. The move proved highly beneficial to Buddhism, and the city soon became the religion's main centre in all of eastern Asia. New recruits flocked to the faith, and by 518 the city's half a million or more inhabitants were served by 1300 temples and 500 monasteries.

Buddhism reached its peak under the regency of Empress Dowager Ling, who seized power in 515 in the name of her infant son. Among other projects, she ordered the building of the great Yongning Temple, whose bell tower was said to be the tallest structure in China, visible from 80km (50 miles) away. Ling's extravagances soon exhausted the imperial treasury. She was overthrown and killed in 528, and the temple she had created burned down in 534. In the same year, the Northern Wei dynasty itself collapsed, and northern China split once more into rival states.

The aristocratic south

Meanwhile, an aristocratic society developed in southern China, as nobles fleeing the chaos in the north came to dominate the Eastern Jin dynasty ruling from Jiankang. Seeing themselves as the natural heirs of the Han, they brought with them a class-ridden mentality in which family background was more important than talent or achievement. Despite their tightening grip on power, the stream of refugees was never-ending.

In the leisured and refined environment of the Eastern Jin court, Buddhist thought took a new direction. Its aristocratic southern proponents were attracted by the philosophical side of the faith, renouncing the things of this world for the life of the mind. Even senior civil servants came to value the contemplative seclusion of Buddhist monks over their own duties.

China reunited

In 581, a general called Yang Jian succeeded in reuniting all of northern China. He proclaimed himself the founder of a new dynasty, the Sui, taking the sovereign name of Wen. Seven years later he made his intentions clear in 300,000 propaganda leaflets that were distributed across the Eastern Jin lands These spelled out the alleged crimes of the ruling Jin dynasty. Wen then sent an army of half a million men down the Chang Jian (Yangtze), and by 589 all of China was reunited under his rule.

Wen was a ruthless but effective ruler. He set his 48 million subjects to work on the nation's infrastructure, using forced labour to lay roads, build palaces and extend China's Great Wall. He created the Grand Canal, a network of waterways 40m (130ft) wide that stretched from modern Beijing as far as Shanghai. He also had a gigantic storage complex erected near Luoyang so that rice shipped from the south could be distributed quickly around the northern provinces.

Wen's public works revived the failing Chinese economy and spread some prosperity, but it was achieved at a terrible human cost. Men and women alike were forced to work on pain of death, and many thousands died anyway. Eventually the effort proved more than the nation could bear. When Wen's successor, Yang, imposed compulsory military service in order to fight a disastrous war against the Korean kingdom of Koguryo, the Northern peasants rebelled. Li Yuan, one of the empire's military governors, then led a coup, forcing Yang to flee to Yangzhou near the coast, where he was murdered in a bath-house in 618. Taking the soverign name of Gaozu, Li Yuan then took power as founder of the great Tang dynasty.

A solemn pose
This statue from the time of the Sui dynasty is unusual in that it depicts the Buddha standing. It is thought to represent Amitabha, the saviour Buddha, often shown wearing a monk's robe.

The Sassanids of Persia

Taking power from the Parthians in AD 224, the kings of Persia's Sassanid dynasty created an empire to rival that of Cyrus the Great in classical times. Yet incessant warfare weakened the kingdom, which fell to the Arabs in 642.

Radiating splendour Intricate glass inlays surround an image of Khosrow I engraved on rock crystal at the bottom of this golden bowl. The king's pose, sitting with his legs spread, is typically Sassanid.

The year was 464 and the Sassanid king Firuz was in deep trouble. His immediate surroundings were regal enough: he was seated on soft cushions in a splendid tent where tea was served on an inlaid table. Yet despite the luxury, Firuz and his son Kavad had just been defeated by the fearsome White Huns, who had invaded Persia from the steppe lands to the northeast. Now the two were prisoners, trying to negotiate their release.

Firuz's attempts to buy the Huns off with money had failed, for his captors did not operate a cash economy and had no use for foreign coins. Only after much hard bargaining were they finally persuaded to accept a ransom paid in precious metals. Even then, Kavad had to remain a hostage until the ransom arrived. Firuz failed to learn from his humiliation, starting a fresh war against the White Huns two decades later. The campaign ended in 484 in a terrible defeat and Firuz's death. In the wake of this disaster the Sassanids were temporarily reduced to the status of vassals of the White Huns, forced to make yearly payments of tribute.

Companion of the stars

The White Hun invasions marked a low point in the fortunes of the mighty Sassanid dynasty, whose kings were earthly representatives of the gods: the king's formal title was 'King of Kings, Companion of the Stars, Brother of the Sun and of the Moon'. Although the kings claimed descent from the gods, in practice there was an elective element to the succession. A king could designate his heir, but his choice had to be confirmed by a council of leading noblemen. In general, only powerful rulers could impose their will over the succession.

In addition to the royal house itself, which took its name from its founder Sasan, six other families made up the highest echelon of Persian society. All had grown great thanks to feudal grants of land earned by holding important offices, mostly provincial governorships. Both land and office continued in the family after the holder's death – a situation that weakened the king's standing by creating rival power bases.

According to the Sassanians' own account, society below this topmost level divided into four separate estates. The highest was made up of priests of the Zoroastrian religion, including temple guardians, teachers and judges. Next came the warriors. The third estate comprised civil servants along with physicians, accountants, poets and astronomers. The fourth estate – and by far the largest – consisted of peasants and artisans. Although state propaganda made much of the peasants, who were promised lavish heavenly rewards in the Zoroastrian holy book, the Avesta, their lot on Earth was never easy, for they bore the brunt of the tax burden and also of the public work duties demanded by the king.

In the wake of Firuz's defeat, the peasants' situation became harder still, as they ended up bearing most of the tribute payments that the White Huns demanded. Poverty and famine brought the kingdom to the edge of internal collapse.

The Mazdakite revolt

Popular discontent found expression at this time in the Mazdakite movement. Its leader, a Zoroastrian priest called Mazdak, preached a form of primitive communism, demanding that property should be distributed equally across the entire population. Initially the new king,

Kavad I, was slow to act against the rebels, probably because he too distrusted the wealth of the great landowners, whose power had come to rival his own. The result was a wave of unrest that swept across Persia between 494 and 496, during which many aristocrats were killed.

Kavad's apparent complicity in the Mazdakite rebellion was, however, a dangerous strategy, for the uprising quickly threatened more than just the over-powerful nobles. It also targeted the privileges of the Zoroastrian priesthood, who controlled vast estates from temples that had accumulated great wealth.

Gentle carnivore This stucco piece of a lion at its ease once formed part of the decoration in a Sassanid royal palace.

The Zoroastrian faith

Persia's religion traced its origins back to the preachings of Zarathustra, the founder of Zoroastrianism in the 6th century BC. This viewed the world as a battleground between the forces of good and evil, represented by the supreme god Ahura-mazda and the evil Ahriman, the precursor of Satan in the Judaeo-Christian tradition.

All humans were free to follow one principle or the other, but if they chose to live their lives according to Ahriman's path of untruth they risked ending up suffering eternal damnation.

Fire was sacred to the Zoroastrians, representing Ahuramazda's purifying force. Priests called magi presided over fire altars in the temples. The priesthood was hierarchically structured and enormously influential; the king personally nominated its highest dignitary, the *mobadanmobed* ('priest of priests'). The magi were dangerous adversaries, and now they turned against Mazdak, hating him all the more as a renegade from their own ranks.

Unsettled times

The combined forces of the priesthood and aristocracy finally brought the Mazdakite disturbances under control, and temporarily toppled the king. Kavad was deposed and exiled to a fortress in Khuzistan, known as the 'Castle of the Forgotten'. After a couple of years, however, he escaped to the land of the White Huns, and there he forged an alliance with his former enemies, marrying their leader's daughter. With the Huns' support, he reclaimed the Persian throne in 499.

Once back on his throne, Kavad proved to be an energetic ruler. He restored order across the country and then sought to unite his divided realm by declaring war on Persia's old enemy – the Byzantine Empire. In 520 he proclaimed his son Khosrow as his successor, and when Kavad died in 531, during the course of the renewed hostilities against the Byzantines, the young man duly took power as Khosrow I.

Rich harvest Sassanian silver-smiths excelled at relief work and often partially gilded their wares. The bold relief decoration on this 6th-century silver wine jug from northern Iran shows prolific vines and a labourer harvesting grapes.

> ## EVERYDAY LIFE
>
> ### Marriages and marriage treaties
>
> Under Sassanian law women could be married off while they were still minors, although not against their will. Traditionally, they became part of their husband's family, breaking off all legal ties to their own parents, although this did not apply in cases where a couple wed of their own free will rather than as a result of a legal contract. Men were allowed to take several wives.
>
> Women could only conduct business if their marriage contract permitted it. The agreement also set out the amount of the dowry to be paid to their family and the provisions to be made for the widow and orphans in case of the husband's death. In Sassanian times a husband could even place his wife, together with her possessions, at another man's disposal for a specified period of time.

Khosrow ruled Persia for 48 years, until 579, and in this time Sassanid Persia reached a political and cultural peak. He crushed the last remnants of the Mazdakites, setting himself up as a champion of the orthodox Zoroastrian priesthood. To control the nobility, he curtailed the power of the highest officer of state, the Grand Vizir, and abolished the position of army commander in chief, instead dividing the empire into four military areas, each with its own leader. He also won the loyalty of the lesser nobles by turning those who served the state in the army or courts into salaried officials, exempting them from taxes and rewarding them with small land-holdings in return for their services rendered.

Khosrow's golden age

One of Khosrow's most important reforms was to shake up the tax system. The register on which tax assessments were based had grown cumbersome and out-of-date. Khosrow ordered a fresh census that counted such assets as date palms and olive trees as well as arable land. In place of payment in kind, he instituted cash settlements, providing the state with a regular income that enabled it to greatly expand its powers.

Khosrow's reign also saw an upsurge in economic activity. The empire's merchants dominated foreign trade in the Indian Ocean, in Central Asia and in southern Russia. The king furthered this development by building roads, caravan stations and bridges, by improving harbour facilities in the nation's ports, and by building fresh trading posts in distant outposts of the empire such as Oman and Yemen.

A taste for magnificence

To Persians of later ages, Khosrow would enter legend as Anushirvan – 'He of the Immortal Soul', the very model of a just king. Under his enlightened rule the kingdom flourished intellectually as well as politically, becoming a crossroads for the exchange of knowledge between East and West.

Literature blossomed in the form of poetry, folk tales and historical epics, which traced the nation's history all the way back to a mythical first ancestor called Gayomard, an Iranian Adam said to have had a body of metal. The king also encouraged medicine, art and education. When the Byzantine emperor Justinian closed down the celebrated Academy at Athens in 529 because of its pagan associations, Khosrow happily provided a sanctuary for the philosophers and scholars who had been displaced.

The king also embellished the Sassanid capital of Ctesiphon on the River Tigris in what is now Iraq. The city's most remarkable landmark was a palace whose central feature was the Taq-i Kisra or 'Arch of Khosrow'. This was an audience hall, opening onto a courtyard, with a vaulted roof rising 35m (115ft), making it one of the largest vaulted structures ever built.

Sassanid taste for great pomp and splendour, was expressed in elaborate stucco decorations, frescoes, mosaics and marble-clad walls. A huge silk carpet decorated the throne room of the Taq i-Kisra; embroidered in gold and precious stones to resemble a paradise garden, it won enduring literary fame as 'Khosrow's Spring'.

The court also became noted for its hunting bowls – impressive silver vessels with finely worked decorations that the king presented to dignitaries at festive occasions. Sassanian silver vessels were treasured as far afield as China and the central Ural region, where they even found their way into the tombs of local chieftains as prestige grave goods.

The expanding empire

Khosrow devoted much of his energy to foreign policy, seeking to expand his empire. In 540 he launched a fresh war against Byzantium that dragged on for 22 years, after which the Byzantine ruler, Justinian, finally agreed to buy peace with a substantial annual tribute. In the east, Khosrow forged an alliance with a new

Hilltop citadel According to legend, before ascending to the throne every Sassanid king journeyed to Tahkt-i Sulaiman (the 'Throne of Solomon'), an important ceremonial site in northwestern Iran, seen here from the air. There he worshipped at the fire altar, which lay in the middle of the larger complex of buildings, clustered at the side of a lake some 70m (230ft) deep.

power, the West Turks, combining with them to destroy the White Huns in about 560. Yet for all his talents as an administrator and military leader, Khosrow could not bring lasting security to the empire. In his later years war broke out again with Byzantium, and after his death in 579 the nation was shaken by internal conflict. His son and successor, Hormizd IV, was deposed in 590 (and soon after murdered) following a defeat by the Romans. His grandson was then proclaimed king as Khosrow II, but needed help – ironically, from Byzantium – to win his throne.

The dominating feature of the second Khosrow's reign was a renewed war against the Byzantines, marked by major reversals of fortune. At first Persian troops were victorious on an unprecedented

scale. In the first two decades of the 7th century, Khosrow's armies conquered the entire eastern Mediterranan shore, capping their achievement in 619 by occupying Egypt. For a brief moment the Sassanid realm rivalled the ancient Achaemenid empires of Cyrus and Darius, stretching from the Nile to the Indus River and from the Indian Ocean to the Black Sea.

Yet Khosrow's reign was to end in a tragedy of his own making. Even by the standards of the time he was a lavish ruler whose court became a byword for luxury. He built vast palaces at Dastagird and Kasr-e Shirin for his favourite wife, Shirin, an Armenian Christian, and was said to have a golden throne supported on ruby-encrusted legs. He was feted for his love of poetry, music, art and philosophy. The income that he needed to indulge his passions came from the taxes provided by his grandfather's reforms.

Khosrow presided over a glittering court whose fashions can still be glimpsed in Sassanian rock reliefs, paintings and embroidery. Female courtiers wore long tunics, some sleeveless and gathered in under the bust, others with long sleeves and a veil that was either fastened over the shoulder with a brooch or else drawn over the head. The queens dressed in long-sleeved tunics, girdled at the waist, made of flowing, transparent fabrics, presumably silk or fine linen. A light cloth or cloak fell from the shoulder down to the knee, and was held in place at the breast by a pin. A pearl or bead necklace was worn around the neck.

The Sassanid kings themselves favoured apron-like tunics, equipped with rings and straps to allow them to ride in comfort. Beneath they wore wide trousers, or else tight leggings fastened to a belt with straps and buttons. They donned a silver breastplate as a symbol of royalty.

Glory and disaster

Every Sassanid ruler had his own specially designed crown. Khosrow's was made of gold and decorated with pearls, rubies and

Zoroastrian monument Located at Naqsh-i Rustam, 7km (4 miles) from Persepolis, this limestone tower, which stands about 12m (40ft) tall, is thought to date from the time of Darius I. Archaeologists are still unsure whether it was built to serve as a tomb or a fire temple.

emeralds; at 91kg (200lb) it was far too heavy for the king to wear unaided, so it had to be suspended from the dome of his throne chamber by thin golden chains that were invisible to visitors. Royal audiences were conducted in accordance with a strict court etiquette designed to instil awe in all who took part in them. For general audiences and at mealtimes the ruler sat behind a veil, which was only drawn back for the lucky few granted a private hearing. Supplicants entering the royal presence had to fall to their knees and touch their face to the floor; when they rose, they were expected to cross their hands over their chests and proclaim: 'May you live for ever!' They could then cast their eyes on the king, whose glittering appearance recalled his legendary descent from the Sun god; even his beard was dusted with powdered gold.

The quasi-religious ceremonial surrounding the king had the effect of isolating him from all but a handful of trusted confidantes. In the circumstances, it was easy for a ruler to get out of touch with the realities of the world around him. Maybe some such factor contributed to the tragic debacle that marked the end of Khosrow's reign.

The Byzantine forces rallied under a new emperor, Heraclius, who set out to regain the lands that Khosrow had won. Heraclius launched a series of assaults deep into the Sassanian heartland, none of which was adequately countered. In 624 he invaded northern Persia, destroying the great Zoroastrian fire temple on the shores of Lake Urmia where Zarathustra himself was said to have preached. Three years later he swept into the Tigris Valley, threatening Ctesiphon itself and causing Khosrow ignominiously to flee.

An abrupt end

Now old and sick, Khosrow seemed paralysed by the turn of events. When he attempted to put the blame for the defeats on his generals, ordering the execution of his commander in chief, a palace faction rose in revolt. In 628 he was overthrown and killed, and his eldest son was set on the throne in his place.

In the ensuing peace, the Byzantines regained all the lands they had lost over the previous two decades. Yet the long wars had fatally sapped the strength of both powers. Neither was capable of countering the new threat that arose in the 630s when mounted Arab warriors, inspired by the prophet Muhammad, swept out of the desert intent on conquest. In 637 Islamic forces brushed aside a Sassanian army at al-Qadisiya on the western borders of Mesopotamia, going on to capture Ctesiphon itself. The last Sassanid ruler, Yazdegerd III, took refuge in Persia, but the Arabs followed him there, winning a decisive victory at Nehavand in 642. Yazdegerd again fled east with the Arabs at his heels. He was finally assassinated in Merv, near the border of Afghanistan, in 651, and the Zoroastrian Persia of the Sassanids died with him.

Much-travelled coins These silver coins were found in a tomb near Turfan in western China, providing evidence of trade relations between the Sassanid Empire and East Asia. They bear the image of Khosrow I's son Hormizd IV, who ruled Persia from 579 to 590.

Artistry in glass Spiral whorls decorate this Persian glass beaker (left), thought to date from the Sassanid era.

India's minor kingdoms battle for power

After the fall of the Guptas, rival states vied for supremacy across India. Although this made it a time of conflict and disruption, the period witnessed the creation of some of the subcontinent's greatest architectural monuments.

Sweet sounds This terracotta tile showing a musician playing a lute-like instrument was created for a Hindu temple towards the end of the 5th-century, as the Gupta era was coming to a close.

The years from 505 to 511 saw the downfall of the great Gupta kingdom of northern India, brought about by the incursions and depredations of the White Huns – horsemen from the steppes, distinguished from the other Hunnish peoples by their pale complexions and non-Mongoloid features. The last Gupta rulers were only able to hold onto their thrones by giving away royal lands to ambitious local nobles, seeking to bind them to the crown by feudal obligations. As the external threat grew, however, central authority weakened and these aristocratic vassals went their own way. In time, a new stratum of minor rulers evolved, and these regional kings maintained an effective balance of power among themselves, resolutely resisting any attempt to reunite their lands into a larger kingdom.

There was to be only one further serious attempt at empire-building in northern India before the establishment of the Delhi Sultanate in the 13th century. It had its roots in the small kingdom of the Vardhanas, whose capital lay at Thaneshwar, about 150km (100 miles) north of modern Delhi. In 606, a young

man called Harsha, no more than 16 years old, ascended the throne. He turned out to be unusually talented and politically far-sighted, briefly succeeding in reuniting much of the north under his control.

Harsha started his reign with a series of conquests, defeating the neighbouring states, which were quarrelling among themselves, and integrating them into his kingdom. In six years he won supremacy over much of northern India. The territory he ruled extended more than 3000km (2000 miles) from Bengal almost to the west coast. Its capital, Kanauj, lay in a central location about 400km (250 miles) southeast of Thaneshwar.

A people's ruler

To control the conquered lands, Harsha introduced a centralised administration that was as far as possible under his own personal control. He travelled constantly around his lands, talking to civil servants, inspecting local administrations and even functioning as a judge. His subjects thought him a wise, just and benevolent king who cared for the poor and supported them from his private purse.

Harsha also introduced new religious influences, actively encouraging Buddhism instead of the Hinduism that had dominated the Gupta period. India's secular ruling classes had traditionally been

Hindu monument to piety
The Bhuthanatha temple (below) is just one of the many impressive monuments created by the Chalukya dynasty to promote Hinduism and to adorn their capital of Badami on the Deccan Plateau.

Pilgrimages to the Ganges

Hinduism underwent significant change from the 7th century on, when scholars of the Vedas – the ancient Hindu scriptures – came to the conclusion that some underlying presence must unite the thousands of deities in the traditional pantheon. According to the new, monotheistically inclined doctrine, people seeking release from the eternal cycle of reincarnation needed to address their worship directly to this supreme unifying being. The bhakti movement arose in response, emphasising the importance of piety and humility and stressing the significance of pilgrimage as a form of worship. The River Ganges became a favourite destination for people hoping to speed their spiritual progress by immersing themselves in its sacred waters, in line with a scriptural injunction that those who did so would become one with God.

Devout bathers This detail from a Mamallapuram temple relief shows pilgrims bathing in the River Ganges, a practice that continues to this day (background image).

attracted to Buddhism, resenting the influence of the Brahmans, the powerful Hindu priestly caste. Harsha endowed innumerable Buddhist monasteries, more than 100 of which were in his capital of Kanauj alone.

A great deal of revenue also flowed into the university–monastery of Nalanda, an important Buddhist centre on the lower course of the River Ganges. Scholars came to Nalanda from all over East and Southeast Asia to study medicine, astronomy, mathematics and rhetoric; others came to read for themselves the Buddhist texts in their original language. The university offered places to an amazing 10,000 students, providing not just lectures but free accommodation and facilities for studying, and above all a unique library said to contain some nine million manuscripts.

Among the visitors to Nalanda was a Chinese monk called Xuanzang, who studied there for three years before setting off on a five-year voyage around Harsha's kingdom in search of Buddhist manuscripts to take back to China. Xuanzang later set down his impressions of the country in a work entitled 'Record of the Western Regions', which has become a priceless source of information on northern India at this time.

A citadel of medicine

Indian medicine was particularly advanced. The subcontinent's physicians had a comprehensive understanding of the workings of the human body and were even able to follow the development of a foetus in the mother's womb. Perhaps most remarkable of all, they had found a way of innoculating people against smallpox by exposing them to the cowpox virus through a small cut in the arm, a method that remained unknown to European doctors until the 18th century.

The end of Harsha

For all his successes, Harsha failed to establish his Vardhana dynasty on lasting foundations. The king never won control of the Indus Valley and India's west coast, and so his land remained cut off from the great trade routes linking the subcontinent with Persia and the Mediterranean. As a result, he could not pay for his generous social policies. The empty treasury may have been the trigger for the plot, engineered by army officers, that put an end to his reign and his life in 647. With his death, Vardhana rule in northern India collapsed and rival petty kingdoms – Xuanzang counted no fewer than 70 of them – once again vied for supremacy.

One dynasty that stood out was that of the Gurjara–Pratiharas, who led the fight against the Arab incursions that followed the birth of Islam in the 7th century. Mounted Muslim warriors swept into the subcontinent in 711, conquering the entire Indus Valley and establishing the twin kingdoms of Multan and Mansura in what is now Pakistan. They were prevented from pushing farther east into India itself by the Gurjara–Pratihara armies, which effectively held back the Muslim advance for almost three centuries. When their power was eventually broken by the Muslim conqueror Mahmud of Ghazni in the years after 1000, Hindu resistance was finally breached and all northern India opened up to Muslim rule.

Dynastic wars

In the course of the 7th century, India's political and cultural centre of gravity shifted to the south, where the Chalukya and Pallava dynasties engaged in a prolonged struggle for supremacy. From their fortified capital of Badami, the Chalukyas created a powerful kingdom in the central Deccan Plateau. The Pallava had their power base on the east coast in the region of modern Madras.

The Chalukyas held power for 200 years before they were eclipsed by the Rashtrakutas in about 760. Paradoxically, their downfall stemmed from a victorious campaign against the Indus Valley Arabs. Barred from expanding eastwards by the Gurjara–Pratihara armies, the Muslim forces instead probed south, down India's west coast. Chalukya forces managed to hold them off long enough for their Rashtrakuta allies to arrive, and together the joint Indian forces were able to stop the Islamic advance. The Rashtrakutas demanded independence in return for the assistance they had offered. The Chalukyas refused, and in the ensuing struggle the Rashtrakutas gradually got the upper hand, founding their own dynasty in about 760.

The temples of Ellora

The most important Hindu works of art in the whole huge Deccan Plateau were created at Ellora, the Rashtrakuta capital, which lay at the junction of two important trade routes about 250km (150 miles) northeast of present-day Mumbai. Here, in the mid 8th century, Indian architects chiselled a complete temple, 30m (100ft) deep, out of solid rock. They had to remove over 200,000 tonnes of stone to finish the work, which stood open to the sky. This method of building was popular at the time, because in spite of the huge costs involved, it still worked out cheaper than erecting free-standing buildings of a similar size. The Ellora complex became a cultural as well as a religious centre; singers, dancers and poets all performed there.

All the southern Indian rulers backed Hinduism, which adapted well to a land of many small kingdoms. The faith had no overall leader to impose a dominant orthodoxy; instead it offered a pantheon populated by thousands of gods. Often a particular god would be worshipped only in certain areas, or would be considered sacred to the local dynasty, helping to legitimise its rule.

The Ajanta cave paintings

At a time when Buddhism was on the rise in China, it was losing ground fast in its homeland of India, and by the mid 8th century its influence was much reduced. Hindus had absorbed Buddhist teachings, and even found a place for the Buddha

Animal pilgrims This detail from a carving in a temple at Mamallapuram, dating from about 600, shows elephants and other forest creatures making their way to the waters of the Ganges.

himself among their many gods. The religion only preserved its own identity in a few areas on the fringes of the subcontinent, notably in Sri Lanka and Tibet.

Buddhism's decline may explain why the unique Buddhist cave temples of Ajanta, about 50km (30 miles) north of Ellora, lay forgotten for centuries. Buddhist artists created the last of the fabulous wall paintings there in the Chalukya period, using a special technique to prepare the walls. First they applied a paste made of pulverised rock, clay or cow dung mixed with chaff and molasses as a foundation layer on the rock surface. Smoothing this mixture down while it was still moist, they then added a layer of distemper – fine lime plaster. Once this had dried, they applied the colours, which were prepared from various plant and mineral substances. Finally, the work was polished to create a glossy finish.

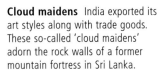

Cloud maidens India exported its art styles along with trade goods. These so-called 'cloud maidens' adorn the rock walls of a former mountain fortress in Sri Lanka.

The Pallava lands

Meanwhile, the eastern part of the subcontinent was ruled at the time by the Pallava dynasty, with its capital at Kanchipuram, about 70km (45 miles) southwest of Madras. Military victories over their neighbours and lucrative trade with Sri Lanka and East Asia enriched the ruling family and a small upper stratum of society. Most of their subjects led a simple life, cultivating palms and bananas in the river valleys and rice in the plains, where paddy fields yielded three harvests a year. People claimed that the land of the Pallavas was so fertile that all it took to feed a family of seven people was the space an elephant needed to lie down in.

The Pallava rulers used some of their wealth to commission imposing rock temples in Kanchipuram in honour of the Hindu gods Vishnu and Shiva. The Kailasanantha Temple, the oldest to survive, is also one of the most beautiful. The port city of Mamallapuram was also endowed with fine monuments – including temples and sculptures dedicated to various Buddhist divinities – all chiselled out of the rock. Mamallapuram's temples soon attracted pilgrims, who took Indian culture and trade goods back with them to Sri Lanka and Southeast Asia.

The rise of the Cholas

Pallava ascendancy was short-lived. The dynasty's decline was closely connected with the re-emergence of the Cholas, an old-established dynasty that had spent the previous 200 years as Pallava vassals. As the 9th century dawned, they started to show signs of insubordination. Vijayalaya Chola saved the town of Tanjore from a siege imposed by a minor warrior clan, then, as the Pallavas were distracted keeping other restive minor kings in check, he held onto the town for himself. Vijayalaya's audacity paid off, for in only three generations the Cholas managed to win vassals of their own, extending their territories and gradually consolidating their power. By the mid 10th century, the Pallavas had been reduced to vassal status, while the now mighty Chola dynasty was ready to launch southern India on a new phase of cultural and political resurgence.

TIME WITNESS

A pleasant kingdom

In his travel journal, 'Record of the Western Regions', the Chinese pilgrim Xuanzang left a glowing account of northern India under Harsha's rule:

'The ordinary people are generally light-hearted, but also genuine and honourable, honest in their dealings with money and thoughtful in legal matters. The Indians are never deceitful and disloyal towards others, but keep their word... Criminals and rebels are few and one rarely has to suffer from their actions.'

Of the king himself, Xuanzang had his to say:

'He was tireless, and the day was too short for him. He barely found time to sleep, for all his efforts and striving to do good works.'

Muhammad and the caliphs

Following a series of visions, Muhammad founded the new religion of Islam. Inspired by his message, Arab warriors burst out of the desert to carry the faith across large swathes of the world.

The Dome of the Rock
Built in Jerusalem between 685 and 691 on the orders of the Umayyad caliph Abd al-Malik, the mosque known as the Dome of the Rock is the oldest surviving example of Islamic architecture and one of the most beautiful.

In the Arab month of Ramadan in the year AD 610, a prosperous and trusted merchant named Muhammad had gone on retreat, as he did every year, to spend time in fasting and prayer in the desert outside Mecca, an oasis town midway down the Arabian peninsula. There, in the solitude of a remote cave, the archangel Gabriel appeared before him.

Place of worship This mosaic in the Umayyad Mosque in Damascus (above) shows a many-pillared public building backed by a garden. The mosque itself (background) started life as a Christian cathedral under the Byzantines, but was converted for Islamic worship in 705.

The Angel of the Lord held out a cloth that looked like brocade, and said, 'Read!'

'I cannot read', answered Muhammad.

Then the angel pressed the cloth hard on him so that he was afraid he would suffocate. 'Read!'

'I cannot read!'

Once again the archangel forced the cloth on Muhammad whereupon, in fear of death, he cried out, 'What is it I am supposed to read?' As he spoke, he realised that he could read: 'Read this, in the name of the Lord, who created mankind from a clot of blood. Read! Your Lord is the Most Bounteous who, with a pen, has taught humans things they did not know.'

The angel's injunctions, preserved in the 96th surah (chapter) of the Koran, Islam's holy book, represent the earliest of the prophet's revelations which he passed down to generations of Muslims. The word 'Koran' itself means 'reading' or 'recitation'. To begin with, Muhammad did not understand the meaning of the encounter, but then he heard a voice saying: 'Muhammad! I am Gabriel and you are the messenger of God!'

This summons by the archangel hit Muhammad like a thunderbolt. Totally overwhelmed, he reacted as so many prophets had before him: he was terribly afraid, doubting his own abilities and the reasons for his selection. But after a period of inner torment he accepted his vocation. He would indeed be a *rasul allah*, a messenger of the Lord.

Family bonds

Muhammad was 40 years old when he had his vision. Born in Mecca in around 570, he was orphaned early in life and was brought up in the household of an uncle, Abu Talib. A strong bond existed between the two, as the older man never ceased to support him, even in the difficult times that lay ahead.

The prophet's full name – Muhammad ibn Abdullah ibn Abd al Muttalib ibn Hashim ibn Abd Mauaf al Qureysh – clearly indicates the importance of family connections in the Arab world at the time: it means Muhammad son of Abdullah, son of Abd Al Muttalib, son of Hashim, son of Abd Mauaf al Qureysh. In his home town of Mecca, everyone knew that he belonged to the Hashim family of the Qureysh tribe. Being a member of the family carried a multitude of obligations, including a duty to protect and shelter fellow Qureyshis.

Tribal allegiance also tended to dictate how a person earned his living, so it was natural enough that Muhammad should become a merchant, following the tradition of his clan. Mecca was a significant mercantile centre at the time, owing its importance to its position on the caravan routes leading from southern Arabia to the great cities of Syria and Babylonia to the north. Its importance was boosted by the fact that it also attracted pilgrims, for people came from far and wide to worship at a shrine in the city's central square known as the Kaaba – this box-like structure contained a black meteorite that was held sacred and dedicated to local pagan deities. The Qureysh tribe were particularly active in long-distance trade and had business connections all the way from southwest Arabia to Syria.

When he was 25, Muhammad married a wealthy widow called Khadija, some years older than he was, who conducted her own business affairs as far away as Syria. The couple remained close until Khadija's death in 619; Muhammad took no other wives as long as she was alive, although local custom would have approved if he had. The couple had two sons who died in infancy and four daughters. Khadija immediately accepted Muhammad's religious vocation and had a considerable hand in his success, as she used her wealth to defend him against the increasing hostility of his own tribe.

A hostile reception

With great enthusiasm, Muhammad threw himself into his vocation as a messenger of God, publicly recounting his visions to the citizens of Mecca. He vehemently opposed the pantheism of the pagan Arab tradition and condemned the idea that the acquisiton of wealth was the most important goal in life.

His fellow-tribesmen at first had difficulty deciding how to react to his sermons. A few people viewed him as a wonder-worker with super-natural powers; others considered him a seer or a poet, this last because of the lofty style in which his revelations were expressed. The general reaction, however, was hostile – and not surprisingly so, as the monotheism that Muhammad preached threatened the foundations of Arab society at the time.

Paganism was deeply embedded in the Arab tribal structure, with each tribe taking its identity partly from the worship of its own gods, along with heroic legends of clan founders. Muhammad's own tribe, the Qureysh, venerated three goddesses: al-Lat, who was revered by shepherds and caravan leaders; al-Manat, who ruled over fate; and al-Uzza, worshipped in trees and sacrificial animals. The trio were regarded as daughters of Hubal, the supreme god of Mecca, whose principal shrine was the Ksaba. By Muhammad's time, this deity was already being addressed as al-Ilah, meaning Lord or God – the root of the name 'Allah' given to the single god of Islamic faith.

It was not just Muhammad's rejection of the tribe's gods that attracted criticism. He also offended tribal leaders by criti-cising the mercantile activities in which they excelled, along with the obsession with profit. The Qureysh were not just proud of their trading skills but also of the tact and diplomacy that went with them, considered necessary to smooth business negotiations.

Messenger of God This Islamic miniature shows Muhammad, with the flame of inspiration, riding al-Borak, the mythical horse given to him by the archangel Gabriel to carry him to paradise. He is accompanied by the first three caliphs.

FRANKISH
KINGDOM

Cordoba

BLACK SEA

BYZANTINE EMPIRE

MEDITERRANEAN SEA

Kairouan

Damascus   Kerbela

Cairo

Kufa   Basra

Medina

Mecca

ARABIA

RED SEA

CASPIAN SEA

SASSANID PERSIA

Euphrates   Tigris

Samarkand

Kabul

INDIA

Indus

ARABIAN
SEA

■ Spread of Islam under Muhammad

■ Islamic empire of the Umayyad Caliphate

● Important cities and Islamic centres

This led to Muhammad being seen as a trouble-maker by the tribal authorities, a view compounded when he demanded that all families should pay the *zakat*, an obligatory 2.5 per cent tax on their excess wealth to support the poor. At first his demands were met by ridicule, then by open hostility, and finally by active persecution of his supporters.

The first followers

It was hardly surprising, then, that Muhammad's teachings enjoyed little support or understanding, and in the early years of his ministry he failed to win over the majority of even his own tribespeople to his cause. His first supporters were his family, in particular his wife Khadija and his cousin and future son-in-law Ali, the son of Abu Talib. Other early converts included Zaid, a freed slave who was a trusted companion, and a wealthy textile merchant named Abu Bakr.

In time, however, the prophet's following began to spread beyond his immediate circle. His message appealed particularly to younger sons, who faced the prospect of occupying subordinate positions in their own extended families.

The flight to Medina

Matters came to a head in 619 when Muhammad not only lost his most influential backer with the death of Abu Talib but also saw a fierce opponent rise to the leadership of his own clan. Worse still, the prophet's beloved wife Khadija died that year. He and his followers decided they had no choice but to leave Mecca and find a new home.

It took them three years to fufil their ambition. Their salvation came from the oasis town of Yathrib, 300km (200 miles) from Mecca, a community rent and divided by strife not just between the town's two main Arab tribes but also its sizeable Jewish community. Hearing Muhammad's message while on a pilgrimage to Mecca, the town's elders invited him there, hoping that he might be able to arbitrate between the warring parties. In return they promised to follow his teachings and to protect him as one of their own. So Muhammad and his followers went to Yathrib in 622. This event, known as the *hijra* or 'flight', marks the date from which all subsequent Arab years are

A desert retreat The Umayyad caliphs often spent the summer months with their families in desert castles such as this one at Qasr al-Kharana in Jordan, built in 710 by Caliph al-Walid. The apparent austerity is deceptive: the buildings were often luxurious within.

counted. Yathrib itself would later be renamed Medina, the 'city of the Prophet'.

Muhammad undertook his new role with energy. In 623 he issued a code of conduct, designed to apply to all the town's citizens, that set down rules governing such matters as marriage, family life, inheritance, alms-giving and slavery, and also abolished usury. This brought him into conflict with Medina's principal Jewish clans, which regarded his claims to speak as a divinely inspired prophet with scorn, not least when he insisted that all citizens of Medina should face Mecca when praying, not Jerusalem as Jewish tradition demanded. Muhammad reacted fiercely. Two of the Jewish clans were driven from the town, and in 627 the third, accused of abetting Medina's enemies, was ruthlessly eradicated, the men were put to the sword and the women and children sold into slavery. Smaller Jewish groups who accepted Muhammad's rule continued to live in the city, however, and were expressly incorporated into the *ummah*, or Islamic community.

Return to Mecca

From 625 to 630 a state of warfare existed between Mecca and Medina, marked by raids and attacks on caravans. Muhammad turned out to be a natural military leader, employing a traditional fighting tactic with great success: during an assault, individual groups of fighters would move off in different directions then attack the enemy from several sides. The purpose of the raids was not just to win booty but to intimidate other tribes, forcing them to throw in their lot with Medina's Muslims.

By 630 the Medina Arabs finally gained the upper hand, and the prophet rode back into Mecca at the head of a victorious army. He cleansed the Kaaba of its pagan idols and dedicated it to Allah, the one true god, justifying his action with a revelation that the holy shrine was a gift from the Old Testament patriarch Abraham and his son Ishmael.

The five pillars of Islam

Muhammad did not have long to savour his victory. He died two years later in Medina, after a short illness, on June 8, 632. He left behind him a new faith that, then as now, obliged all believers to fulfil

five essential requirements – the five pillars of Islam. The first was to accept the *shahada*, the Islamic creed stating that 'There is no god but Allah, and Muhammad is his prophet'; new converts had to publicly pronounce this statement in front of witnesses before they could enter the Islamic community. The second was the obligation to pray five times a day at prescribed hours. A Muslim may utter the prayers wherever he or she happens to be, although certain ritual ablutions need to be performed first. Every prayer ends with the declaration *Allah akbar*, 'God is great', and with the salutation of peace, *Salam alaikum*, 'Peace be with you', addressed to bystanders. The

New motifs With its images of elephants, this dichromatic or two-coloured glazed tile hints at the exotic influences to which the Arabs were exposed during their expansion into Africa and the borders of India.

third pillar was the giving of alms; this obliged all Muslims to share their wealth with the poor. The fourth pillar required believers to keep holy the month of Ramadan, in which Muhammad received his first divine revelations; it was to be a time for reflection and penance, involving abstinence from eating, drinking, smoking and sexual relations between the hours of sunrise and sunset, although certain exceptions were made for invalids, travellers, pregnant women and nursing mothers. The final pillar was the *haj* or pilgrimage to Mecca, which every adult male Muslim was expected to make at least once in his life, providing his health, wealth, and the safety of the roads allowed.

Finding an heir

Muhammad's unexpected death in 632 left his followers with a dilemma. The Koran stated that no further prophet would appear after him, and he had made no clear provisions for a successor, yet a new religious and political leader had to be found. One obvious candidate was Muhammad's son-in-law Ali, whose wife Fatima was the prophet's only surviving child. But the elders of the community decided to pass over Ali's claims, choosing instead the prophet's old companion Abu Bakr, whom they appointed as *khalifa*, or successor. This title was adopted by later Arab leaders claiming to rule in direct line of descent from Muhammad, and has entered the English language as 'caliph'.

Abu Bakr had been a close friend of the prophet and had accompanied him to Medina at the time of the hijra. After the death of Khadija, Muhammad married Abu Bakr's daughter, Aisha, and she had become the favourite wife of his later years. Muhammad turned to Abu Bakr both to lead the pilgrimage to Mecca in the last year of his life and to serve as prayer-leader during his final illness.

Abu Bakr now initiated the collection and writing down of Muhammad's revelations, which had previously been passed on primarily by word of mouth. He used his authority to calm the rivalries that broke out between different sets of followers on the prophet's death, and when persuasion failed he used force to drive restive tribes back into the Islamic fold. In 633, the Ridda rebellion (*ridda* means a falling away from the faith) was smashed by Abu Bakr's general Khalid ibn al-Walid, known as the 'Sword of Allah'.

BACKGROUND

The holy Kaaba of Mecca

The Kaaba, Islam's holiest shrine, was a sacred site long before Muhammad was born. It stands in what is now the courtyard of the Mecca's Great Mosque. Muslims turn in its direction whenever they pray, and Muslim men are expected to make a pilgrimage there at least once in their lives. Non-Muslims are not allowed to approach the shrine.

The sanctuary is about 11m (36ft) high, with a flat roof, slightly inclined so that rainwater drains off to refresh the tombs of Hagar and Ishmail, wife and son of the biblical patriarch Abraham, which are said to lie beneath it. The four corners of the building are oriented with the points of the compass and a sacred black meteorite, said to have been given to Adam on his expulsion from Paradise, is embedded about 1.5m (5ft) up in its southern corner; pilgrims touch and kiss the shrine in the course of the *haj*. For most of the year the shrine is covered with an enormous black brocade cloth, decorated with verses from the Koran, but at times of pilgrimage a white cloth replaces the black one.

A single door, set about 2m (6ft 6in) above the ground and reached by a wooden ladder, gives access to the marble-floored interior. This is empty except for three columns supporting the roof and a number of gold and silver lamps hanging from the ceiling; the walls are covered with Koranic inscriptions.

A divine message
The gold embroidery on the black cloth covering the Kaaba displays verses from the Koran together with the statement: 'There is no god but Allah, and Muhammad is his prophet.'

The forward march begins

Abu Bakr survived Muhammad for just two years, dying in 634, and Umar ibn al-Khattab was elected caliph; he too had been a father-in-law and friend of the prophet. A strong personality, he considered it his duty to spread the new faith, if necessary by the sword, and so he became, after Muhammad himself, the true founder of the Islamic empire. In the 10 years of Umar's caliphate, Muslim armies conquered Byzantine Palestine, Syria and Egypt, as well as Mesopotamia and Persia, destroying the Sassanid Empire in the process. This wave of conquest – one of the most dramatic in world history – brought a multitude of people of different faiths under Muslim rule.

Within the conquered territories, separate categories of non-believers were treated in different ways. The choice for pagans was conversion to Islam or death. Jews and Christians, however, were regarded by Muslims as 'Peoples of the Book', and were granted freedom to practice their religions if they placed themselves under the protection of the state and paid a head tax, although they were subject to some dress restrictions and could not carry weapons or ride horses.

Umar was a wise ruler, leaving much of the administration of the conquered lands in local hands; in many cases he actually reduced the tax burden paid by his new subjects. He separated the Arab soldiers from the rest of the population by settling them in garrison towns; as soldiers of the faith, their principal concerns would be war and religion.

An early crisis

In 644 Umar was assassinated, stabbed by a Persian slave with a poisoned dagger. Following his death Ali was yet again passed over as caliph, this time in favour of Uthman, Muhammad's other son-in-law. Uthman belonged to the Umayyad clan of the Qureysh tribe – its wealthiest and most powerful branch, particularly well represented in Mecca's trading community.

Uthman had a reputation for piety, and the definitive version of the Koran was commissioned at this time. Under his rule, however, the Meccan establishment tightened its grip on the Islamic empire, arousing resentment among other sections of the Arab community. The caliph himself was accused of favouritism for showering governorships and other key appointments on his Umayyad relatives. Revolts and mutinies followed as the troops who had won the empire for Islam saw the rewards of their victories given away to wealthy non-combatants. Matters came to a head in 656 when a delegation from Egypt came to demand the resignation of the 80-year-old caliph. When Uthman refused, the tribesmen stormed his palace and cut him down.

The fourth caliph

With the death of Uthman, Ali's turn had finally come. He had the backing of a substantial group, the Shia Ali or party of Ali, the term from which the word 'Shiite' would later be derived. But Ali had also made enemies who raised the flag of resistance against him. Soon Muslims were fighting Muslims.

Ali also managed to offend the powerful Umayyad clan, who found a champion in Muawiya, the governor of Syria and Uthman's cousin. Muawiya commanded the strongest army in the empire and had considerable support across the Arab world. In order to avoid a civil war, Ali agreed to negotiate with his rival, thereby triggering the first great split within Islam. Some of his own followers rebelled in protest at his decision, winning the name of Kharijites ('seceders'). Ali's moral authority was badly shaken by their defection, and although he managed to

Graceful dancer Vivid frescoes including this dancer (above) decorate the walls and ceilings of the small castle of Qusair Amra in Jordan (background), built as a summer palace by Caliph al-Walid in about 700.

Coins of the caliph This gold dinar (right) bears the image of the Umayyad caliph Abd al-Malik, who ruled from 685 to 705.

Meeting-place for the faithful The mosque in Sana'a, capital of present-day Yemen, is one of the oldest in the world, dating back to the 7th and 8th centuries.

suppress their uprising, he fell victim soon after to a Kharijite assassin's dagger.

The Umayyad dynasty

Ali's murder in 661 marked the end of an era – that of what later Arab chroniclers would call the 'rightlyguided' caliphs or 'companions of the prophet'. Ali wassucceeded by his old opponent, the Umayyad Muawiya, whosecentre of power lay in Syria. The supporters of Ali were never reconciled to Muawiya's accession, and their dissatisfaction turned to outright fury in 680 when Ali's last surviving son Husain, a grandson of the prophet, was ambushed and killed by Umayyad forces near Karbala, in what is now Iraq, while on his way to join an anti-Umayyad revolt.

The deaths of Ali and Husain led to the greatest schism in Islam's history. Their followers, the Shiites, won the support of Muslims disturbed by the worldliness of the Umayyad regime, who expected their caliphs to be religious as well as secular leaders. The Shiites viewed sin, remorse, repentance and punishment as essential elements of the faith, and after Husain's death a cult of martyrdom also became embedded in their world view. The dead leader's

tomb at Karbala became the Shiites' main place of pilgrimage. The majority of the Islamic community backed the Umayyads, however, and they made up the Sunni or 'traditionalist' arm of the faith. The Sunnis were happier to accept the division of religion and politics, and were also much more emphatic than the Shiites in their insistence that a ruler must always be obeyed, even if he acted in a tyrannical manner. Under Muawiya's rule, Damascus replaced Medina as the capital of an increasingly wealthy and cosmopolitan Arab world, and the caliphs of the Umayyad line who came after him enjoyed an aristocratic lifestyle. Highly educated and proficient in music and poetry, they were generous patrons and benefactors of the arts.

Enthusiastic builders

Architecture flourished as a result of the Umayyad's mosque-building activities, which included the construction of the Dome of the Rock in Jerusalem. This was commissioned by Abd al-Malik, caliph from 685 until 705, as a counterbalance to the sacred sites of Mecca and Medina, whose influence he hoped to diminish.

The Umayyad rulers showed an equal enthusiasm for secular building. Damascus was often swept by epidemics, so for their own health's sake they built magnificent palaces on the desert's edge to which they would repair for tribal councils and major festivals and celebrations. In the prevailing atmosphere of assassination and insecurity, these complexes were designed as castles, complete with defensive towers. The rooms radiated off a central courtyard which, in the smaller palaces, was surrounded by roofed ambulatories.

The residences

were furnished with fine mosaics, wall paintings, stone reliefs and sculptures.

Life for the ruling Umayyads was luxurious and refined – a long way from the rugged simplicity of Islam's roots. The contrast created discontent – in particular among the Bedouin tribes – that was only kept in check by continued military success.

As long as the Muslim world continued to grow, surplus energy could always find an outlet channel in military campaigning. But the days of expansion came to an end after 714. By then the empire had reached its peak: it extended from the Indus Valley in modern-day Pakistan to the Pyrenees on the border of Spain and France; most of Spain fell to Islamic forces in the years after 711.

Internal political unrest in the empire eventually led to the Umayyads' downfall. In theory, all believers were equal in the eyes of Allah, but in practice, Muslims of Arab origin were regularly favoured over non-Arab converts who, in the wake of the great conquests, had come to greatly outnumber the Arabs. Discontent came to a head in 750, when a rebellion linking Muslim converts in eastern Persia with dissident factions in the Umayyad heartland brought the dynasty down. Eighty Umayyad princes were murdered with their families at a banquet; only one, Abd ar-Rahman, managed to escape to Spain, where he founded a rival caliphate. A new dynasty, the Abbasids, now came to power, inaugurating a new era in the world of Islam.

Mounted warrior This 6th-century miniature shows the legendary poet and warrior Anatara ibn Shadad al Absi, son of a Bedouin sheikh and an Ethiopian slavegirl, accompanied by his wife. The Arab tradition of mounted warfare predated Islam.

The glories of the Tang dynasty

The Chinese Empire reached its greatest extent in the 7th and 8th centuries, but internal strife eventually brought down the brilliant Tang civilisation.

Court beauty
The Tang ideal of feminine beauty, captured in this clay statuette, included a small mouth, an intricate coiffure and a voluptuous figure.

In 618 the last emperor of China's Sui dynasty directed his final order to his successor to the Dragon Throne: Li Yuan was to place the state crown with its 12 cords, the symbol of royal dignity, on his own head and raise the standard of the Son of Heaven. Three times Li Yuan made a show of resisting the order, then finally did as he was urged. This act completed the ceremonial preconditions for establishing his own rule, and the Tang dynasty formally took power from the Sui. Li Yuan and his successors were to rule the Middle Kingdom – the Chinese name for their land, which they saw as the centre of the world – until 907.

This carefully staged handover of power threw a cloak of legitimacy over a regime change that had already happened. A scion of an aristocratic clan of northern China, Li Yuan had risen to prominence as a top general in the service of the Sui. After China suffered defeat by the Korean kingdom of

Koguryo, civil war broke out and the last-but-one Sui emperor, Yangdi, fled south. Li Yuan seized the capital, Chang'an, and set a child from the Sui clan on the throne as a new emperor. At first he ruled in the boy's name, but after Yangdi was murdered the following year, the youngster was forced formally to hand over power. As the first Tang emperor, Li Yuan took the name Gaozu, 'Exalted Ancestor'.

Li Yuan had shown himself to be a skilful politician, but in fact the driving force who had propelled the Tang to power was one of his sons, Li Shimin, who had led the assault on Chang'an at the age of just 16. Nine years later, Li Shimin staged a family coup. He shot his elder brother, the crown prince, with an arrow and had a younger brother and ten nephews killed. He forced his father to abdicate, putting him under house arrest, and became emperor himself. As Emperor Taizong, 'Great Forefather', he ruled for 23 years, until his death in 649, and his reign saw China firmly ensconced as the world's greatest power.

An industrious emperor

Taizong had much to thank the Sui for, as their massive public works paved the way for the advances made in his reign. New canal and road systems eased traffic and communications; a fair system of land distribution ensured an effective agrarian economy and boosted taxes; state exams for prospective civil servants ensured plenty of qualified administrators.

With fiery enthusiasm, Taizong flung himself into the task of consolidating his empire, even papering his bedroom walls with administrative memoranda so that he could absorb useful facts as he dressed. His commitment paid off, and at his death he passed on a nation secure enough to enjoy an entire century of peace and stability. His work was continued by his son Li Zhi, who ruled as Emperor Gaozong, 'Exalted Forefather'. In a 34-year reign, he made additional reforms and expanded the power of the dynasty and empire.

Consolidating power

These first Tang emperors created a model centralised state that enabled them to override interference from the aristocratic clans. They set up a governing council whose 12 members answered directly to the emperor. Six of them, as office-holders by merit, had a purely advisory function. The other six were placed in pairs in charge of the three main governmental departments: the imperial secretariat, which issued the emperor's edicts; the imperial chancellery, which controlled access to the ruler, broadcast the imperial commands, received reports and advised the emperor at audiences and ceremonies; and the state chancellery which controlled day-to-day affairs and watched over the ministries for civil servants, finances, the armed forces, justice and public works.

The Tang dynasty also introduced a new institution, the censors' office, whose role was to check the activities of other departments and to investigate complaints from the public. The 30 censors were

Shifting perspectives Chinese painting sometimes combined different perspectives in a single picture. This detail from a landscape scroll includes a downhill view of a courtly procession with an uphill view of the mountainside in the background and a towering cliff in the foreground.

A talented official This detail from a silk scroll painting known as *The Thirteen Emperors* (right) is attributed to Yan Liben, a high-ranking court official who won a reputation as an artist specialising in figure-painting. The extract here shows one of the emperors with female attendants. *The Thirteen Emperors* was Yan Liben's masterpiece, although only seven of the rulers depicted are thought to be his work.

responsible for political and moral standards and looked into allegations of corruption, fraud, or misappropriation of funds. It was easy to make enemies in such a job, and many ended their careers by being demoted – or even executed.

The central bureaucracy was based in the Imperial City – the name given to the government quarter in Chang'an (today's Xi'an, in Shaanxi province). It was here that the strings of power came together, controlling the 360 districts and sub-districts into which the nation was divided.

Alongside the civil service stood a parallel military hierarchy working through 53 regional headquarters. The military commanding officers took precedence over the civilian administrators in their designated areas. This military power base would later cause major problems for the Tang, eventually bringing about the dynasty's downfall.

Careers for the well-connected

There was a constant need for educated staff to run the complex administrative system with its nine separate ranks of civil servants. Two institutes of higher education, in Chang'an and Luoyang, trained the cream of the crop. Students enrolled between the ages of 14 and 19 in one of six different faculties, depending on their social origins. Three faculties trained the sons of the privileged classes in literature, philosophy and the Confucian classics; the other three, for middle-class students, concentrated more on practical disciplines such as mathematics. As the sons of the wealthy increasingly sought civil-service careers, more and more candidates put themselves forward for places in the colleges. Many civil servants, however, by-passed the system altogether, instead relying on family connections to get them jobs.

The Tang education system required standard texts and exam papers, so Taizong

Metal mirror Lacking glass, the Chinese used metal plates as mirrors. They favoured bronze alloys with a high content of tin, lead and, especially, silver. This bronze example from the 9th century has a decorated back.

BACKGROUND

Crowning glories – hair styles and make-up

Women's hair has rarely been teased, trained and tugged into such elaborate and outlandish shapes as it was in Tang times. Court beauties might choose to wear their hair combed up into a horn, or in two carefully shaped knots rising above the forehead, or trained in two large loops over their ears.

Other popular styles included egg-shaped buns arranged over the hairline; 'knife blades', which consisted of ridges of hair lined with sideburns hanging in long points; and 'bee's wings', created by plaiting the hair into twin ponytails rising up from the top of the head that were then let down and arranged in loops.

Those not blessed by nature with luxuriant tresses to indulge such exuberant flights of fancy relied instead on artificial hairpieces. Ribbons, brooches and pins were used to secure 'hair clouds' that required long and intricate arrangement. Kingfisher feathers, prized for their metallic, greenish-blue hue, were specially imported from Vietnam to crown these masterpieces of artifice.

To avoid disturbing their hairstyles, court ladies put aside soft feather cushions in favour of hard ceramic neck supports to serve as head rests.

Cosmetics came second only to coiffure in preparing a face to

meet the world. Face powder made of ground lead or tin and rouge produced from plant substances provided a base.

An aspiring beauty might then paint her mouth cherry-red in a heart-shaped bow and highlight her plucked eyebrows in bluish-black willow charcoal above the narrow, almond-shaped eyes demanded by fashion. Black beauty spots positioned at the corner of the mouth provided the final touch.

Girls of noble family were taught beauty techniques from an early age, for long practice was considered essential if they were to compete with fashionable court rivals in later life.

commissioned a fresh edition of the Confucian classics. In 653 the *Wujing Zhengyi*, or 'Correct Interpretation of the Five Classics', became compulsory course material for all civil-service exams.

Graduates were expected to apply the maxims of the Confucian canon in their subsequent careers. Over time, the standardised curriculum produced a homogenous group of administrators sharing the same fundamental attitudes and ways of thinking – a development that helped to blur the distinctions between different social classes.

Crime and punishment

China's oldest collection of laws to have survived intact was created during the Tang dynasty between 624 and 653. The Tang Codex contained more than 500 articles designed to form a complete code of criminal justice. It defined offences – such as acts against a person or property, trespass, or violations of marriage laws – and set penalties to deter perpetrators. The punishments it prescribed ranged from beatings with a reed or bamboo cane, to forced labour or banishment, to death by strangulation or beheading.

The severity of the sentence depended in part on the class status of the crime's perpetrator and victim. At one end of the scale, servants who abused their masters were treated very harshly; at the other, top-ranking civil servants and members of the imperial household stood entirely above the law. Judgment was in the hands of district or sub-district officials, who also served as magistrates, prosecutors and defence counsels. In cases of doubt they were encouraged to lighten the punishment rather than exonerate the accused.

The farmer's lot

Agriculture played a vital part in the economic prosperity of the Tang era. Farming families worked land allocated to them by the state and in return paid taxes in the form of grain, raw silk or hemp cloth. In addition, they were required to give 20 days' free labour each year on public works. They were also expected to supply much of the manpower for the imperial armies.

In the year 636 there were 633 separate local military units on call, and men from the ages of 20 to 60 were liable for service in them. Detachments consisted of either 800, 1000 or 1200 men. The troops had to provide their own supplies, but were at least spared from paying taxes while on active duty. Conscripts, however, needed to return to their farms at regular intervals to bring in the harvest, so the army also recruited a nucleus of full-time professionals drawn from the ranks of the old military aristocracy, supported by mercenaries.

The road to empire

The first Tang emperors embarked on a series of military conquests. A first assault on the East Turks in 630 won parts of Mongolia for China, and this initial victory was soon followed by other offensives striking deep into the heart of Central Asia. In 648, the resistance of the Western Turks was overcome, giving Taizong control of all the oasis kingdoms of the Tarim Basin and putting the famous Silk Road almost entirely in Chinese hands.

Tang forces subsequently ranged far to the west, crossing deserts and mountains, to extend Chinese rule briefly into what are now Uzbekistan and Afghanistan. Some units ranged farther still, probing into Pakistan and northern India and even reaching Kish, near Baghdad in modern Iraq. In 668, the kingdom of Koguryo was finally vanquished, bringing northern Korea under the control of the Tang emperors; Vietnam followed in 679.

Tomb rider This glazed statuette of a mounted soldier was found in a Tang dynasty tomb. The Tang era was a golden age for the arts in China, expressed not just in small-scale ceramic figures like this one, but also in monumental sculptures such as the Buddhist monuments decorating the caves of Longmen, near Luoyang in what is now Henan province (background).

China attained its greatest extent at this time. The marginal regions of its vast territory had administrative centres staffed by Tang officials who helped to spread the Chinese influence. Japanese, Arabs, Persians, even Byzantines were all in contact with the empire at this time, trading along the Central Asian trade routes, particularly the Silk Road, and in the port cities of the east coast.

Emergence of an empress

This great age of imperial expansion fell in the reign of the third emperor, Gaozong, by all accounts a weak and sickly ruler, who could take little of the credit for the successes of his reign. The power behind the throne was Wu Zhao, the ambitious daughter of a former wood merchant. The merchant had been ennobled, given the post of Minister for Public Works, and had married a girl of the Sui imperial line. Their daughter, Wu Zhao, entered Taizong's harem, where she attracted the attention of the emperor's son, becoming his concubine.

When the old emperor passed away, Wu Zhao, like the other harem widows, shaved her head and entered a Buddhist nunnery, but her lover, now the emperor, had not forgotten her. Within a year she was restored to the imperial harem, and soon dominated the weak-willed ruler. By a series of intrigues she supplanted the childless empress in his affections and, in 655, Gaozong formally elevated her to the position of first wife. Soon after she had her predecessor and another minor wife killed; other rivals were banished. At that point the

Huntsman on horseback The delicately engraved figure on this silver drinking goblet is shown hunting with the double-curved Turkic bow.

Filigree jewellery Two gilded pendants provide evidence of the refinement of the goldsmith's art in Tang times (right).

emperor suffered a stroke that left him temporarily paralysed, and Wu Zhao seized the opportunity to strengthen her position further. From then on she was the true ruler of China, and Gaozong's later feeble attempts to control her came to nothing. The empress's hold on power even survived Gaozong's death in 683. The couple's third son inherited the throne as Emperor Zhongzong, but after a few months his mother banished him to the south, replacing him with his younger brother, Ruizong, who ruled as his mother's puppet until 690.

The only daughter of heaven

In later centuries Wu Zhao was demonised by historians, who disliked the notion of a female ruler. She was indeed a despot who brooked no dissent. Suspecting the powerful Li clan from northwestern China of plotting against her, she launched a reign of terror in which hundreds of high-ranking civil servants and their relatives were killed. She forced one of her own sons, Zhanghuai, to commit suicide, and later in her life she had her grandson and heir to the throne, Yide, beaten to death.

However, such behaviour was little different from that of the male rulers who preceded her. There is evidence that Wu Zhao was a popular ruler, worshipped by many of her subjects, if not by the aristocratic clans whom she affronted. Politically acute and sensitive to the concerns of the people, in 674, under Emperor Gaozong, she introduced reforms to benefit farmers and lower civil servants by improving salaries, reducing taxes and prohibiting the building of costly ostentatious palaces. Ten years later, at the time of Ruizong's accession, she granted a general amnesty and declared a national holiday for troops on frontier duty.

Wu Zhao staged her greatest coup in 690, when she forced Ruizong to abdicate and took power in her own name as the founder of the short-lived Zhou dynasty. Taking the name of Wu Zetian, 'Striving for Heaven', she became the only woman ever to occupy China's imperial throne in her own right.

To secure her grip on power, the empress moved to Luoyang, 250km (170 miles) east of Chang'an, where the aristocratic families who were hostile to her had less influence. She selected her top officials and provincial governors from the ranks of the civil service, choosing people from non-aristocratic backgrounds who were loyal to her, with no military power base of their own. In so doing, she vastly increased the power of the bureaucracy, creating an apparatus of State power that was finally separate from the aristocracy.

Even so, Wu Zetian's hold on power was fragile at best. She alienated general support by surrounding herself with a narrow clique of favourites, and was even accused of sexual deviance for appointing her young lovers to high office. The last straw came in 705 when she pardoned two of her protégés who had been found guilty of serious misdemeanours. The noble Wei clan staged a palace coup, storming the empress's private quarters and murdering her hated favourites. Wu Zetian herself was allowed to take to her bed. Later in the same year she died peacefully in her sleep at the age of 82.

A stylish metropolis

Nominally restoring power to Ruizong, the hapless son Wu had deposed 21 years earlier, the Wei clan then set themselves up as the power behind the throne. A period of political infighting followed, ending when Wu Zetian's grandson, Minghuang, seized power in 712.

This emperor, who reigned under the name of Xuanzong or 'Profound Fore-father', ruled China until 756, presiding over the Tang's artistic golden age. Xuanzong was a patron of the arts,

a talented calligrapher, and a poet and musician. He moved the imperial capital back to Chang'an, a city built by the Sui emperors that stretched almost 10km (6 miles) from east to west and 8km (5 miles) north to south. Within its walls, 110 densely packed neighbourhoods were laid out around ruler-straight main avenues, each between 70 and 150m (230–500ft) wide. The city's main artery led directly

from the South Gate to the Imperial City, where the government and administrative quarters lay.

The emperor himself lived in the 'Palace of Great Clarity', built with the aid of forced labour from 634 on; to finance the building project, all civil servants were compelled to forgo a month's salary. The palace, whose outer walls were over 5km (3 miles) long, housed some 30 state chambers used for public audiences and receptions, as well as private residential quarters for the emperor and his wives.

Decapitated dignitaries Stone dignitaries provide a guard of honour for Emperor Gaozong along the sacred way leading to his burial site. The statues' heads may have been deliberately removed as a gesture of disrespect after the death of Empress Wu, his wife and imperial successor, who was also buried in the same complex.

Helping hands Avalokitesvara was the most popular of all the many boddhisatvas, or Buddhas-to-be. Full of compassion, he was often depicted with many arms to symbolise his wide-ranging powers. By the 10th century the figure had undergone a profound evolution in China, eventually entering the traditional pantheon as the revered goddess of mercy, Guanyin.

Tolerant and cosmopolitan

Up to 2 million inhabitants lived in the city of Chang'an – along with Byzantium, it was the world's largest conurbation of the time. Merchants and diplomatic delegations from much of the Eurasian world gathered in its streets and courts, bringing with them not just foreign goods and fashions but also new religious ideas, all of which were hospitably received in the cosmopolitan atmosphere of the capital.

The Tang ruling classes showed off their wealth in luxurious lifestyles, indulging a taste for the exotic and a fashion for ostentatious display. Aristocrats lived in huge mansions with living and reception areas partitioned by screens inlaid in gold and silver; the floors were covered with felt carpets to muffle the sound of footsteps. Courtiers and concubines reclined on couches upholstered with silk mats and cushions, and in cold winter months they enjoyed a warm night's sleep in beds shrouded by gold-embroidered curtains. In summer, they often slept on reed or bamboo mats to the sound of bead curtains rustling in open windows. Chests and cupboards decorated with gold, silver, mother-of-pearl, ivory and semi-precious stones guarded clothes made of heavy brocade – eunuch craftsmen in the palace workshops created the finest brocade of all for the emperor and imperial court ladies. Courtiers perfumed their clothes with incense kept in silver-filigree containers, or hung them on a frame near a slow-burning fire to absorb the scent of aromatic woods.

The good life at court

Woodsmoke and incense also mingled at court banquets where guests were served ice-cooled melons, pomegranates, walnuts, figs, almonds and such exotic fare as the feet and humps of camels on platters of agate, glass, rhinoceros horn, bronze, silver and gold. Wines made of bamboo leaves as well as grapes were served from jugs shaped to resemble the leather bottles of Central Asia's mounted nomads. Guests were also sometimes offered cow's milk, an unfamiliar curiosity for the Chinese and not to everyone's taste.

The exquisite workmanship of the dining vessels demonstrated the skills of the nation's gold and silversmiths, who introduced novel hammering and engraving techniques borrowed from Persian craftsmen at this time. If the emperor himself was present, servants would be on hand in summer to cool his brow with large fans made of peacock feathers. At open-air entertainments in winter, when the court sometimes repaired to a nearby spa famous for its hot springs, courtiers huddled under sable furs provided to protect them from the cold.

Guests at banquets were entertained by dancers and musicians of both sexes; Emperor Xuanzong employed no fewer than 30,000 of them, trained in four conservatoires devoted to dancing, singing, instrumental performances and court music. This last was slow and stately, played by musicians squatting on their heels; female dancers would contort their bodies sinuously to its measured beat. A very different musical style, tracing its origins back to military roots, was also popular, accompanying sword dances in which the participants would whirl around courtyards and gardens under the gaze of breathless spectators.

Horses, pottery and porcelain

The favourite sport of the Tang aristocrats was polo, which had reached China from Iran. In 667, in order to preserve the game's exclusive pedigree, an imperial decree forbade artisans and merchants from riding horses. At the same time, there was a rise in interest in horse-breeding, with Mongolian and Tibetan ponies, Kirghiz steeds and pure-bred Arab stallions all providing bloodstock. By the mid 7th century, the imperial house was said to own more than 700,000 horses, stabled in large stud farms in the present-day provinces of Gansu and Shanxi.

The equine cult also had a significant effect on art, for Chinese nobles, like their 18th-century English equivalents, liked to have mementoes of their favourite animals. Images of thoroughbreds found their way into paintings, clay sculptures and even stone reliefs in imperial tombs.

Clay sculptures were particularly popular at this time, although few have survived. Sometimes the sculptors simply coated their works with a layer of white lime and then painted them, but glazing was more common – at first in monochrome but from the late 7th century on in three colours, usually amber, green and transparent white. The so-called *sancai* (three-tone) effect was created by firing two or more metal oxides, such as copper or cobalt, in a lead glaze at a low temperature to provide a variety of different hues.

Tang potters drew on the accumulated experience of thousands of years of making ceramics to create the first porcelain. The transition from stoneware, fired at very high temperatures, to true porcelain – defined in the West by its translucence and in China by the ringing sound it makes when struck – happened gradually from Sui dynasty times on. The fine white pottery was used to make tableware that rapidly became popular not just in court circles but also in town markets. Zhejiang province, south of the Yangtze Delta, was the centre of porcelain production, along with Henan. One contemporary poet described the ware as 'whiter than frost and snow' and sounding, when tapped, like 'jewellery made of precious stones'.

Of temples and tomes

Buddhism flourished under the Tang. The reign of the Empress Wu in particular witnessed a boom in temple-building. Chinese architects adopted the pagoda form from India and Central Asia, where the

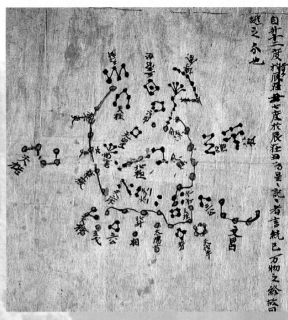

Star symbols This star chart (above) depicts the night sky seen from the northern hemisphere, using Jupiter as its point of reference. Tang dynasty scientists exchanged knowledge with their counterparts in India and Byzantium via the Silk Road and the trade centres along its route (background).

EVERYDAY LIFE

Tea becomes the national beverage

Tea had been brewed in southern China since the 3rd century AD, but the Tang fashion for health drinks made it popular. Northerners learned to drink it first for its medicinal properties and then as a stimulant to meditation before finally getting used to the idea of serving it simply for pleasure.

At first the leaves were imported from Southeast Asia, but a local industry soon developed in the southern provinces of Anhui, Zhejiang, Fujian and Sichuan.

In later Tang times, when the state was plagued by financial problems, tea was a way of raising revenues. In 793 the trade became a state monopoly, boosting taxes, but also setting off a surge in smuggling.

Seated in state This detail from the scroll known as *The Thirteen Emperors* shows one of the Tang rulers surrounded by his retinue. A Tang emperor is similarly depicted in all his pomp and circumstance in a cave at Dunhuang.

Stone warrior High-ranking Tang military officials were often buried with statuettes like this one (right), designed to commemorate their rank and status in life. Sometimes tombs also included an accompanying figure of a senior civil servant.

to translate 1300 texts from Sanskrit into Chinese. He also wrote an account of his travels, his *Record of the Western Regions*, which 900 years later inspired China's best-known comic novel, Wu Cheng'en's *Monkey: A Journey to the West*.

Buddhist teachings, along with the Daoist and Confucian classics, became widespread thanks to the invention of wood-block printing – another Tang innovation, partly inspired by craftsmen's experience in cutting seals. The oldest surviving printed book is a copy of *The Diamond Sutra*, a volume of Buddhist wisdom, dating to 868.

To produce a page of script, the printer first drew the relevant characters with a paintbrush on a sheet of paper – in use in China since the 1st century BC – that he glued face down on a woodblock. He then cut away the surrounding wood, leaving the symbols standing out in relief. Next he coated the characters with ink, then laid another sheet of paper over the top and pressed down evenly. The paper the printers used was made from plant fibres (bamboo, hemp and rice, among others) that were soaked in tubs then boiled in saltwater solutions to make them soft. The pulp was sieved off in thin layers and dried. Tang manufacturers used starch paste as a binding agent and coloured their products with dyes.

tower-like structures had originally been used to hold the bodies or relics of holy men. The most distinctive feature of the pagoda was that each storey was smaller than the one below, creating a tapering effect. At first the buildings were made of timber, but later bricks and stone were used. Some rose to 120m (390ft) changing the skyline of China's cities.

Chinese Buddhists kept contacts with India, the religion's homeland, and some intrepid monks journeyed there to study the Buddha's teachings. The most famous was of these Xuanzang, who spent 16 years travelling in search of Buddhist manuscripts. He returned to China in 645 and spent his remaining 21 years working with a team of scholars

A society under strain

For all its apparent prosperity, it was not long before the Tang state was bleeding to death from its pomp and splendour. The luxury-loving imperial court soaked up more and more of the nation's taxes at a time when the sources of income were threatening to dry up. The land distribution system was under strain as a growing population meant that hardly any free land was left.

Buddhist monasteries owned huge tracts thanks to donations from wealthy backers, but they paid no taxes. The nobility also largely managed to bypass paying taxes, controlling vast estates that grew by taking up the holdings of peasants who could no longer meet their tax demands. The bulk of the tax burden fell on the remaining free farmers, who increasingly abandoned their lands, either to work on the big estates or else to squat illegally to avoid being entered on the tax rolls.

The militia system, which had been largely staffed by peasants, was dissolved in 722 in favour of a professional army that had to be paid for from taxation. This further strengthened the influence of the military class and the provincial governors, who developed strong regional power bases and sometimes refused to pass on the revenue they collected to the capital.

Matters came to a head in 755, when General An Lu-shan, previously a favourite of Emperor Xuanzong, seized Luoyang. Chang'an itself fell the following year, and the emperor fled south. It was left to Xuanzong's son and heir-apparent to win back the capital with the aid of Tibetan auxiliaries and other mercenaries, after which he had himself proclaimed emperor under the name of Suzong. The uprising was finally smashed in 763, but marginal areas continued to break free from the empire, which was left weakened both politically and militarily. The glory days of the Tang had passed.

The twilight years

The dynasty held on for another 150 years, and under strong emperors it even enjoyed temporary revivals. Successive rulers tried to raise fresh revenues by creating monopolies in alcohol, tea and salt – this last eventually made up half the imperial income. The traditional forms of taxation were also reformed, with ground rent replacing the poll tax from 781 on.

From 843 to 845 a fanatically Daoist emperor launched an all-out assault on the Buddhist establishment, secularising the monasteries and confiscating their lands and treasures. The move forced 260,000 monks and nuns into secular life and added a further 150,000 slaves working the monastic estates to the tax registers. Although many of these measures were soon rescinded, Chinese Buddhism never fully recovered from the blow, and its decline was accompanied by the fading of the cosmopolitan, liberal culture of the Tang golden age.

In the later Tang years, the ruling establishment was riven by battles between the old aristocratic clans, the newly empowered middle classes who had risen to prominence in trade, and the civil service, who were themselves now sometimes large landowners. The imperial government was also less and less able to keep the restive military governors in check, not least because the bureaucrats who staffed the civil service were not prepared by their Confucian training and education to deal with violent confrontation. In addition, the civil servants were engaged in intrigues of their own. Court eunuchs, originally employed as harem guards, grew more influential in both the civil and military hierarchies, at times reducing even the emperors themselves to the role of pawns in their complex power struggles.

The final blow came in 874 when peasants, driven to desperation by a series of disastrous harvests, rose up under Huang Chao, a would-be state employee who had failed his civil-service exams. Up to 600,000 strong, the rebel army marauded across China without meeting any significant resistance and ended up occupying Chang'an itself. Even though the peasant uprising was eventually suppressed, the Tang court had lost virtually all its remaining power. The empire fell into the hands of rival warlords who eventually toppled the last of the Tang emperors in 907.

A safe repository The Buddhist manuscripts brought back from India by the pilgrim monk Xuanzang were stored in the Wild Goose Pagoda in Chang'an (modern Xi'an). The entire temple complex, containing almost 2000 rooms for about 300 monks, was built by Emperor Gaozong in honour of his mother.

The Silla kingdom of Korea

Established in 668, the Silla kingdom was the first state to unify and encompass all of Korea. Over the next 250 years, architecture and art flourished, while stonemasonry and bronze-casting reached a peak of artistry.

I n 676, Emperor Gaozong of China's Tang dynasty dispatched a great army to conquer the upstart Korean kingdom of Silla. China was at the height of its power, and he expected to have very little trouble in bringing this small state, a one-time ally, to heel.

Silla's ruler Munmu, realising that the very existence of his young kingdom was at risk, came up with an extraordinary strategy to ward off the attack. He ordered his subjects to make a model of a temple out of coloured silk, thereby calling down divine protection on their nation. He even hoped – vainly – that the silken sanctuary might persuade the Chinese to call off the invasion, seeing that the gods favoured the Sillan cause.

With or without divine aid, however, and against all expectations, Munmu's troops emerged victorious and pushed the Chinese army back beyond the River Taedong on the kingdom's northern border. A typhoon destroyed a Chinese fleet sent to support the troops, further convincing the people of Silla that the gods had indeed come to their aid.

In the wake of his great victory, Munmu was able to unify Korea for the first time in its history. For the previous 300 years, the peninsula had been divided among three separate kingdoms: Koguryo to the north, along the border with China; Paekche in the southwest; and Silla to the southeast, facing Japan. Silla had been the smallest and weakest of the three.

The Tang alliance

Silla owed its rise partly to an alliance forged by King Muyol earlier in the 7th century with the nation's future enemy, the Tang. By linking his country with this rising power in the great days of its expansion, Muyol gained great economic, cultural and military advantages.

Aiming for supremacy within Korea, in 660 Muyol used Chinese help to conquer neighbouring Paekche, a country with an ancient Buddhist tradition and a great artistic legacy. Just eight years later, Muyol's son Munmu successfully continued his father's grand design by subjecting Koguryo. It was in the wake of this victory that he was able to found Great Silla, the first unified Korean state, in 668.

Thereafter the relationship with China quickly soured. Emperor Gaozong had no

Fantasy guardians These two figures in the form of fabulous beings once guarded the entrance to the Punhwang-sa pagoda temple in Kyongju.

desire to see a strong power established on his northern border. Incensed when the Sillans moved to occupy Paekche and southern Koguryo in 670, he soon began to make demands for the restoration of the conquered territory. The result was the war of 676, which ended in disaster for the Tang and confirmed Silla's hold on the entire Korean peninsula.

A Buddhist monarchy

Although many ordinary Koreans continued to worship ancestral tribal gods, the kings of Silla were Buddhists and used Buddhist teachings to legitimise and stabilise their rule. Like their counterparts in China, they used the Buddhist concept of a just universal ruler to promote the view that the king was, in some fashion, an incarnation of the Buddha.

As Buddha's earthly counterpart, the king was expected to behave honestly and perform meritorious actions in the earthly sphere. The inhabitants of Silla firmly believed that their land was the true land of the Buddha and so a veritable Heaven on Earth, an attitude that boosted national self-confidence, not least because it provided Silla with a supernatural buttress against its enemies.

Temples and a national shrine

Munmu himself encouraged this belief by giving Buddhism enthusiastic state support. Three years after his victory over China he began construction of the Temple of the Four Kings of Heaven at the foot of Mount Nang outside his capital of Kyongju near Korea's east coast. Another temple in the environs of Kyongju, built in an exposed position on a

high plateau overlooking the sea, was specifically intended to protect Silla from invasion by the Japanese. The temple lived up to expectations: there was no Japanese assault until the 16th century.

Munmu died in 681 before the temple was completed, but his son, Shinmun, continued the work. Accordingly, the building was named the Kamunsa, the Temple of Filial Piety, when it was

An eye for detail This sword hilt was cast in bronze and then gilded. It is decorated with the head of a bird, perhaps an eagle or a phoenix.

EVERYDAY LIFE

Chinese astrological year-signs in Sillan tombs

Among the many cultural influences to reach Korea from China was the folk tradition of associating each year with one of 12 animals on a 12-year cycle, so that individuals born in a given year – the Year of the Horse, the Year of the Rat, etc – would inherit characteristics associated with that animal. The animals achieved symbolic status early on, and by the time Great Silla rose to power, the tomb-mounds of kings and nobles were sometimes surrounded by so-called 'protective stones' bearing their images, which were thought to protect the deceased from negative influences.

Among the many legends describing the origins of the year signs is a Buddhist version that ascribes the animals' elevation to the Buddha himself. The story tells how he called all the beasts to him shortly after the Creation, but only 12 species turned up. The reward for each one was to lend not just its name to a year in the cycle but also its particular characteristics and qualities, which were supposed to influence events in the course of the 12 months and also the fate of people born within their span.

The first year was assigned to the rat, followed in turn by the ox, the tiger, the hare, the dragon, the snake, the horse, the goat, the monkey, the cockerel, the dog and the pig. Each animal in this ancient zodiacal system also symbolised a fixed point in the sky.

An age of temple-building
The Silla kingdom left an impressive legacy of Buddhist temples. The best-known are probably the Pulguksa temple built around 751 outside Kyongju (background) and the cave sanctuary at Sokkuram nearby, with its great statue of the Buddha (below).

finished a year later. It became a national shrine dedicated to Korean unity and the well-being of the royal house. Within its portals the people of Silla could pray for the soul of the founder of their kingdom.

Following the example of their kings, the Sillan nobility also actively embraced Buddhism. Those who could afford to do so subsidised the building of temples, monasteries and pagodas, while the less wealthy contented themselves with commissioning statues and other cult objects. Largely thanks to their patronage, Great Silla reached a cultural peak in the middle of the 8th century, marked by the construction of further splendidly furnished state temples.

The Sokkuram shrine

One building stood out from the others as one of the most remarkable sacred buildings of the entire Buddhist world. This was the cave sanctuary of Sokkuram, created to the east of Kyongju near Mount Tohan on the orders of King Kyondok, who reigned from 742 to 785.

The inspiration for the building came from outside Korea, in the many cave temples dotted across East Asia. These reflected an abiding Buddhist fascination with mountains and caverns, which provided the remote solitude considered ideal for meditation and the quest for enlightenment.

Most of the Korean peninsula lacked natural caves, so Kyondok decided that an artificial grotto would have to be created. The task presented no great problem for Silla's architects, who had inherited a long tradition of working with stone, stretching back to the very earliest times. In the centre of the sanctuary at Sokkuram, an unknown sculptor fashioned a huge statue of the Buddha, 3.5m (11ft) tall, out of a single block of white granite. The work, which shows the Buddha seated in the lotus posture, his eyes closed in tranquil meditation, is considered a masterpiece of Buddhist art, radiating majesty and an omniscient calm.

The temple of Pulguksa ('Land of Joy'), was built nearby on the slopes of Mount Tohan at about the same time. The temple – which was largely destroyed by Japanese invaders in the 16th century but has recently been restored – seems to grow naturally out of its rocky mountain background. Its many stepped pagoda roofs are a prime attraction for visitors to Korea to this day.

Ancient traditions

Alongside the state religion of Buddhism, older traditions survived among the common people, including an ancestor cult and a belief in spirits and the shamans who claimed to be able to communicate with them. Nearly every home in the land contained a shrine dedicated to the spirits of the family's ancestors. In most Sillan villages there were enormous cairns that grew steadily as passers-by added stones to the top, seeking the favour of protective spirits. People also erected large wooden posts that were colourfully painted and adorned with terrifying faces; like totem poles, these were thought to be the homes of ancestral spirits who protected the local community from misfortune and disease. Many Sillans called on the powers of female shamans as healers. They sought to trap the evil spirits causing disease either in doll-like images of the sick person or in various kinds of artificial snare.

The shaman's power

Some shamanistic rituals were conducted in public for the good of the community as a whole, seeking perhaps to bring rain or a good harvest. The shamans apparently had royal backing, to judge from a mysterious, bottle-shaped stone tower set in the middle of Kyongju. For a long time the building was thought to be East Asia's oldest astronomical observatory, winning the name 'Star-Gazing Tower', and savants do seem to have studied the heavens from its roof in order to devise a calendar to establish the correct time for sowing and harvesting. Nowadays, however, most scholars think that its main purpose was ceremonial; priests may have conducted state-sanctioned rituals within its walls, the most important being sacrificial rites each spring and autumn.

Further evidence of the power and prestige of the shamans at this time comes in the form of splendid golden ceremonial crowns that have survived from the days immediately before the foundation of the Silla kingdom. The crowns probably represented stylised antlers, branches and feathers – typical shamanistic attributes that were no doubt connected with early Korean beliefs about the afterlife.

Following the Chinese model

After Munmu's victory over Tang China, amicable relations were soon restored between the two neighbouring countries. Silla distanced itself politically from its former mentor, but trade and cultural contacts remained unaffected. Many Koreans went to China to study classical and Buddhist literature or to learn about state administration – an important

Star-gazing tower Long considered to have been an astronomical observatory, Kyongju's Cheomseongdae or 'Star-Gazing Tower' is now thought to have served primarily as a cult temple.

advantage for Silla, as the nation's structure of government exactly followed the Chinese model.

Seeking to establish an absolute monarchy like that of China's own Sons of Heaven, the Sillan kings saw a competent and independent civil service as a useful counterweight to the political influence of the powerful nobility. With that in mind, they introduced an examination system along Chinese lines to select suitable candidates to staff the service. The exams, which were held once a year in front of a government-appointed committee, were open to all students who could read and write and had a good standard of general education.

Only about one in ten of those who took part were successful, but for these it opened up a route to a respected and potentially lucrative career. Wealth, status and good family connections continued to play an important part in the political scene, however, and it was often the sons of the nobility who obtained the highest positions in the administration and in government.

Friendly guardians This small wooden lion, known as a 'Korean dog', seems to be observing passersby through its large glass eyes. The figure probably once stood guard at a palace or temple door.

Easy living in Kyongju

For the first century of its existence, Great Silla enjoyed unusual political stability. The kings retained unchallenged authority and both they and Kyongju, their capital, prospered. The city was built on a fertile alluvial plain watered by three rivers and sheltered by a trio of mountain chains to the north that allowed it to take maximum advantage of the warm climate of the southern part of the country.

Seeking to rival the Tang metropolis of Chang'an, Munmu endowed the city with an array of splendid temples, palaces and pagodas that made it one of the finest cities of East Asia. A huge wall studded with 20 gates protected the inhabitants from external attack. Within the walls the city was built to a grid plan, with 25 streets running from north to south, crossing 20 streets oriented east to west. The royal palace sheltered behind a wall of its own in the heart of the city, on the bank of the southern-most of the three rivers. Known as the Moon Fortress, it formed a small town in its own right, made up of many different buildings.

Palace pleasure garden

In 674 Munmu laid out a pleasure garden stocked with rare animals and exotic plants and landscaped with hills and an artificial lake that covered 1.5 hectares (4 acres). Courtiers amused themselves by taking boat trips on the lake, admiring the wild geese and ducks that flocked there, and enjoying the peace and tranquillity of the islands set within its waters. Others preferred to contemplate the scene from pavilions built on jetties along the lake's west bank, where they drank tea, passed the time playing dice or board games, and enjoyed musical performances.

Golden crown Found in one of the Silla royal tombs, this elegantly decorated royal crown dates from the Three Kingdoms period immediately preceding Korea's unification in 668.

From time to time the king would hold huge banquets in the pavilions, at which he played host to foreign delegations.

In recent years archaeologists have excavated the gardens, unearthing some 15,000 everyday objects that provide ample evidence of the garden's popularity in Sillan times. The finds include numerous images of the Buddha and Buddhist saints, which were probably thrown into the lake as offerings.

Expert craftsmen

The golden age of the Silla Kingdom was a time of wonderful artistic creativity by its potters, goldsmiths and other craftsmen who fashioned some remarkable works of art. Bronze-casting in particular attained a high level of technical accomplishment, which is still evident in the giant Buddha sculptures made for the new temples.

To create these huge works of art, the metalworkers made use of the lost-wax technique. First they modelled the figure in clay, strengthened with iron wire to provide extra stability. Then they covered the clay model with a layer of wax about 3cm (1in) thick, incising the wax with delicate patterns, before coating the entire figure with a second layer of clay. The figure was heated and the layer of wax sandwiched in the middle of the clay layers melted away. Molten bronze was then poured through prepared channels into the space left behind.

Once the metal had cooled, the bronze-workers broke off the outer clay mould and extracted the inner clay nucleus before adding the finishing touches by hand. Countless sculptures of the Buddha were prepared in this way, each of them unique in its individual detail.

The Emille Bell

The technical accomplishments of the Silla metalworkers also included the casting of gigantic bronze bells, the largest of which, according to tradition, weighed an astonishing 330 tonnes. The so-called Emille Bell, which was cast in 775 and is now preserved in the Kyongju National Museum, is almost as monumental. Standing 3.75m (12ft) high, measuring 2.3m (7ft 6in) across and decorated with human figures and lotus flowers, it is still among the largest and most impressive bells in the world.

Kyongdok commissioned the Emille Bell in memory of his deceased father. A sad folk tale recalls the creation of the bell. Supposedly, when the first castings proved unsatisfactory, the king consulted soothsayers, who advised him to offer up sacrifices to the gods. Royal messengers were duly dispatched across the land to collect precious objects from his subjects to succour the great project. Most people handed over metal figurines, but one poor widow who owned nothing but the clothes on her back offered up her only child. The little girl was brought to the capital and, to the chanting of prayers, was thrown into the molten mass of bronze.

The story, which is no doubt fictional, may have been invented to explain the bell's name, which means 'mother'. Even today, Koreans still claim to hear in its booming the plaintive note of a young child calling for her mother.

The potters' art
Silla's sophisticated court circles provided a ready market for elegant luxury objects to decorate private homes. In the last phase of Silla rule, ceramics with a celadon glaze were in particular demand. This greyish-green, impermeable stoneware, fired at temperatures of 1200°C (2200°F), was uniquely elegant. Its special beauty lay in the nuances of colour found in each piece, for the exact tint could vary from a light bluish shade to a deep dark green.

The colour variation depended on the amount of oxygen piped into the furnace as a piece was fired, and on the iron content of the feldspar glaze, which was itself colourless. Wine jars, vases, cosmetic boxes and incense burners were all produced in a variety of shapes and, by the end of the Silla period, entire palaces were sometimes decorated with jade-green celadon tiles.

Great Silla's decline began in the 9th century when the discrepancy between the luxurious lifestyle of the upper classes and the poverty of the peasants led to serious social unrest. Many farmers were forced to leave the land and drifted into a life of banditry. The provincial nobility took advantage of the weakening of central authority to establish power bases of their own; one local lord was said to control a private army of 10,000 men.

Eventually, one of the rebel leaders declared himself king, forcing the last Silla ruler to abdicate in 935. He called his new kingdom New Koguryo or Koryo, a word that eventually entered the English language as Korea.

Temple bell This bronze bell from the Pulguksa Temple was commissioned by King Songdok in 771. The ornamental bands around the top and bottom are typically Korean in style. Large bells such as this could be heard for many miles around.

A golden age in Japan – the Nara period

The Nara period was named after Japan's first purpose-built capital city. It was a time in which Chinese and Korean influences created a cultural peak in Japan.

The Todaiji temple Nara's Great Temple was built in a very Japanese style that still accommodated foreign influence. A Brahman from India consecrated the giant bronze statue in the great hall, while musicians from Southeast Asia accompanied the ceremony.

For some time farmers on the Nara Plain, not far from the imperial residence at Asuka, had been watching odd goings-on. Men, whose dress clearly marked them out as scholars, had been taking measurements and noting down the results. From time to time, in deep discussion, they compared their conclusions. Eventually, they returned to the imperial court and consulted with officials. The men were geomancers, and they were checking whether the topographical conditions in the area were in harmony with the spirit world.

The Empress Gemmei – one of several women to rule Japan in the 7th and 8th centuries – needed their services because she had made a momentous decision. With China's example in mind, she had decided that her country – traditionally a nation of landed estates and villages – needed a central seat of government. She had decided to build a capital city.

In China's shadow

Asuka, where the emperors had resided until now, resembled a large village more than a city, but it mirrored the structure of Japanese society, which was divided into clans. Japanese tradition had previously dictated that a new palace had to be built whenever an emperor or empress died, for the Shinto religion regarded sickness and death as defiling. The only way for the heir to the throne to escape the taint of bodily corruption from his dead predecessor was to shun the dwelling, too.

With the adoption of Buddhism and Confucianism alongside the indigenous Shinto faith, such attitudes lost some of their force. Then again, the new Chinese form of administration that the emperors had recently adopted, complete with a centralised imperial bureaucracy, made the idea of moving the seat of government much more difficult.

So, in 710, the empress decided to create a new, permanent capital on the Nara Plain. The new city had much in common with Chinese models. Over the preceding centuries, numerous Japanese delegations, sometimes up to 500 strong, had journeyed to China on fact-finding missions, soaking up information on religious, scientific and cultural matters that could be put to use back in Japan. Chang'an – the Tang capital and one of the two largest cities in the world at the time – particularly impressed them.

Coming from an agricultural society, they had no major urban centres of their own to compare. The Japanese adopted a grid plan for their new capital. It measured 4.5km by 5km (about 3 miles in each direction), with the main axis running south from the imperial palace.

Shaping a capital

Japan had few raw materials at her disposal, and the mountainous terrain of its four main islands meant that barely 15 per cent of the total land area was fit for cultivation. As a result, the construction of the capital involved an immense effort for which all the energies of the state had to be mobilised. The area around Nara quickly became a vast construction site. Huge quantities of timber were brought down from the hills and cut into beams and planks for the countless wooden buildings of which the city was made.

In imitation of Chang'an, the imperial palace and the main government buildings were placed in the north of the city. Chinese models also served as templates for the architecture of the palace buildings and the residences of the court nobility, with houses built around an inner courtyard that also served as a garden.

Noble offerings The Japanese upper classes expressed their piety by donating works of art to the temples, among them this 8th-century sutra roll recounting the life of a priest, Sakyamuni (above), and an elegant statue of a six-armed goddess (background, left).

Scenes in black and red
Japanese artists were particularly fond of motifs from nature in their wall paintings. This example comes from the Horyuji Temple near Nara, whose main hall is the world's oldest-known intact wooden building.

richly adorned with paintings and statues of wood or bronze. The decorative arts played such an important role in the Japanese economy that special government departments were created to train and supervise workers employed in textile weaving, bronze-casting and lacquerwork. Craftsmen from Korea and China were encouraged to come to Japan to pass on their skills to Japanese apprentices.

The great temple

The religious centrepiece of the city was the Todaiji or Great Temple of the East, whose influence extended across the nation. Emperor Shomu and his wife commissioned the temple in the 740s to commemorate the death of a young son. Two seven-storey pagodas advertised the temple's presence, but its main attraction was a gigantic statue of the Buddha, donated by the emperor in keeping with a vow he made when seeking divine aid to bring a smallpox epidemic to an end.

Standing 16m (52ft) high and weighing 550 tonnes, the Todaiji Buddha was the largest bronze statue in the world at the time. After several failed attempts to cast it in one piece, it was finally made in several pieces that were then fitted together under the supervision of a master-craftsman specially brought in from Korea. Initially, it seemed that resource-poor Japan would not be able to provide the 230kg (500lb) of gold needed to gild the statue, but at the last moment, as if by divine intervention, a new source was found in a remote northeastern province. The hall that housed the statue was equally impressive: at the time, it was the largest wooden building ever constructed, 87m (280ft) long, 66m (215ft) wide, and 60m (195ft) high.

In 752, festivities took place across the capital to celebrate the consecration of the statue, which soon became famous well beyond Japan's borders. The enormous cost and effort involved provide eloquent testimony of the profound impact that Buddhism had had on the country.

The main residential quarters where the clan chiefs had their dwellings were positioned to the south.

Nara was not just a home for the emperor and the great noble families, it was also the administrative centre of the country and its religious heart, endowed with Buddhist monasteries and temples

The old Shinto faith retreated into the background at this time, although it never completely lost its influence, for the imperial house continued, as it had always done, to derive its claim to rule from the Shinto sun goddess Amaterasu, the legendary progenitor of the imperial line.

Temple treasures

The Todaiji temple was a windowless wooden structure, designed to make the most of the natural properties of the timber of which it was made: in hot weather the planks shrank, providing some ventilation, but in wet conditions they expanded, preventing damp from getting in. This made the building suitable for storing important manuscripts and other documents, so it became the state treasury. Buddhist relics and liturgical objects, including those used to consecrate the temple itself, were kept there, as well as countless art treasures, most of them donated by noble families and in particular by Shomu's widow.

Many of these objects have survived to this day, providing a fascinating insight into the Nara world. Although the majority came from Japan and China, there are exotic works from as far afield as India, Iran and Central Asia. These imports reached the imperial court via China, after the Tang dynasty rulers had vastly extended their nation's frontiers, opening up contacts with lands as far away as the Middle East.

A thriving courtly culture

Cultural life flourished in the new capital, again reflecting Chinese influence; the fashions of the Tang court affected dress, etiquette and nearly all areas of life. But the Japanese were also finding their own way. Chinese pictograms had long been used for writing the Japanese language, despite the fact that the two tongues were very different in both structure and sound. Now, scholars started to develop a syllabary system called kana, by which the characters were assigned phonetic sounds,

and this considerably simplified the task of transcription. The beginnings of Japanese literature also came in the Nara period: the nation's two oldest historical works, the *Kojiki* and the *Nihon Shoki*, both date from this time. Between them they spell out the nation's ancient foundation myths, providing an invaluable source for Japan's early history.

Mainland influences also affected other areas of life. Early in the 8th century a Buddhist monk of Korean descent, named Gyoki, rose to prominence in Japan, designing roads, bridges, harbours and dams. He also drew the oldest known map of the country.

An upsurge in craft production stimulated a demand for raw materials, encouraging more economic development. As the use of metal grew, the mining industry expanded and new mines were sunk. Rich deposits of copper were discovered, permitting Japan to mint its own coins for the first time. Precious metals, however, continued to be reserved for the exclusive use of the court and the temples.

Japan made great strides towards a centralised administration at this time, but the emperors' attempts to expand their rule over the whole country were only partially successful. In the provinces, there were hardly any

Hokkaido

SEA OF JAPAN

HONSHU

PACIFIC OCEAN

SILLA KINGDOM

Biwa-ko

Fuji-San

Nara

Shikoku

Kyushu

■ The Nara Kingdom

→ Japanese expansion

◄ ∙ ► Contact with Korea and China

Courtly pastime This wooden gaming table, with a precious ivory inlay, was preserved in the treasury at Nara's Todaiji Temple. The rules of the game are not known.

towns that could function as centres of state power. Economic activity was also still localised by Japan's fragmented topography and poor communications; a nationwide trading network did not really exist. In addition, the aristocracy and the monasteries were tightening their grip on the country's farm land. In theory, all of it belonged to the emperor, who allocated it to the people who worked and paid taxes in return. In practice, the nobility and the Buddhist monasteries held large estates. Often, farmers holding land from the emperor actually preferred instead to enter the service of a nobleman or a monastery, as the rent for a tenancy could be less than the taxes demanded by the emperor's agents. Other farmers lost their land because of debts incurred following bad harvests.

Prince Shotoku Prince Shotoku, imperial regent from 593 to 622, first forged the cultural link with China that did so much to shape the Nara world.

The dispossessed

The great estates built up by the aristocracy enabled nobles to lead a comfortable life, mostly centred on the new capital. The city's cultured lifestyle was supported by the efforts of the rest of the population, some of whom were forced into slavery, while others laboured to the point of exhaustion on state building projects. For many farmers not tied to the great landed estates, robbery was the only alternative to starvation. Armed bands of roaming landless peasants presented a constant threat to law and order.

In the wild border country north of present-day Tokyo, a state of chronic warfare existed between the ethnic Japanese population and the Ainu, an indigenous people of uncertain origin. It was an unequal conflict that saw the Ainu slowly but steadily pushed back northward. A warrior caste was born of this struggle, and it came increasingly to provide the emperor with the backbone of his armies. This further reduced the political influence of the peasantry, who had hitherto supplied him with fighting men in times of crisis.

Political shortcomings

The cultural brilliance of Nara was not enough to cover up its fundamental political weaknesses. The influence of Buddhism and the wealth of the monasteries grew steadily thanks to donations and legacies from the nobility, and this wealth was further swollen by the tax-exempt status that the monks enjoyed. One temple in Nara owned 46 separate estates covering a total of some 5000 acres of prime agricultural land. Separate monasteries were in the hands of different Buddhist sects, encouraging competition in the economic and political as well as religious sphere, and adding to the tensions that increasingly split the state.

A presumptuous monk

The Todaiji Temple exerted enormous economic power that gave it an ever greater say at the imperial court. In the mid 8th century, its influence peaked in the career of a monk called Dokyo, who managed to win the confidence of the Empress Koken through flattering dream interpretations and predictions. Promoted to chancellor, the ambitious monk finally went too far by claiming to have had an oracular vision indicating that the gods wished him to become emperor. This was too much for Koken. Mindful of the ancient Shinto tradition that only someone of imperial lineage could ever mount the throne, she rejected Dokyo's suggestion and withdrew her favour.

After Koken's death in 770, Dokyo was banished from court and exiled to the small island of Ajawi. The state council, which decided on the rules of succession to the throne, then decreed that no woman should henceforth be allowed on the imperial throne – a ruling that, with just two exceptions, has been followed throughout the history of Japan to the present day.

The end of an era

The power of the Buddhist clergy had by that time become so great that, in 784, Emperor Kammu, another strong personality, decided to move the capital to Nagaoka, which lay 50km (30 miles) to

the north. Oracles and geomancers confirmed its position as propitious, and a labour force 300,000-strong was assembled to create another new capital out of nothing. But a number of accidents occurred during its construction, which were seen as bad omens. Work on the city was discontinued and a fresh site was sought. This time the geomancers settled on the nearby region of Yamashiro and, in 794, the foundation stone of Heiankyo, the future Kyoto, was laid. A new era was about to dawn, although not one that would live up to the new city's name, which meant 'Capital of Peace'.

Theatrical mask Gigaku was a form of theatre featuring mime, music and dance that reached its peak in 8th-century Japan. This wooden gigaku mask of an old man was used for court theatrical performances in Nara times.

The temple-building kingdoms of Java

Some of the world's greatest surviving Buddhist and Hindu monuments were created on the high plateaus of central Java more than a thousand years ago.

Place of contemplation
Seventy-two separate bell-shaped stupas – Buddhist shrines – line the three uppermost terraces at Borobudur. Some have been partly demolished, revealing stone images of the meditating Buddha inside.

Powerful eruptions shook the centre of the Southeast Asian island of Java (now part of Indonesia) in AD 1006. Vast masses of lava and ash from the Merapi volcano buried large parts of the island – and along with it some 2000 Hindu and Buddhist shrines. Among them was one of Buddhism's largest and most important sites: the temple complex of Borobudur, built early in the 9th century. Java's luxuriant jungle vegetation had already begun to reclaim the hill where the temple complex stood; after Merapi's eruption, Borobudur sank into oblivion for centuries.

In honour of Shiva

Java owed its temples to a wave of economic prosperity that washed over the island and its neighbour Sumatra from the 3rd century AD on, when the collapse of China's Han dynasty disrupted overland

trade routes westward from China. Instead, an increasing amount of Chinese merchandise travelled by the sea routes south, and Java and Sumatra became important trading posts where Chinese and Indian merchants met to exchange goods. The new wealth flowing into the islands encouraged the growth of native kingdoms. In Java these started in the west and by about 500 had spread to the island's centre. Their rulers followed the Hindu faith, which had been brought to Java by Indian traders.

One of the most powerful of these local dynasties was the Sanjaya, who seized power in central Java around the end of the 7th century. Sanjaya kings commissioned the first Hindu temples and chose for their location the Dieng Plateau, a mystical landscape, framed by volcanoes, where clouds of vapour drift across the black rocks and jets of hot steam shoot up, releasing heat from deep within the Earth. In honour of Shiva, their

A bird's-eye view The temple-mountain of Borobudur in central Java has a base area of 2000m^2 (21,500sq ft) and rises to about 35m (115ft) above the Kedu Plain. It was declared a UNESCO World Heritage Site in 1991.

most venerated deity, the Sanjaya built a city in this remote but evocative area, calling it the 'Home of the Gods'.

In about 780, the Sanjaya were pushed out by the rival Sailendra dynasty, whose kings ruled central Java for the next 70 or 80 years, reducing the Sanjaya to vassals in the eastern part of the island. The origins of the Sailendra are unknown, but they self-confidently styled themselves 'Lords of the World Mountains', and they succeeded in creating a short-lived maritime empire that temporarily took in Sumatra and much of coastal Malaya as well.

Building the temple-mountain

The Sailendra rulers built their palaces on elevated sites, in keeping with the local

Rising from the Kedu Plain beside the River Progo in central Java, Borobudur is a temple-mountain at whose core lies a natural hill. The court astrologers of the Sailendra kings chose the site in about 780. Local belief held that building a temple was an act of conception, so they sought out a location where, in their view, the 'male Sun penetrated the female Earth'.

A mandala in masonry

For the next 50 years or so, tens of thousands of stonemasons and other workers laboured to complete the project. The raw materials for its construction – some 55,000m³ (1.65 million cubic feet) of volcanic stone – came from the nearby riverbed. The boulders were cut to size before being transported to the temple site, where a small army of labourers were waiting to set the blocks in place; about two million blocks were fitted together without mortar. By the year 830, when the work was finally finished, the entire hill had disappeared under a cloak of masonry.

The finished temple was a terraced pyramid: six rectangular storeys lead up to three superimposed circular levels, crowned by a central stupa – a dome-shaped structure

Battle of the gods This wall relief (above) is in the Javanese temple complex of Prambanan (background). It illustrates a scene from the Ramayana, India's great Hindu epic, and shows a god firing an arrow at a demon.

view that kings were god-like beings imbued with a special spiritual force that compelled loyalty from their subjects. In contrast to the Hindu Sanjaya, the Sailendra were Buddhists and they sought to express their faith by building the great temple of Borobudur.

traditionally used to house Buddhist relics. Each terrace has a gallery-like walkway, with niches in its walls for sculptures – there were more than 500 in all. The temple got its name from these statues of bronze and stone, for Borobudur, roughly translated, means 'many Buddhas'. In addition, some 1500 sculpted stone reliefs on the walls depicted episodes from the life of the Buddha and his followers. The whole complex took the form of a gigantic mandala – a geometric design that symbolises the universe, used by Hindus and Buddhists as a meditation aid.

A symbolic ascent to Nirvana

Climbing the temple-mountain of Borobudur was intended to be an act of worship; ascending it symbolised the path to enlightenment. Pilgrims made their way up a path that stretched for more than 5km (3 miles), spiralling clockwise up to the stupa shrine at the top. In doing so, they metaphorically moved upward from the everyday world to the peak of Nirvana – for Buddhists, this is a state of freedom from worldly concerns attained through enlightenment.

In keeping with the concept of a spiritual ascent, the stone reliefs on the lower levels of the temple illustrated edifying maxims and scenes from the life of the Buddha, but the three circular terraces near the summit were not decorated at all, suggesting a state of pure meditation in which all earthly concerns were left behind. Instead, pilgrims made their way past a number of bell-shaped stupas, each containing a stone statue of a meditating Buddha.

The stupa crowning the structure enclosed two small sealed chambers, both now empty; reports indicate, however, that they once contained relics, thought to have been removed soon after the structure was discovered by Europeans early in the 19th century. One suggestion is that the temple may have been built to

BACKGROUND
The stupa

The first stone stupas were built in India to house the remains of the Buddha; the domed shape seems to have been borrowed from pre-Buddhist burial mounds. Later the monuments were used to shelter Buddhist relics and to mark sacred sites or landmarks. Early Buddhism disapproved of worshipping images or icons, and so the stupas themselves sometimes became objects of worship. Believers expressed their faith by circling round them in the direction taken by the sun.

When stupas spread beyond India's borders, they sometimes lost their uniform dome-like appearance. Bell-shaped stupas emerged in Sri Lanka as well as Java, whereas in China and Japan the stupa form evolved into the pagoda.

house relics of the Buddha released from India by Emperor Asoka in the 3rd century BC as a way of sharing the heritage of Buddhism with the rest of the world.

The Sanjaya comeback

Not long after Borobudur was completed, the star of the Sailendra kings began to set. The Sanjaya, who had been driven away to eastern Java, had now regrouped and were mounting a fresh challenge. Old legends give a hint of how these changes in the dynasties' fortunes came about. According to the stories, in about the year 850 the Sailendra prince, Balaputra, set out to put the renascent Sanjaya in their place once and for all, but his great project failed. The Sailendra lost the ensuing power struggle and were forced to flee to the nearby island of Sumatra, leaving Java once more to the Hindu Sanjaya kings, who now called their kingdom Mataram.

A rival project

Borobudur continued to be a pilgrimage site up to the time of the Merapi eruption, but with the fall of the Sailendra, Buddhism had passed its peak in Java. No doubt intending to outdo their predecessors, the Sanjaya rulers immediately set about constructing a rival Hindu temple complex. Their chosen site was at Prambanan, some 80km (50 miles) to the southeast of Borobudur, where the Sailendra kings had already begun to build Buddhist temples. Eventually, Prambanan would hold more than 200 separate monumental structures.

Elephant bell This 8th or 9th century bronze 'elephant bell' is a musical instrument. When struck it produced a gong-like tone that was used in religious processions and dance ceremonies.

Guardian of order Made of delicately hammered gold, this precious 9th-century image shows the god Vishnu surrounded by four of his symbols: a prayer wheel, a conch, a mace and a lotus flower.

The legend of Prambanan

A Javanese folk tale is said to relate to the building of the Prambanan temples, and may contain a kernel of truth beneath the many fantastic elements in the story. It tells how a Sanjaya king planned to marry his daughter to a Sailendra prince who was one of his subjects. But the beautiful Princess Loro stubbornly refused to accept her intended bridegroom and used all her cunning to find a way of avoiding the marriage. She took advantage of a Javanese custom of the time that allowed a bride to set a challenge for a prospective suitor in order to prove his worth. With this in mind, she insisted that she would only agree to marry the prince if he succeeded in building 1000 temples in a single night.

By all human standards this was, of course, an impossible task, but unbeknown to Loro, the Sailendra prince had magical powers that he could call on. He set to work with a will, and the princess watched in astonishment as temple after temple appeared from nowhere on the designated site.

As dawn approached, she realised that her cunning plan would come to nothing as the requisite number of shrines would soon be in place. So, in a final attempt to thwart her would-be lover, she came up with another ruse. Waking all the cockerels in the vicinity, she set them to crowing, announcing the arrival of the new day before its expected time – and, crucially, just before her suitor was able to put the last block in place.

The prince was understandably frustrated and angry, and he took a cruel revenge. He used his magical powers to turn Loro to stone. To this day, guides point out her statue in the Prambanan temple precinct.

A popular faith

Hinduism eventually outstripped Buddhism in popularity among the Javanese people, perhaps because it was easier to reconcile with local pagan traditions of pantheism and ancestor worship. Like Buddhism, the Hindu religion contained the idea of liberation for the spirit and salvation from continued earthly existence. It had no overriding central authority, no hierarchy, no direct divine revelation and no rigid moral code, but it did have a huge number of gods, the most important being Brahma (the Creator) and Shiva (the Destroyer), with Vishnu (the Preserver) who mediated between the two.

When the Sanjaya kings determined to build Prambanan, they decided to dedicate it to all three of the principal Hindu gods. They even changed the course of the River Opak to make enough space to build three separate, generously planned temple precincts. They spared no expense, spurred on by the desire to put Buddhist Borobudur in the shade.

As ever, the bulk of the work fell to the lot of the peasants living in the area, who, over a 50-year period, had to drag stones to the site and then construct the temples. Shiva, as the supreme Javanese Hindu god, had the tallest and most elaborate temple: the structure built in his honour rose all of 47m (150ft) high. The inscription marking the temple's consecration in 856 described the building as a 'beautiful residence for the god'.

In the end, even the gods could not save the Sanjaya dynasty. A contemporary source recounts that their rule ended in 928 as the result of an unspecified catastrophe – possibly a volcanic eruption or an earthquake, or perhaps a devastating epidemic. All that is known for sure is that central Java sank into political insignificance after their demise, and the centre of power on the island shifted decisively to the east. There, three centuries later, a mighty new dynasty would rise to power: the Singhasari.

Empire of 1001 nights – the Abbasid caliphate

The Abbasid dynasty seized power in the Islamic world by a rebellion. Led by Caliph al-Mansur and Harun al-Rashid, the dynasty built Baghdad and made it an international centre of culture.

A caliph's gift This ivory chess piece was a present from Caliph Harun al-Rashid to Emperor Charlemagne. Exotic gifts from Baghdad were much prized at the Frankish court.

Standing in the pulpit in the Mosque of Kufa in what is now Iraq, Dawud gazed out across the congregation gathered before him. Then he raised his voice to make an historic announcement.

'Praise be to God, with thanks, thanks and more thanks! Praise be to He who has destroyed our enemies and has returned our inheritance from Muhammad. God's blessings and peace be with you! Right has returned among men from the family of your Prophet. God has allowed you to see what you have so long been waiting for and looking forward to. He has allowed a caliph of the family of Hashim to appear before you.'

With these last words, he stretched out his hand to point at his brother, Abu al-Abbas, first ruler of the Abbasid caliphate.

The road to power

The new Abbasid dynasty seized power over the vast Islamic Empire in 750. They traced their descent back to another Abbas, an uncle of the prophet, Muhammad. The dynastic connection was important, for one of the rallying cries of the rebels who had overthrown the previous Umayyad dynasty was that it lacked legitimacy in not tracing its descent from Muhammad's own direct family.

The Abbasids had twin power bases – one around Kufa in southern Iraq, the other in Khorasan in central Persia, extending eastward into Central Asia. The city of Merv (now in Turkmenistan) was their eastern headquarters, and it was from there that they spread the propaganda that helped to prepare the revolt.

Khorasan was fertile ground for discontent, for it was home to many muwalis – Muslims of non-Arab origin. Nearly all Islam's more recent converts fell into this group, and they had come to

EVERYDAY LIFE

The Hammam – reports from the bath-house

When an Arab traveller reported on conditions at the court of Emperor Charlemagne, he referred with a shudder to the dismal state of personal hygiene that he found there. Courtiers bathed only once or twice a year, he reported, and then only in summer.

Things were quite different in Baghdad, a city that was equipped with several hundred bath-houses, or hammams. Today, we have a good idea of what these hammams were like, because the activities there were a favourite subject for manuscript illuminations in Arabic books.

The hammams were quite dark and semi-subterranean, and visitors had to carry candles. Before entering the bath-house itself, bathers removed their clothing which was left with an attendant in a cool dressing room; there were also pallets here to rest on after bathing. After undressing, they wrapped towels around their waists and proceeded to the hammam proper,

which was marble-clad and beautifully decorated with patterned tiles.

There were two separate pools – a large one for bathing and a smaller one that the guests sat around, making themselves comfortable in the heat, while employees poured water over them, massaged their backs, or even washed their hair. People went to the hammam to relax and meet friends or to conduct business.

Relaxing at the baths
Some hammams, like this one in present-day Tripoli, in Lebanon, were quite beautifully decorated. Visitors to the baths set great store by refined architecture and a pleasant and sociable atmosphere.

fiercely resent the way in which they were discriminated against, socially and legally, under the empire's Umayyad rulers, regardless of their status within their own communities. Because of this, the Abbasids were able to win massive support for their message of revolution among the Muslims of Persia.

The Abbasids chose a general called Abu Muslim to organise the revolt. He mustered support against the Umayyads in the name of the house of Hashim – the branch of Mecca's ruling Qureysh clan to which Muhammad himself had belonged, as had his son-in-law, Ali. In doing so, he played on a division that had split Islam from its early days: this was the divide between the Sunni majority of Muslims – who had initially accepted the claims of the Umayyad caliphs, even if now they found them wanting – and the Shiite minority, who had long held that the rightful line of descent for the caliphate was through the family of Ali.

Abu Muslim never mentioned Abu al-Abbas by name to the Shiites; he spoke of an agreed candidate 'of the House of Muhammad' who would replace the hated Umayyads, which the Shiites took to mean a descendant of Ali. By such ruses Abu Muslim managed to unite disparate groups around the standard of revolt and gathered together an army.

The end of the Umayyads

In June 747, Abu Muslim raised two flags bearing the Hashimite colours at Merv, and the banner soon became a symbol of the revolution. Abu Muslim used verses from the Koran to call his followers to war:

'Those who fight because an injustice has been done to them are permitted to take up arms, and Allah has the power to grant them victory.'

The rebel army drove the Umayyad governor out of Merv, then turned westward. In 750 they defeated the last Umayyad caliph, Marwan II, at the Battle of the Zab, fought near Mosul on the eastern banks of the River Tigris. Marwan subsequently fled, and eventually met his death in Egypt. Meanwhile, Dawud had duly proclaimed Abu al-Abbas caliph in Kufa. For the

Shiites, he was not the direct descendant of Ali that they had expected, and they felt badly betrayed. Over the next 50 years they would repeatedly take up arms against the Abbasids, who had won their support by deception.

An elite force

The Abbasids owed their victory to the army raised by Abu Muslim, which inspired admiration and terror in equal measure for its fighting skills, its unity and the rigid discipline of its troops. The soldiers won the respect of the general population by not harming civilians, refraining from sexual excesses and obeying their commanders' orders. One Persian observer reported enthusiastically that no army like it had ever been known in the Islamic world.

Oath of loyalty

All soldiers in this unusual force had to take an oath of loyalty to Islam and the caliph, swearing on the Koran, on the traditions of the faith, on the words and deeds of the prophet Muhammad, and on their duty to the prophet's kin. They also vowed not to demand their pay or keep until their general chose to provide them, and not to incite their enemies to attack before their officers had given the command to start fighting. Previous Arab armies had often been paralysed by tribal rivalries, but Abu Muslim took care to see that his troops were firmly committed in their loyalties. The army's devotion gave him great personal power – too much, as it turned out, for after Abu al-Abbas's death in 754, his brother and successor al-Mansur had the general murdered.

Building Baghdad

Shiite discontent flared up regularly in armed revolts, making life uncomfortable in Kufa, so in 760 al-Mansur decided to build a new capital near the old Sassanian royal city of Ctesiphon. He named the new foundation Medinat as-Salam, or 'City of Peace'; later it would become

Religion and art This 9th-century parchment from the time of the Abbasid caliphs shows a fragment of verses from the Koran (left). The Abbasids extended the Great Mosque at Damascus built by the Umayyads (background).

known as Baghdad. The new metropolis quickly became not just the political heart of the Abbasid realm, but also a centre of excellence for science, literature and art, and it retained its fame as a cultural centre long after it lost its political pre-eminence.

Baghdad lay in a strategically favourable position on the banks of the River Tigris, which linked it to other Mesopotamian centres as well as with northern Syria and the Persian Gulf. Important land routes led from the city to southern Syria and eastward across the Iranian highlands towards the mountains of the Hindu Kush and onward as far as distant China.

Over the following centuries, the Abbasid city would disappear under later constructions, but it is still possible to reconstruct its appearance with the help of descriptions by Arab writers. It was circular in shape, measuring 2700m (8800ft) across, and was surrounded by a bank and ditch and double brick walls.

Romantic warrior An Arab miniature dating from the 16th century paints a romantic picture of Caliph Harun al-Rashid. In reality he was a competent and refined but cruel ruler, who had his longtime friend and adviser Gafar al-Barmaki executed.

Muslim currency The words 'In the name of Allah' circle the rim of this gold dinar. The coin was struck in the year 165 of the Muslim calendar, equating to AD 781. The inscription in the centre of the reverse face reads, 'Muhammad, Messenger of God'.

Ornamental Art Stylised palm-leaves decorate this long-necked Abbasid ceramic jug from the 8th or 9th century (right).

Four gates pierced the walls, with the entrances slightly staggered to make it difficult for attackers to force their way in with battering rams. Above the gateways were domed chambers used by the caliph for public audiences. From them, the city's four main thoroughfares, lined with shopping galleries and soldiers' barracks, led to the city centre.

Within the walls, the city's outer ring was divided into 45 neighbourhoods arranged in a fan shape and separated from one another by radial dividing walls; each one was assigned by the caliph to a particular tribe. A network of paths and alleyways cut through these residential districts, linking up to a ring road that circled the inner city and housed the royal palaces, the main government buildings, the state treasury, an arsenal and the police headquarters. The original plan was that the city's population should be relatively small so as to keep the caliph at a safe distance from his subjects, so no bazaars were allowed within the city limits. In time, however, densely-packed suburbs grew up outside the walls, complete with a merchant's quarter, craft workshops and a large army camp. Soon crowded residential districts pressed so closely on the town centre that even the government quarter was no longer securely shielded.

The Persian presence

Al-Mansur, together with his son and successor al-Mahdi and his grandson Harun al-Rashid, established a new ruling elite for the Islamic world and pushed through radical changes in the way their lands were governed. Their Arab predecessors had inherited from the Sassanid rulers of Persia an efficient administrative system staffed by competent civil servants, most of whom they kept in office, although Arabic replaced Persian as the official language of government.

Under the Abbasids, the influence of these Persian civil servants, many of whom were only recent converts to Islam, expanded considerably. One family in particular, the Barmakids, played a crucial role as grand viziers to successive caliphs. Freed slaves from Africa and Central Asia who had been trained for palace service also played a growing part in helping the caliph carry out his administrative duties.

Codifying the Sunna

In addition, al-Mansur reformed the legal system. Under the Umayyads, the peoples of the Islamic Empire had lived with a great deal of inequality before the law, as provinical governors and their representatives tended to give judgments that reflected their own prejudices or local traditions, rather than the words of the Koran. Now the caliph decided to create a code of laws that would be applicable equally to all his subjects. He turned to a high-ranking government official, Ibn al-Muqaffa, who suggested that a comprehensive survey of past judicial decisions be carried out so that these could be compared with the Sunna – the body of traditional law based on the words and doings of Muhammad. A system of jurisdiction could then be drawn up to put the Sunna into practice. The work was mostly done at a school named after its founder, the jurist Abu Hanifa.

One of its students, Abu Yusuf, attained high rank under Harun al-Rashid, compiling a work on ground rents.

A profane poet

At its peak, Baghdad formed a cultural centre for the Islamic world, buzzing with ideas and creativity. But by no means all the intellectuals who gathered there were pious scholars. A group known as the Zindiqs preached an epicurean doctrine of pleasure. Taking their inspiration from Persian traditions, they viewed the Islamic prohibition of wine and disapproval of music and song as small-minded and restrictive. Such views found expression in the work of the poet Abu Nuwas, whose witty, cynical verses not only extolled life's pleasures but even encouraged vice, urging his readers to 'accumulate as many sins as you can'. Abu Nuwas moved in high court circles, forming an unholy trinity with Harun al-Rashid and his vizir, Gafar al-Barmaki.

The Zindiqs had a marked impact in court circles, encouraging wealthy nobles to adopt a sophisticated lifestyle that did not take the Islamic prohibitions too seriously. At the same time, they enriched Islam itself by forcing it to engage in rationalist debate, encouraging a school of thought that was prepared to look outside the faith itself to find arguments in its defence.

Courtly opulence

Less happily, long-held Persian traditions of autocracy also influenced court ceremony. Appointed officials controlled all access to the caliph, who at audiences sat on a throne of ebony dressed in gold-embroidered robes. An executioner stood nearby, ready to put the ruler's judgments into immediate effect.

The ostentatious and indulgent lifestyle of the court caused some resentment, not least among orthodox scholars who thought that it clashed with the ideals of simplicity and spontaneous piety adopted by the prophet Muhammad.

Their dissatisfaction was shared by a large proportion of the Baghdad population and found expression in a rash of anonymous pamphlets. Harun al-Rashid was sufficiently concerned by the criticisms to abandon the capital in 796 for Raqqa in Syria – which also provided a convenient base for the military operations he was waging at the time against the Byzantine Empire. Baghdad was not restored to its position as capital until 808, a year before the caliph's death.

Al-Rashid reinforced the fortifications around Raqqa and the neighbouring town of al-Rafiqa and also commissioned the construction of a splendid palace complex that covered 10km² (almost 4 square miles) and comprised 20 individual buildings, most of them made of mudbrick reinforced with fired bricks.

Ascending ramp The spiral minaret of the Abu-Dulaf mosque in Samarra, some 125km (80 miles) north of Baghdad, is said to have taken its inspiration from Babylonian ziggurats. Now ruined, the mosque, dating from the 9th century, is said to have been one of the largest in the world.

Fluid colours This brilliant red and yellow ceramic bowl was found in the palace of Samarra. The city became the Abbasid capital in 836 and remained so for 56 years.

The largest, located in the middle of the settlement, was the Qasr as-Salam or Palace of Peace, which measured 350 x 300m (1150 x 1000ft); around it lay other buildings housing Harun al-Rashid's family, his courtiers and his troops. The caliph did not stint on the interior furnishings. Craftsmen covered much of the palace with white stucco decoration, often featuring vine-tendril motifs. Walls were adorned with murals depicting court pleasures, such as hunts and banquets, along with female dancers and singers. Polo, adopted from the Persians, was another popular diversion.

The weavers' art

Wooden furniture was almost unknown in the Middle East at the time. Courtiers sat on the floor, so floor coverings, cushions and throws made from precious textiles were important furnishings. The caliph's retinue were also provided with outfits to suit the seasons, which were kept in vast costume stores. Harun al-Rashid's will gives some idea of their extent: the stores held 8000 mantles, 10,000 shirts, 10,000 caftans, 2000 pairs of underpants, 4000 turbans, 5000 headcloths, 1000 wraps and 1000 hooded cloaks.

Not surprisingly, textiles featured prominently in Islamic arts and crafts, and an entire branch of the economy was based on their production. Linen came from the Nile delta, cotton from Mesopotamia, Iran and India, and precious silk was imported from China. The art of weaving silk was already established in Syria in pre-Islamic times, but under the Abbasids production increased abruptly, and the finished products were exported as far as Africa and Europe.

The fabrics destined for the caliph's household, designated *tiraz* from a Persian verb meaning 'to embroider', were marked with his name or that of his vizier. Some bore other messages calling down blessings on the caliph's head, along with marks identifying the date and place of their manufacture and the way in which they were produced. Apparently, careful laundry lists were kept.

A war between brothers

Harun al-Rashid was only able to enjoy the splendours of Raqqa for 12 years. He returned to Baghdad in 808 to confront a revolt that was shaking Khorasan. A year later, fighting off illness, he travelled to the province in person, accompanied by his

Pleasure palace The massive walls of the fortified palace complex at Ukhaidir, 75km (50 miles) southwest of Baghdad, once enclosed audience chambers, courtyards, living quarters and a mosque. The palace was built in 774.

son al-Mamun, whom he had made governor of the eastern part of his empire. The caliph's condition worsened on the journey, and he died at Tush, near modern Meshed, in 809.

After al-Rashid's death, civil war broke out between al-Mamun and the designated successor, al-Amin, who governed the western provinces of the empire. Al-Mamun emerged victorious in 813 and ruled until 833. In his reign the Abbasid caliphate attained fresh cultural heights. He set up a library and academy in Baghdad, the House of Wisdom, that was a centre for the translation of Greek philosphical and scientific works, and favoured the Mutazilite movement of Islamic scholars who espoused rationalism and intellectual openness.

New ideas and lasting influence

The Mutazilites were particularly eager to explore the classical heritage of Greece and Rome, and in so doing they helped to liberate Islamic philosophy and science from the restrictive influence of conservative theologians. The first important Islamic philosopher was al-Kindi, and he was strongly influenced by Platonic thought; in all, he wrote over 200 works on subjects as diverse as mathematics, medicine, chemistry, physics, astronomy, music and philosophy.

Other scholars of the time made valuable progress in astronomy – Caliph al-Mamun established observatories for their use – and medicine, while others

BACKGROUND

Stories from the Arabian Nights

No work of Middle Eastern literature is better known than the Arabian Nights – actually something of a misnomer, since the bulk of the stories contained in the work came not from the Arab-speaking world but from Persia, which always held a certain exotic appeal for its Arab conquerors.

The Sassanid rulers of Persia provided a pseudo-historical background for the story that frames the other tales: that of the cruel king Shahriyar and the wise and gifted storyteller Scheherezade, who saved her own life by telling gripping stories to her master each night. The Persian version of this tale was already well known to Arabs of the Abbasid period.

The work as a whole enjoyed enormous popularity across the Islamic world, and new stories were constantly added, some of them from Arab sources.

Among these were several which featured Caliph Harun al-Rashid and his real-life vizir Gafar al-Barmaki. Their popularity suggests that the caliph had already become, for his contemporaries, a personification of the wealth and romance of the Abbasid dynasty at its peak.

Nimble servants Wall paintings from the harem of the Abbasid palace in Samarra show dancing female slaves pouring wine out of long-necked carafes into cups.

developed syncretic philosophical systems designed to reconcile the Islamic faith with the findings of science.

There was also an upswing in the writing of biographies and travel journals. The trade routes of the Islamic world carried not just material goods but also ideas and manuscripts, some of which found their way to Europe, where they had a lasting influence on the growth of intellectual life.

The spread of the world's religions

The religious instinct is doubtless as old as humanity itself. From the earliest times people have sought to explain and come to terms with the great existential questions: Why am I here? Is there life after death?

Religion provides an assurance that life on Earth has a purpose, helping individuals to come to terms with their fate and to accept the prospect of death with composure. The psychological reassurance that comes from belief, and the sense of awe in the face of the unknown, are as much part of the spirit religions of Central and South America as they are of the great monotheistic faiths of Judaism, Christianity and Islam, or the East Asian religions of Buddhism or Hinduism.

A creator god

There are also, of course, crucial differences between faiths that go far beyond the fundamental question of praying to one god or to many. In Judaism, Christianity and Islam, all life is seen as dependent on a personal god who fashioned the Universe out of nothing and who, in his mysterious wisdom, rules according to a plan. In this vision, the time from the creation of the world to its final destruction runs from a fixed starting point to a predetermined goal.

A never-ending cycle

Neither Hinduism nor Buddhism accept the notion of a beginning or end for the Universe. Instead, they propose an eternal cycle of growth and decay that would continue even without divine intervention. These faiths are less concerned with the purpose of the Universe as a whole than with the individual's search for meaning within it.

ZAPOTEC

MAYA
Palenque

Native peoples of Mesoamerica appeased and honoured their gods with frequent sacrifices, not just of foodstuffs and animals but also sometimes of human beings.

The religion of the followers of Jesus Christ, shown here in a mosaic from Constantinople, asserted itself over the paganism of the Roman empire. In the 4th century, Emperor Theodosius made it the empire's offical creed.

Christendom
Jerusalem and Jewish diaspora
Islam
Origin and spread of Buddhism
Buddhism, Taoism, Confucianism
Hinduism
Zapotec
Maya
● Religious centres

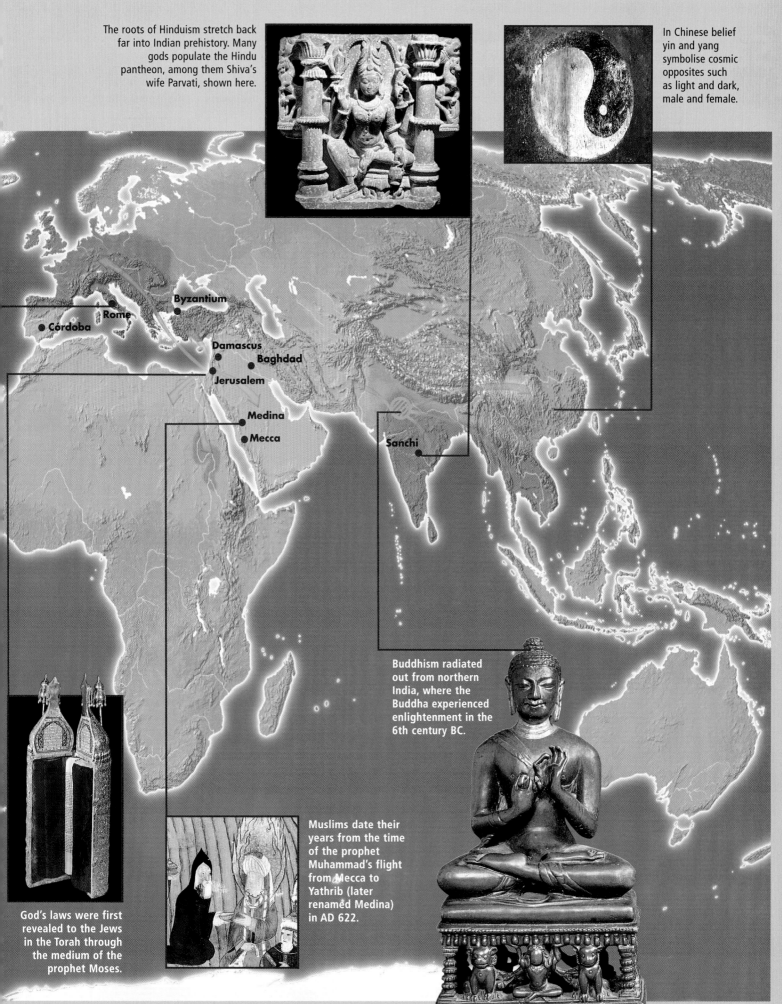

The roots of Hinduism stretch back far into Indian prehistory. Many gods populate the Hindu pantheon, among them Shiva's wife Parvati, shown here.

In Chinese belief yin and yang symbolise cosmic opposites such as light and dark, male and female.

Byzantium

Rome

Córdoba

Damascus

Baghdad

Jerusalem

Medina

Mecca

Sanchi

Buddhism radiated out from northern India, where the Buddha experienced enlightenment in the 6th century BC.

God's laws were first revealed to the Jews in the Torah through the medium of the prophet Moses.

Muslims date their years from the time of the prophet Muhammad's flight from Mecca to Yathrib (later renamed Medina) in AD 622.

Sacred sites and cult objects

Stupas originally took their form from Indian burial mounds. Later the basic shape was adapted to make tombs and reliquaries that were holy shrines for Buddhists.

The great religions have many elements in common, among them a reverence for sacred sites and symbols. Believers of almost all denominations regularly come together at special sites for prayer or worship. For Christians, Jews and Muslims, religion is communal; the faithful gather in churches, synagogues and mosques to express their faith as part of a congregation of the like-minded. For Hindus and Buddhists, faith is more of an individual commitment, but both still have places of worship – temples for Hindus, stupas for Buddhists – where people can go to be close to their god.

Places of worship

The architecture of the world's religious buildings mirrors the greatness of the gods they serve. Spires and minarets stretch up to the sky, symbolising the ascent from the earthly to the celestial realm. Buddhist shrines are often located high up, and the faithful can only reach the sanctuary by climbing steps. Places where people have seen visions or where miracles have happened have a special aura of holiness and believers flock to them: Christians are drawn to Lourdes in southern France, for example, while Buddhists make pilgrimages to the bodhi tree in Bodh Gaya, which is believed to be descended from the very tree under which Buddha found enlightenment.

Symbols of belief

Religious symbols can be quite as important as physical places of worship in helping believers to focus their faith. It would be hard to imagine Christianity without the crucifix or Judaism deprived of the seven-branched candlestick known as the menorah, while the image of the meditating Buddha is an ubiquitous icon of Buddhism. Most religions also retain a special veneration for relics of holy men and women.

The deep sense of reverence that such objects arouse has a powerful unifying effect, bringing together the community of the faithful.

This golden arm was fashioned to hold the hand bones of a Christian saint. Relics of holy men were hugely important to Christians in the Middle Ages. People would travel many miles to see and touch them in the hope of winning spiritual advancement or finding miracle cures for physical ailments.

Each mosque has a tall minaret from which the muezzin calls Muslims to prayer five times a day. The minaret above is part of the Great Mosque in Tunisia's holy city of Kairouan, an Aghlabid foundation dating back to the 9th century.

Hewn from a single massive block of stone, the Sun Gate is the main surviving feature of the city of Tiahuanaco, to the south of Lake Titicaca in Bolivia. The relief in the centre of the stone shows the 'staff-bearing god', whose cult attained its greatest extent between AD 600 and 1000.

The menorah, a seven-branched candlestick, is one of the Judaism's most important symbols. It originally formed part of the furnishings of the tabernacle in the wilderness, and then of the temple in Jerusalem before the temple's destruction in AD 70.

Benedictine monks spread Christianity through the Germanic kingdoms of Europe and church-building was an important part of their mission. This chapel in Spain was built in the time of the Visigoth kingdom there. It was consecrated in AD 661 and dedicated to John the Baptist.

The basic elements of faith

While the tenets of primitive religions were passed down purely by word of mouth, the great world faiths have to a greater or lesser extent used the written word to spread their message. Priests and religious scholars have traditionally had the task of interpreting the scriptures and explaining them to the rest of the population. Christians believe in the message of divine salvation as set out in the Old and New Testaments. God gave the people of Israel the Torah, whose holiest scriptures are contained in the Pentateuch – the first five books of the Old Testament as passed down by God through Moses. For Muslims the Koran is the word of God, revealed in visions to the prophet Muhammad. The sacred text of the Hindus, the Vedas, contains ancient songs, cosmological texts and ritual prescriptions.

Icons and sacred images

Art has been used through the ages to convey the religious message to ordinary people, the vast majority of whom were illiterate. The beliefs of Christians, Buddhists and Hindus alike were reinforced through paintings, statues and sculptures in their places of worship. For the most part, Jews and Muslims were discouraged from making or worshipping images, so synagogues and mosques were decorated almost exclusively with abstract imagery, often featuring floral motifs.

The moral message

Nearly all of the great religions set out basic rules for people to live by; Jews, Christians and Muslims, for example, share the Ten Commandments as revealed to the prophet Moses. For most, an essential cornerstone is the idea that individuals should behave towards others in the way they would like to be treated themselves. Believers of almost all faiths turn to prayer, whether on their own or communally, to seek divine help. However, different currents within individual religions have different priorities. Over the centuries, both Buddhism and Hinduism have taken many different forms. The followers of Islam split between two main groups, the Sunnis and Shiites. Christianity has a long history of heresies and splinter movements, and still divides into Catholic, Orthodox and a variety of Protestant communions.

For Muslims, the Koran is the word of God as revealed to the prophet Muhammad, and many of the faithful learn its contents by heart. This 13th-century Persian miniature (above) depicts the public library in Hulwan near Baghdad.

Many Hindu temples are decorated with colourful frescoes, like the one below, illustrating legends that play an important part in the faith. A favourite source of legends is the Ramayana which, alongside the Mahabharata, is the best-known of the great Sanskrit epics.

For a long time the Buddha's teachings were transmitted orally; they were only written down long after his death. The Buddhist message was spread across Asia by wandering preachers and missionary monks, and reliefs like this one (below), from Borobudur in Java, served as teaching aids.

This miniature from the Vivian Bible (far left), presented to the Holy Roman Emperor Charles the Bald in 846, shows Moses receiving the 10 Commandments.

The Talmud, represented here by a page from a 13th-century Spanish manuscript (left), is a compilation of commentaries on Jewish life and law laying down precepts for correct behaviour.

Paths to salvation – monks and pilgrims

Fasting is an element of all religions. By temporarily going without food, the believer hopes to find spiritual clarity and a better understanding of God. Muslims celebrate the end of the fasting month of Ramadan with music and festivities, as shown in this 13th-century miniature.

Christian pilgrimages symbolised the earthly journey towards a heavenly goal. The decorated water bottle below would have been carried by a pilgrim in the late Middle Ages. Such bottles replaced traditional gourds for carrying water, although the name gourd continued to be used for this essential piece of a pilgrim's equipment.

All religions have special activities or vocations intended to help the faithful get closer to the divine. Pilgrimages to sacred sites, often involving long and sometimes dangerous journeys, have tradition-ally served either as a penance for sins committed or as an exercise in piety. The *haj* to Mecca is one of the duties of every male Muslim. Pilgrimage destinations for Christians include Jerusalem, Rome and Santiago de Compostella in northwestern Spain, where the bones of the apostle St James are supposed to lie. Pilgrims are often readily distinguishable by their clothing and certain symbols, such as the pilgrim's staff carried by medieval travellers. In Europe in the Middle Ages Christian pilgrims would also wear a rainproof cloak and a broad-rimmed hat for protection in all weathers.

The path of self-denial

Fasting, a shared element in all religions, serves both as a penance for sins committed and as a path of self-denial permitting the believer to attain a better understanding of God. The Koran prescribes a prolonged period of fasting for Muslims in the month of Ramadan each year.

A life of contemplation

Incense creates a mystical atmosphere inside the sacred buildings of many denominations, helping to transport the believer into a different mindset. It is also used to aid the practice of meditation, another tradition common to many religions, which aims to free the mind from earthly concerns in order to approach God more closely. For Buddhists, meditation provides a path to Nirvana, the longed-for state of freedom from worldly desires and the cycle of reincarnation. This contemplative element in Buddhism and Christianity encouraged the setting up of monasteries, which have traditionally served as sanctuaries for individuals leading a life dedicated to God, as centres for missionary activities, and as places where study of the arts and sciences was encouraged.

Top: The Seder is a ritual meal consumed in Jewish homes on the first night of the Passover, a feast that commemorates the ancient Jewish exodus from Egypt.

Above: This Buddhist pilgrim is recognisable by the items he is carrying: a fly net in one hand and his pilgrim's staff, the *kakkhara*, in the other.

Left: The *hacha*, an axe-shaped stone blade, was part of the equipment used in the ceremonial ball game which played a part in Mesoamerican religion.

AFRICA

The longest migration – the Vandals in Africa

After a rampage across Europe that made their name a byword for wanton destruction, the Vandals eventually reached North Africa, where they set up the first independent Germanic kingdom on Roman soil.

Vandal horseman This Roman mosaic, which once decorated the floor of a house in Carthage, shows a mounted Vandal nobleman. It dates from about the year 500.

The year was 429, the place southern Spain. The wind direction was favourable and the weather looked ideal for sailing. Gaiseric waited calmly on deck, surveying the armada of hundreds of ships that he had assembled in the harbour of Iulia Traducta (modern Algeciras). When all the ships were loaded and ready, he nodded to the captain of his own vessel. The order to cast off was given, and the first ships set sail. In all, some 80,000 people would be transported across the Strait of Gibraltar to North Africa, the single largest seaborne movement of Germanic peoples ever.

The journey across Europe

In their wanderings across Europe the Vandals were joined by other Germanic peoples, including the Alans and the Quadi, although the Vandals made up the chief component of the horde. In the Roman Empire's early years, the Vandals were one of the largest groups inhabiting the eastern Germanic lands, settled on the broad plains between the Oder and Vistula rivers in what is now southern Poland. The great migrations were triggered by the incursions of the Huns and other peoples from the east. The Vandals abandoned their homelands in about the year 400, crossing the Rhine into Gaul in the winter of 406. From there they moved on to Spain, arriving in 409. Some died in battles with the Visigoths, who challenged them for control of the Iberian peninsula from 416 onward.

The migrants left few mementoes of their stay in southern Spain other than the name Andalusia, meaning 'land of the Vandals'. Yet the two decades they spent near the Mediterranean coast had a marked effect on their own future. In that time they had access to harbours and ships and they mixed with experienced seafarers. They quickly learned maritime skills, encouraged by the lucrative rewards of piracy. In 426 they attacked the Balearic Islands and the Roman province of Mauretania in what is now coastal Morocco and Algeria, and soon after they won mastery over the Strait of Gibraltar.

Control of the seas roused the Vandals' interest in North Africa, which was the most prosperous surviving part of the Western Roman Empire. The authorities in Rome itself were unable to do much to stop them as they were distracted by the threat of the Huns and by their own conflicts over the imperial succession.

The Vandals were under increasing pressure from the Visigoths, who had set up their own kingdom in northern Spain in alliance with the Romans. So Gaiseric weighed the risks against the potential benefits and made the decision to lead his people to North Africa. He had great diplomatic skills and military capabilities as well as strong backing from his people. Long after his death, he was remembered among the Germanic peoples as a wise leader. Yet he was also one of the most unscrupulous rulers of a savage time, regularly breaking treaties and agreements when it suited him to do so.

The conquest of Roman Africa

Having crossed to North Africa, Gaiseric led his people eastward towards what is now Tunisia, the wealthiest and most urbanised part of Roman Africa. Some sources assert that the Vandals were invited to the province by the Roman commander Boniface, who had ambitions to set up a kingdom of his own there, but this view is challenged by other scholars.

Whatever the facts of the matter, Boniface could hardly have bargained for the outcome of the invasion, for the 20,000 or so warriors in the Vandal ranks proved more than a match for his own legions, and he was quite unable to halt

Costume jewellery Decorated with precious stones and hammered squares of sheet gold, this brooch would have once served to hold a nobleman's cloak in place. It was found in a Vandal tomb near Carthage.

their progress. In June 430 the Vandals arrived outside Hippo Regius (present-day Annaba in eastern Algeria) and besieged it for 14 months. The city's bishop, the great church father, St Augustine of Hippo, died of a fever with the invading army encamped outside the walls. When Hippo finally fell, Gaiseric made it his headquarters, conducting further campaigns eastward as far as the walls of the Roman capital of Carthage.

In 435 Gaiseric negotiated a peace treaty with Rome that gave him control of all the western shoreline except for Carthage and its immediate surroundings. Four years later he tore the agreement up and seized Carthage itself in a surprise attack. At the time the city was second only to Rome in size and wealth, with some 200,000 inhabitants; contemporaries compared it with the Egyptian city of Alexandria, one of the chief glories of the Byzantine Empire.

In the years following the capture of Carthage, the Vandals extended their grip, wielding destruction and terror on a

BACKGROUND

A Vandal legacy in central Europe

In the course of the 4th century, when the Vandals were still living in the eastern Germanic lands, the tribe was divided into two sub-groups, the Asdings and the Silings, each with its own separate ruling house. The Siling Vandals settled in southern Poland, and the Asdings on the River Tisza, further south in Hungary.

When, at the beginning of the 5th century, the Vandals set off on their great migration across Europe to Africa, the Silings left a significant reminder of their stay in the area in the word Silesia. The name is used to this day to describe the region of Poland that borders on Germany and the Czech Republic.

fearsome scale. In 442 Rome was forced formally to acknowledge Vandal control of all Roman North Africa. Gaiseric agreed to pay tribute to Rome in return for the recognition, and also to send one of his sons as a hostage to the imperial capital. He considered this a price worth paying for the official establishment of the first independent Germanic kingdom on Roman soil.

In the years that followed, King Gaiseric used his enhanced prestige to change the way in which Vandal leaders were selected. Previously, military success had been the only criterion, but Gaiseric introduced the principle of hereditary succession. He made Huneric, his eldest son, his heir and in 445 strengthened the younger man's position by arranging his engagement to Eudocia, a daughter of the Roman emperor, Valentinian III.

Rich pickings from Rome

In 455, Valentinian was murdered by assassins in the pay of a rival candidate for the throne, and Gaiseric sent his forces to sack Rome. The raiders returned to Carthage bearing rich booty and bringing with them many experienced craftsmen, Roman senators, and even the emperor's widow Eudoxia, together with her daughters Eudocia and Placidia. There, Eudocia was belatedly married to Huneric in 462. In return, Eudoxia and Placidia were freed to settle in Constantinople. Eight years later Eudocia also left Africa, with or without her husband's consent, eventually finding her way to Jerusalem, where she died in 472. By that time the Eastern Empire itself was on its last legs, and the imperial heiresses had lost what

Transfer of ownership This inscribed cedarwood tablet records the sale of a property in the province of Africa by Iulius Restitus and his wife Donata to one Geminius Felix in the year 494.

value they had once had as chesspieces in Gaiseric's complex diplomatic games.

On their arrival in North Africa the Vandals found a flourishing, well-governed land that was the breadbasket of Rome. Its fertile agricultural lands were divided into huge estates, some of them in imperial hands while others belonged to the Church or to private owners. Gaiseric seized the imperial lands for himself, while most of the Roman landowners lost their estates to Vandal noblemen. Some were allowed to remain as dependent tenants of the new owners, but others were expelled or chose to leave. The lifestyle seduced the incomers, who in many cases adopted the Roman culture in its entirety. The administration of the kingdom was also left largely in Roman hands, as the Vandals themselves were relatively inexperienced in the day-to-day business of government.

The Arian persecutions

One major barrier preventing the assimilation of the Roman and Vandal populations was religion. Although the Vandals were Christians, like many other Germanic peoples they subscribed to the Arian sect. Unlike orthodox Catholics, Arians did not accept the absolute unity of the three elements of the Holy Trinity, maintaining instead that Christ had been created by God, a view that had been condemned as heretical at the Council of Nicaea more than a century earlier.

Now, Gaiseric used this doctrinal division as a pretext for extending Vandal control over the area. Landowners who would not convert to Arianism were turned off their estates, and Catholic churches were plundered of their treasures. Many clerics and laymen were banished, and the king used his power to prevent bishops being appointed to vacant Catholic sees, bringing the work of the native Church almost to a halt. The persecution stirred up revolts, particularly

among the Berber tribes, but all were put down. Gaiseric himself died in 477, but the policy of Catholic repression was continued under his heir, Huneric, who ruled until 484.

An abrupt exit from history

In 523 a new Vandal king, Hilderic, came to the throne, intent on improving relations with the Roman people and with Rome itself, by now under the control of the Ostrogoth, Theodoric. Hilderic's attempts at assimilation failed, however, partly because of the growing power of the Berbers in the western regions of the kingdom, but also because his reforms stirred up resentment in the Vandal community. When Hilderic went down to defeat in battle with the Berbers in 530, he was deposed.

Vandal coin This metal coin, shown from both sides, dates to the reign of Gunthamund, a nephew of Huneric, who reigned from 484 to 496.

Hilderic's successor, Gelimer, renewed the persecution of the Catholics, attracting the hostile attention of the recently enthroned Byzantine emperor, Justinian I, a fierce opponent of Arianism who was also intent on resurrecting the old Roman Empire. In 533, Justinian sent his brilliant general Belisarius to North Africa at the head of an imperial army. Gelimer capitulated in 534 after a brief campaign, and the first Germanic kingdom on Roman soil disappeared from history, leaving behind few permanent traces.

Gold, salt and slaves – the kingdom of Ghana

Desert caravan This 14th-century illustrated map offers a European view of a trading caravan crossing the desert. The Arab merchants who plied the Sahara seeking gold and slaves relied on experienced local guides to see them safely through their journey to Ghana's prosperous trading towns.

Strategically located at a crossroads of several busy and lucrative caravan trade routes, and set in a fertile savanna landscape, the West African land of the Soninke people developed into a powerful and wealthy state.

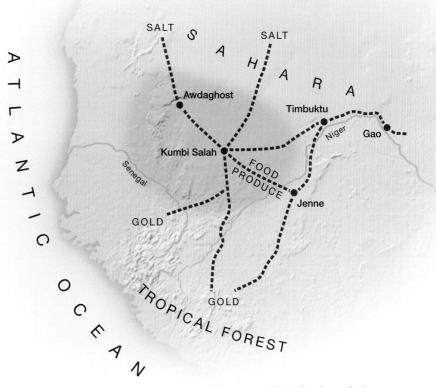

The much-travelled Arab chronicler, al-Bakri, visited Ghana in the 11th century and was granted an audience by the king. In his account of his travels, *The Book of Roads and Kingdoms*, al-Bakri left a description of that meeting:

'The king has a palace with many domed rooms, surrounded by a kind of city wall... He adorns himself with jewellery like a woman, with a necklace round his neck and bracelets on his lower arms. On his head he wears a tall hat that is decorated with gold and wrapped in a turban of finest cotton. When he gives audience to his people or listens to their complaints, he sits in a domed pavilion surrounded by ten horses bearing gold-embroidered trappings. Behind him stand ten pages with gold-embossed swords and shields, and at his right hand are the sons of the vassal kings of his country, wearing splendid robes and with their hair braided with gold.'

The realm that this splendid monarch ruled lay in the fertile savanna south of the Sahara Desert, extending from the great bend of the River Niger westward to the River Senegal. The area under his sway extended across parts of present-day Mauritania, Senegal and Mali, but did not include the modern Republic of Ghana, whose borders were drawn up by European colonial

- Kingdom of Ghana
- ---- Trade routes
- ● Towns and trading centres

powers in the 19th century, without consideration for African associations and connections, either historical or cultural.

Fertile ground

The old kingdom of Ghana was the most ancient of the three great West African empires: Ghana, Mali and Songhay. According to al-Bakri, it was known to its inhabitants as Wagadu, while *gana* was originally the title of its kings. A central feature of the landscape was the land-locked delta of the Niger, one of the world's few inland river deltas, which played a part in giving the region a more humid climate than today. This helped to support an agricultural economy whose rich harvests served to feed the ruling dynasty and its civil servants, as well as an active class of merchants and craftsmen. Ghana was also an important trading centre; within its borders, the caravan routes from North Africa to the Guinea coast crossed those from the Atlantic seaboard to Lake Chad and the Nile. The Soninke people inherited all these advantages when they settled the region in about the 5th or 6th century AD.

The earliest records to mention Ghana date back to the late 8th century and were penned by Arab historians and geographers. They report that, in about 790, a Soninke ruler name Kaya Maghan Cisse founded the Cisse Tunkara dynasty, which ruled until the 11th century. The kings soon grew rich by taking control of the trade in Saharan salt as well as the traffic in gold, a vital source of revenue as the goldmines of Bambuk, in present-day Mali, lay not far away between the Faleme and Bafing rivers.

A city rich on gold

The Ghanaian kings were less interested in mining gold than in controlling the gold trade. Records of the time show that they used every trick in the book to keep the exact location of the mines a secret. The kings also took other precautions to control supply and keep the price high: for instance, al-Bakri reports that they kept all the gold nuggets discovered in their lands locked up in the royal treasuries, as otherwise there would have been 'too great a quantity of gold and it would lose its worth'.

The ruler sent troops to guard the trade routes, which extended from the headwaters of the River Senegal along the River Niger, passing close by the site of the later city of Timbuktu, and then on into the Sahara. Ghana's sphere of influence extended from its capital – the trading town of Koumbi Saleh – for hundreds of miles in all directions.

Soninke art This wood carving of a woman, found at Dogon in Mali, is strangely reminiscent of modern sculpture. The Soninke people of West Africa grew wealthy on the Saharan salt trade (background).

Koumbi Saleh itself lay on what is now the border between Mauritania and Mali, about 320km (200 miles) north of Bamako. Another Arab writer, Edrisi, reports that it consisted of two cities set about 10km (6 miles) apart. One lay on the plain, and was inhabited mainly by Arab traders; the other was the royal residence where the king's palace lay, surrounded by sacred forests. The royal settlement has yet to be discovered, but the trading town has been found and partially excavated.

Town of traders

The excavations suggest that Koumbi Saleh's trading station covered about 3km² (1.2 square miles) and may have had up to 30,000 inhabitants at its peak in the 10th century. Straight roads cut through residential districts of stone houses, two or more storeys high, with central courtyards and slate-slabbed floors. The ground floors were shops or storerooms, with living quarters upstairs.

There were many mosques in the town, and most of the corpses buried in the cemeteries faced east towards Mecca – a sign that the settlement was mainly populated by Arab traders, just as the literary sources suggested. Archaeological findings have provided evidence for this view in the form of glass weights, which were used for measuring out gold; shards of pottery from the Mediterranean world; and stones inscribed in Arabic with verses from the Koran.

Literally, a golden age

Ghana grew wealthy on the trade in gold and also in slaves, and its kings used its prosperity to finance an extensive administration. The kingdom was divided into a number of provinces that were in turn subdivided into districts, all of them with governors and military commanders. In addition, al-Bakri records that the king had a 200,000-strong army at his disposal, staffed by soldiers who received land and trading privileges in return for their services. Only the ruler and his immediate entourage were allowed to wear gold ornaments; everyone else had to make do with copper jewellery, made from metal imported from the lands north of the Sahara.

Of gods and ancestors

Burial mounds in present-day Mali provide evidence of the unequal distribution of wealth and the differentiated social structure of ancient Ghanaian society. Most people were buried with just a few modest grave goods, but members of the upper class could afford to be buried in large burial mounds, or tumuli, surrounded by enduring evidence of their wealth. The tumuli were constructed in different ways in different parts of the country. Around the Niger Delta, they were built up of layers of soil. In the savanna regions, however, they were cut out of the rocky subsoil and then covered over with earth.

The Soninke believed in various creator deities, including rain gods to whom they

sacrificed cattle during periods of drought. There was also a cult of tribal ancestors, who were thought to keep a watchful eye on their descendants, rewarding or punishing them depending on whether or not they observed the expected rites to propitiate the dead. The ancestors themselves were thought to live in a shadow

EVERYDAY LIFE

Trade and the salt caravans

At the time of Ghana's ascendancy, the market towns of the Sahel region, between the Sahara and the savanna, were busy centres of trade. In places like Awdaghust and Oualata, North African textiles and salt from the Saharan desert – which was essential at the time for preserving as well as flavouring food – were exchanged for leather goods, peacocks' feathers, slaves and, above all, gold, for which there was a constant and seemingly insatiable demand. Caravan leaders would endure great hardships to obtain the precious metal.

A description of just such a desert caravan was left by a Spanish Moor, Abu Hamid al-Andalusi. He recounted how the traders fetched the salt on camelback from the deposits where it was mined. Starting from Sidjilmassa in what is now southern Morocco, they carried their precious cargo across the desert, relying for navigation on experienced guides who could find their way by the shapes of distinctive rocks and the stars of the night sky.

The caravan carried provisions to last for six months. When it finally reached Ghana, the traders would weigh out the salt and exchange it for gold, the exact amount varying from time to time depending on the market and the state of supply.

Human merchandise As shown in this Arab manuscript (below), traders exchanged their salt not just for gold but also for black slaves, who were much in demand in the North African lands.

world that largely mirrored that of the living. In preparation for the afterlife, dead kings were said to be laid to rest with all their robes and jewellery and large stores of food, and some of their followers were sacrificed to provide them with a retinue of servants beyond the grave. However, no royal tombs have yet been discovered, so much remains speculative or unknown about such burial rites.

Grave attendant
This mounted ceramic figure was found in a Soninke burial mound in present-day Mali.

Journey's end for the caravans

One of the most important trading towns was Awdaghust, in southeast Mauritania. This lay at the start of the most travelled of the trans-Saharan caravan routes, which led across the desert to the trading post at Sidjilmassa in what is now southern Morocco. Here, merchants exchanged slaves and gold for textiles, leather goods and copper from the Mediterranean, as well as for salt from the Sahara itself. According to Arabic sources, the town of Awdaghust was founded by the Sanhadja, a Berber tribe, in the 7th century, and the rulers of Ghana were not able to bring it into their kingdom until the late 10th century.

The houses in Awdaghust were built to a rectangular plan around an inner courtyard housing a well that provided the dwellings' water supply. The oldest known mosque in Mauritania was situated in Awdaghust. Al-Bakri visited the town on his travels and left a description of it. He claimed it had the most beautiful gardens of the entire sub-Saharan region, shaded by date palms and fig trees, and it produced the finest cattle, the fattest sheep and the largest cucumbers. He sounded equally impressed by Awdaghust's womenfolk:

'Here one can find young Berber girls with beautiful, light-skinned faces and supple bodies, with firm breasts, slim waists, broad shoulders and large buttocks.'

Threat from the desert

In time the town of Gao – located on the River Niger in the Songhay kingdom, straddling present-day Mali and Niger – came to rival Koumbi Saleh, finally overtaking it in the 11th century thanks to a flourishing trade with Egypt and Morocco. Here, too, the indigenous people and the Islamic traders lived in separate quarters of the town.

As events turned out, the 11th century was a difficult time for the kingdom of Ghana even without the competition from Gao. Climate change caused increasing aridity, which reduced agricultural yields. A more immediate threat, however, came from the Almoravids, a dynasty with roots in the Berber tribes of the Saharan that espoused a fiercely evangelistic form of Islam. Declaring a jihad on their non-Muslim neighbours, the Almoravids first struck north from Mauritania, eventually conquering southern Morocco and Spain as far north as the River Ebro.

Empire's end

In 1054 the Almoravids took Awdaghust, and in 1076 Koumbi Saleh itself fell to them. The royal palace and much of the town were completely destroyed, and all the inhabitants who would not convert to Islam were put to the sword. The king of Ghana managed to retain control of what was left of his kingdom, but only by agreeing to make tribute payments to the Almoravid overlords.

In the ensuing decades, the empire of Ghana gradually withered away as subject peoples broke free from its grip. Weakened by the loss of several provinces, Ghana was ultimately unable to offer any resistance to the rise of the Songhay kingdom, whose great ruler Sundiata finally destroyed Koumbi Saleh in 1240. Thereafter, only fleeting memories of the old kingdom of Ghana remained to haunt the imagination of the Soninke people, and in the following centuries they migrated westward into what is now Senegal.

The Maghreb – Idrisids and Aghlabids

Two very different independent Muslim dynasties took power in North Africa at the end of the 8th century. They helped to give the region a unique culture, in which Arab elements mingled with local tradition.

A hall for prayer The Qarawiyin mosque in Fez, one of the oldest and largest in North Africa, is the seat of a famous madrasa (a religious school). The horseshoe-shaped arches are a typical feature of Islamic architecture.

The Maghreb – today's Morocco, Algeria and Tunisia – fell to the Arabs between 665 and 698 and was rapidly Islamicised. At first its rulers loyally acknowledged the authority of the Umayyad caliphs in Damascus, but in the course of the 8th century the caliphate's internal difficulties encouraged the local rulers to build up their own power bases, weakening the central control.

In 789, Idris I set up his own caliphate in Morocco. Idris, a great-great-grandson of Ali, the son-in-law of the prophet Muhammad, was a partisan of the minority Shiite branch of Islam, dedicated to the belief that the succession to the caliphate should have passed down through Ali's family. In common with other Shiites, Idris was bitterly opposed to the new ruling Abbasid dynasty in its capital at Baghdad. He had, in fact, reached North Africa as a fugitive from Abbasid persecution.

Idris died two years after winning power. His son and successor, Idris II, proved to be an energetic ruler in a reign of 37 years. One of his most lasting achievements was to develop the city of Fez, founded by his father. Strategically sited on the caravan route serving the North African gold trade, Fez became a major trading centre. It attracted immigrants from Kairouan, in present-day Tunisia, and from Islamic Spain, who settled in a special quarter and built their own mosque, helping to make Fez an international centre of intellectual endeavour.

Idris II was revered as a saint following his death in 828 and his burial place in Fez – the Tomb of Moulay Idris, begun in his lifetime – became Morocco's most venerated place of pilgrimage. The strength of his kingdom waned without him, however. His descendants divided it up into principalities and it lost much of its importance. From 926 on their lands gradually fell to the Umayyad rulers of Spain, a process that was completed when the last Idrisid ruler died in 985.

Land in transition

Farther to the west, the Aghlabids started an orthodox Sunni emirate in the province of Ifriqiyah, made up of what is now Tunisia and eastern coastal Algeria – a region that, since Roman times, had been the wealthiest part of the Maghreb. The dynasty came to power in AD 800, when an energetic provincial governor, al-Aghlab, was raised by the Abbasid caliph Harun al-Rashid to be hereditary emir. The Aghlabids continued to pay lip service to the caliphs in Baghdad while in practice functioning as independent rulers.

At the time of al-Aghlab's accession, Ifriqiyah was a land in transition. An Arab community perhaps 100,000 strong – by far the largest in the Maghreb – had established itself, yet it was still heavily outnumbered by native Berbers and mixed-race descendants of the Roman population. Islam had made great strides in the region, yet strong Christian and Jewish minorities survived. The Arabic language gradually asserted itself, serving as a conduit for the literary culture of the Middle East. The blending of the different traditions created a predominantly Islamist culture that, however, retained a unique character.

War-like times

The Aghlabids ruled in unsettled days. Their Berber subjects had never entirely

Pulpit decoration This carved wooden panel, found in Kairouan in Tunisia, adorned the pulpit of a Maghreb mosque in the 10th or 11th century.

Fortress of the faith Emir Ziyadat Allah I extended the ribat (fortress) of Sousse in Tunisia in 821, in response to a serious revolt that had shaken his realm.

A cure for heartache

Humans throughout history have suffered the pangs of unrequited love and have sought fast and effective relief for the malady. Al-Gazzar, a famous physician from Kairouan, published a book on the subject, *About Love*, that approached the problem from a medical point of view. Among the opinions expressed in the book are the following:

'Love is one of those illnesses that arise in the brain. It is caused by an excess of desire, combined with restlessness and sensual desire. That is why this sickness is accompanied by great suffering of the soul, as well as severe mental strain and sleeplessness... Sexual healing is recommended for those who have been seized by black bile and frenzy. The sexual act will bring the sick person back to his senses... For sensitive souls love is accompanied by serious side-effects. Sufferers endure considerable mental strain, and their sunken eyes are constantly in motion. The symptom stems from the soul's turmoil, which is caused by restlessness and the desire to see the object causing the suffering...'

In al-Gazzar's opinion, the best way of treating a person sick with love was to prevent him from dwelling on his feelings and sinking into melancholy. The doctor had his own, apparently well-tested, prescription:

'Instead, drink with him, join in song, discuss poetry and enjoy looking at gardens and happy faces.'

Precious verses These lines in golden ink on blue parchment are from a handwritten copy of the Koran, created by a scholar from Kairouan in the 10th century, and today in Tunisia's National Library in Tunis.

accepted Arab dominion and continued to resist foreign rule. In addition, the emirs had to cope with restive Arab militias. In response, they built heavily fortified strongholds called ribats, particularly along the Mediterranean coast. These were sanctuaries for the population in times of danger; in peacetime, they served as retreats where the faithful could find tranquillity. They were also assembly places for Islamic warriors and embarkation points for raids across the Mediterranean.

In 827 Aghlabid forces made the first of many attacks on Sicily that gradually enabled them to wrest control of the whole island from the mighty Byzantine Empire. They also struck mainland Italy, swooping down on Rome itself in 846, when they plundered St Peter's Basilica.

Palaces and aquaducts

With security in mind, Emir Ibrahim I decided to create a new residence for himself outside his capital of Kairouan, calling it al-Abbasiya in honour of the Abbasid caliphs in Baghdad. At the centre of the complex was the Qasr al-Abyad or White Palace, where the emir lived surrounded by his closest confidantes and bodyguards. Later emirs also built themselves palaces, the best-known of which was constructed by Ibrahim II at

Raqqada, some 9km (6 miles) south of Kairouan, complete with an artificial lake.

Some of the building activities were intended to benefit the populace at large. Ahmad, who was emir from 856 to 863, was a distinguished architect who set out to provide a reliable water supply for the inhabitants of Kairouan. He constructed the famous Aghlabid Basins, twin reservoirs from which purified river water was carried by aqueduct more than 40km (25 miles) to a vaulted cistern in the capital, and was then piped around the city.

A brief flowering

The country enjoyed a brief period of political stability and economic prosperity under Muhammad II, who ruled from 863 to 875. In addition to trade with the Islamic countries, economic relations with Christian Europe improved at this time. Ifriqiyah exported wheat and oil to Italy and Byzantium, and cotton, linen and silk textiles to many lands, Kairouan's famous carpets being much in demand. The emir levied tribute and taxes, and used the revenue to finance his own trading fleet.

Kairouan benefited from this economic upswing, becoming a centre of culture and scholarship. The emirs endowed it with a fine library and also a hospital with a lepers' ward that became the seat of a famous medical school. The spiritual focus was the Great Mosque, which held a celebrated collection of manuscripts.

Ultimately, however, the Aghlabids' championship of Sunni orthodoxy did not serve them well. The luxurious lifestyle of the emirs offended conservative opinion, and opposition to the regime grew. In the last decade of the 9th century a Shiite missionary named Abu Abdallah whipped up revolt among the Berber tribes in the name of the Fatimid dynasty, which would later go on to conquer Egypt. In 909 the Fatimids captured Kairouan, bringing the dynasty to an end. There were many people at the time, even in the orthodox Sunni community, who were prepared to see in their victory the judgment of God.

The Tulunids of Egypt – descended from slaves

Taking advantage of a crisis in the Abbasid caliphate, Ahmad Ibn Tulun, a descendant of military slaves, seized the opportunity to establish his own dynasty in Egypt.

Early in the 9th century, the Abbasid caliphs who ruled most of the Islamic world came to a momentous decision. Short of troops to police their vast domains, they settled on the expedient of buying the services of Turkish slave soldiers. There were obvious advantages to be had in hiring these mercenaries; they were formidable fighters and, in theory at least, owed absolute obedience to the masters whom they served. In practice, however, things turned out rather differently. The Turks' loyalty often went to their immediate commanders, rather than to the distant caliph. The risk was vividly illustrated in 861 in Samarra, then the Abbasid capital, when Caliph al-Mutawwakil sought to

Inside the Nilometer The Nilometer on Rawda Island, now within Cairo's city limits, was used to measure the height of the Nile's annual flood. It was constructed a few years before Ibn Tulun seized power in Egypt, but he restored and improved the device.

restrict the power of the foreign troops, who had been terrorising the city. In response, the Turkish commanders had him assassinated while he was drunk.

By that time, however, the caliphs had become dependent on the Turks. To pay for their services, they developed the *iqta* system, by which Turkish generals were given rights to revenues from specified areas. In 868 one general, Babak, was offered an *iqta* over Egypt. He chose to remain in Baghdad, but sent his stepson, Ahmad Ibn Tulun, in his place.

An energetic ruler

Ibn Tulun was an ambitious man who immediately set about building up his power base. The first step was to create an army made up of his fellow Turks. He also won financial control of the province by taking over revenue-raising from the fiscal officer appointed by the caliph. After a lengthy power struggle he finally got his rival transferred to Syria in 872, leaving him in total control and governing Egypt as an independent ruler. In 877, when he failed to respond to demands from Samarra for the payment of tribute, Caliph al-Mutamid

sent an army to bring him back into line. Ibn Tulun not only beat the incoming force but went on the offensive, invading Syria and occupying its major cities. From then on he made no pretence of holding power in the caliph's name.

Ibn Tulun proved a capable ruler who took measures to boost agriculture and to encourage trade and industry. Under his aegis, Egypt and Syria were also spared the need to transfer funds to the caliphate in the form of tribute. The result was an economic boom that made Ibn Tulun's reign a time of great affluence, expressed in an ambitious building programme.

The fruits of prosperity

Soon after coming to power, Ibn Tulun added a new district to Egypt's capital, al-Fustat, located in what is now an outlying section of modern Cairo. He built it over an old cemetery that bore the name al-Qatai, 'the plots', gracing it with a palace, a barracks for his troops, a horse-racing track and an aqueduct to

A lasting legacy The Ibn Tulun Mosque in Cairo was built by Ahmad Ibn Tulun, founder of the the Tulunid dynasty. The minaret was modelled on that of the Great Mosque of Samarra, the Abbasid capital at the time.

conduct water from the Nile. He sent for craftsmen and artists from the Abbasid heartland in Mesopotamia for the construction and decoration of the buildings. The crowning glory of his architectural projects was the Ibn Tulun Mosque, built between 876 and 879, that still stands as a monumental witness to the prosperity of the Tulunid era.

A vast structure measuring 140 x 116m (455 x 377ft) – it is still the largest mosque in Egypt – the Ibn Tulun Mosque was built of red brick and plaster, materials rarely seen before in Egypt, but common at the time in Baghdad and Samarra. The historian al-Qudai claimed that the materials were chosen as a safety measure against the risk of damage by fire or flood. Unusual and distinctive features of the building include the crenellations, which top the colonnades and the complex's outer walls, and the external staircase that spirals up the minaret – the only one of its kind in Egypt – which recalls the Great Mosque of Samarra.

The Nile – a vital artery

Water was a vital concern for any ruler of Egypt because, from the earliest times, the prosperity of the country had been intimately linked to the annual Nile flood. By measuring the height of the flood at its peak, it was possible to predict the yield of the coming season's harvest with surprising accuracy – an invaluable tool for any ruler seeking to calculate the revenues he could expect from the year's taxes. To ensure accurate measurements, Ibn Tulun ordered the restoration of a device known as the Nilometer on Rawda Island opposite al-Fustat. This installation consisted of a rectangular shaft connected to the Nile by two tunnels at

EVERDAY LIFE

A busy marketplace

Egypt's affluence under Ibn Tulun was based in part on long-distance trade. Al-Fustat, the nation's capital at the time, lay in an ideal position on the Nile delta where many trade routes came together. From the south came building materials and grain, ivory, ebony and other exotic products. To the east, the route skirted the Mediterranean coast to Palestine and Syria. An overland route to the west connected with Libya, and large quantities of goods moved back and forth along the Nile to the bustling port of Alexandria. Spices from India, silk from China, copper from the Anatolian mountains and gold from Africa all found their way to the city's markets, to be exchanged there for glass, ceramics, textiles and grain.

Market forces The business of negotiating prices in Egyptian markets has changed relatively little since Tulunid times.

its base. A pillar rising from the centre of the pit was marked with a graduated measuring scale that could be viewed from a flight of stairs descending the pit, permitting observers to keep records of high-water marks down the years.

An abrupt end

When Ibn Tulun died in 884, he bequeathed to his son and successor, Khumarawayh, a prosperous, well-governed land with an overflowing treasury. The new ruler began promisingly enough, proving himself a competent military leader. He won victories over Abbasid forces in Syria and Mesopotamia that compelled Caliph al-Mutadid, in 892, to accept Tulunid rule over Egypt, Syria and northern Mesopotamia for a period of 30 years. To further consolidate his position, Khumarawayh gave a daughter in marriage to al-Mutadid.

Sadly, however, Khumarawayh lacked his father's thrift and the financial surpluses that had been built up were squandered on extravagant living. When his successors encountered problems with dissident Muslim sects, they quickly ran out of money to pay their troops. The result was rapid collapse. The Abbasids sent an army to reconquer Egypt, and in 905 the dynasty came to an abrupt end.

Delicate carving Tulunid art was mostly abstract, featuring arabesques and floral patterns. Representational elements were usually highly stylised, like this elegant bird, carved on a wooden panel in the 9th or 10th century.

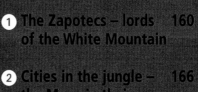

AMERICA

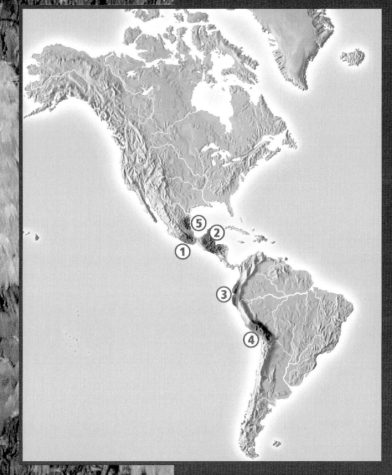

The Zapotecs – lords of the White Mountain

At Monte Albán, in the modern Mexican state of Oaxaca, the Zapotecs created one of the greatest and most enduring temple cities of Mesoamerica.

Bat god This jade mask found at Monte Albán in Mexico is thought to represent Murcielago, the Zapotec god of night and death.

Situated in southwestern Mexico, the valley of Oaxaca is one of the most important ancient American cultural regions. To this day it is the homeland of the Zapotecs, who call themselves the Penizaa, or 'Cloud People'. Zapotec culture was at its peak around AD 500, and its traces can be found in more than 200 different sites that are concentrated around the present-day city of Oaxaca. The most important of these was the ceremonial capital of Monte Albán, the White Mountain, with a subsidiary centre at Mitla, 40km (25 miles) to the southeast.

By that time the Zapotecs had developed what amounted to a centralised administration and a stratified social system, an extensive trade network connected the region with other parts of Mexico and with the Mayan lands.

Little is known of the Zapotecs' early history. Their origins are a mystery, and there is no way of knowing when exactly they arrived in Oaxaca. The earliest traces of their settlements date back as far as 600 BC, when the first phase of development took place at Monte Albán. The site must have seemed a natural one for a cult centre, rising dramatically some 400m

(1300ft) above the valley floor. The hill on which the centre was built formed the highest point of a small chain running on an almost exact north–south alignment.

Labour of generations

The Zapotecs – or perhaps even their predecessors in the valley – went to enormous efforts to level the top of the hill. Thousands of workers toiled with tools of stone and wood to create a flat platform about 800m (2600ft) long and 300m (980ft) wide.

On this artificial plateau they erected their magnificent shrines, using the stone removed from the hill as their building material. The labourers were evidently unable to remove a few very large chunks of rock, which were simply incorporated into the temple mounds.

Construction took place at Monte Albán over more than a millennium, but there seems to have been a peak period between 100 BC and AD 100. Despite this long gestation, the city always remained an architectural unity. Many of the structures were built along parallel axes; those located towards the sides of the platform, where the ground starts to fall away, were built with deeper foundations than the ones in the centre to preserve a uniform overall height profile. One of the temples was approached up a stairway 40m (130ft) wide. Considered to be the largest in all Mesoamerica, it was

The tomb frescoes of Monte Albán show the Zapotec taste for elaborate costume and personal adornment.

A masterpiece in clay Zapotec artists depicted their gods both in frescoes (background) and in clay sculptures like the one above. Dating from the 6th century, it shows the head of a god emerging from the jaws of a jaguar, the top predator of the American jungle. The figure on the animal's head is shown wearing the head-dress of the Zapotec rain god.

plaza, reached via wide staircases, that was overlooked by higher rock formations to the north and south. The plaza – which, in its basic form, may have originated in pre-Zapotec times – housed a central group of temple pyramids.

A galleried observatory

To the south stood an oddly shaped building, fashioned to resemble an arrow pointing to the southwest. This structure had an interior that was honeycombed with galleries, and probably served as an observatory; some scholars have speculated that it was designed to indicate the point in the sky where the star Capella rises on the night of the first zenith passage.

Most of the Mesoamerican peoples were close watchers of the heavens, and the Zapotecs no doubt shared the general fascination with all things celestial. Priests perched on Monte Albán's lofty eyrie, on the platforms at the top of their step pyramids, must have felt very close to the gods on clear nights when the skies were full of stars.

Serious stargazers

Zapotec astronomers carefully recorded the movements of the stars, handing down their observations through a fraternity of initiated priests. The knowledge helped the priests to retain a powerful and respected position in Zapotec society, for they alone were able to predict the courses of the celestial bodies and so, by implication, the will of the gods as expressed in them.

The most important product that the Mesoamerican cultures drew from their astronomical observations was the solar calendar, used to plot the activities of the agricultural year. In addition to this practical tool, the Zapotecs, along with other Mesoamerican peoples, also maintained a second, ceremonial calendar. This divided the year into 260 days, which were split into quarters of 65-days each; the quarters were then subdivided into five 13-day months.

supported by pillars with a diameter of 2m (6ft 6in). The fortifications that now surround the platform postdate the Zapotec era and were almost certainly built in later Aztec times.

The end product of so much labour was a magnificent hilltop acropolis in which brightly-painted, stucco-clad temples rubbed shoulders with palaces and step pyramids, all aligned with the general direction of the chain of hills. In the middle of the complex was a great paved

Writing in the Americas

The Zapotecs were able to preserve their astronomical findings thanks to an invention that was their greatest individual contribution to Mesoamerican civilisation: they devised a written script, the earliest in the Americas. The inspiration may have come initially from their neighbours the Olmecs, who had developed a primitive form of annotation.

The Zapotec system of writing was altogether more complex, comprising a multitude of pictorial and abstract symbols whose meaning varied depending on the ways in which they were combined. The script, which has still not been fully deciphered, formed the basis for the scripts of later peoples such as the Toltecs, Mixtecs and Aztecs. It is likely that Zapotec writing was only comprehensible at the time to a few priests, who gained additional authority from this exclusive knowledge.

Cult centre or city?

In its earlier centuries, Monte Albán was probably a cult centre rather than a city. Its only residents would have been the priests who served the temples and, perhaps, also the king and high nobility, for political power and religious authority were normally inextricably entwined in Mesoamerican cultures.

In later centuries, Monte Albán developed into a true city as well as a ceremonial centre, although only the nobility ever lived on the hilltop itself, inhabiting palaces that were scattered among the temples. Open stairways gave access to the stone buildings, which had living areas grouped around a central courtyard. At the back of each palace was a small private chapel, built over an underground mausoleum where family

Monolithic record
Stone steles like this one erected at Monte Albán bore inscriptions recording the Zapotecs' victories and conquests.

members were buried. Ordinary citizens lived on the lower slopes of the hill or in the valley beneath it and would only have come up to the hilltop for religious festivals when they assembled in the great plazas to worship the gods.

Preparation for the afterlife

The cult of the dead occupied a central place in Zapotec religion, as the elaborate burial vaults found at Monte Albán clearly show. Most had artistically decorated tomb chambers, each with an accompanying ante-chamber. A shaft led down into the tomb itself, which was often cruciform in shape and covered over with large stone slabs. Small niches let into the walls of the chambers were designed to hold vessels containing offerings of food and drink, as well as distinctive ceramic urns shaped to represent the major Zapotec gods. The deities of rain and maize were particularly popular subjects, perhaps

---

POINT OF VIEW

A city without water

For a city that endured for well over a millennium, Monte Albán had one extraordinary feature: the hilltop on which it was built had no water supply. The site had obvious advantages as a cult centre; it was situated high up, with extensive views over the surrounding countryside, and it was easy to defend. But the lack of a well or any other water source raises huge questions about its suitability for residential purposes.

Presumably only limited numbers of people ever lived on the hilltop itself. In later centuries, when Monte Albán became a substantial city, the bulk of the population are thought to have resided in the surrounding valleys, where water was relatively plentiful.

Even so, the nobles who inhabited the hilltop palaces would still have needed water, and they could have obtained it in only two ways.

One possibility is that they had access to cisterns or reservoirs that trapped and stored rainwater. If so, these have yet to be discovered in Monte Albán's remains.

The other, more likely, scenario is that they were serviced by columns of servants who toiled up the hillside carrying water in portable containers, without even the benefit of pack animals or wheeled vehicles to help them in their task. Presumably, the precious liquid was then emptied into storage tanks within the palaces, until it was needed.

because, as figures linked to agricultural fertility, they were also associated with rebirth in the afterlife.

Once the dead person had been laid to rest, accompanied by the requisite grave goods, the tomb was sealed with a stone slab, often beautifully decorated with relief carvings. The inscriptions identified the grave's occupant by their name-day, for Zapotecs took their names from the day in the ritual calendar on which they were born. The burial chambers were often reused many times.

A pantheon of nature Gods

The plastered walls of some of the burial chambers were decorated with frescoes that offer glimpses into Zapotec funeral rites and beliefs. They show the façades of temples and

Golden ornament This fabulous necklace, which was found in a tomb at Monte Albán, may be the work of a Mixtec craftsman.

masked images of gods alongside processions of richly costumed male and female figures adorned with magnificent head-dresses and precious jewellery; these possibly represented gods and goddesses accompanying the dead on their journey into the afterlife.

The Zapotec pantheon included a full range of nature deities. The jaguar god, also sacred to the Olmecs, was important to them and was worshipped in animal form. The rain god was a central figure, for his goodwill was vital for the cultivation of maize; he was portrayed as a hybrid being, blending human, feline and serpentine features in his visage, and sporting a forked tongue. Another divinity with a strong connection to agricultural fertility was Pitao Cozobi, god of the harvest and the fruits of the field, who

was depicted in human form with maize plants sprouting from his head-dress.

The gods were represented not just in the funeral urns but also in tomb wall-paintings and in stone reliefs decorating Monte Albán's ceremonial centre.

The role of the priests

Religion played an important part in the life of the Zapotec state. The high priest was equal in status to the king, and also served as chief judge. The Zapotecs called him *uija-tao* or 'Great Seer', as he alone was thought to know the will of the gods. To contact the spirit world, he entered a trance state partly induced by taking drugs.

To protect his privacy, the *uija-tao* lived in strict isolation in his own palace, and ordinary mortals were never allowed to see his face. Women were normally barred from entering his residence, but once a year he hosted a wild and hugely dissipated feast at which he was temporarily released from the vow of chastity that he observed at other times. His successor would eventually be chosen from among the male progeny conceived on these nights of promiscuous passion.

Lesser priests were prepared for their various tasks at special schools. After finishing their studies they were assigned to different functions, for example calendrical studies (used for purposes of divination) or the cult of individual gods.

The ball game

One of the most distinctive buildings at Monte Albán is a stone structure shaped rather like a capital I. This was a specially built court for the sacred ball game, which was played with local variations in all the cultures of Mesoamerica, although no sources have survived to give details of the game as it was played in the Zapotec lands. Stone grandstands that could seat hundreds of spectators line the court's sides, and niches let into the end walls probably held statues of the gods.

The Teotihuacán connection

Archaeological evidence suggests that between about AD 300 and 700 there were close links between Monte Albán and Teotihuacán, the great metropolis of the Valley of Mexico which lay about 400km (250 miles) to the northwest. The influence of Teotihuacán fashion can be seen in Zapotec architecture, stonecarving and pottery. Zapotec merchants had their own quarter in the big city, where they carved monuments in the Zapotec script and buried their dead in Zapotec-style tombs.

Teotihuacán was destroyed by unknown assailants sometime in the 7th or 8th century. Its downfall ushered in a final flowering of Zapotec art and culture, as exhibited in the vivid decorations of the Monte Albán tombs. By that time the influence of Zapotec culture radiated well beyond the valley of Oaxaca itself. The high priest had a second residence at Mitla, a city known to the Zapotecs as Lyobaa, meaning 'Place of the Dead'; in time it came to enjoy equal status with Monte Albán itself.

An unexplained end

Sometime after 900 the Zapotecs abandoned Monte Albán in favour of Mitla, which they made their capital. Why they chose to leave the mountain that had been their cultural centre for over a millennium remains a mystery.

As a ceremonial site, Mitla came to be as important as Monte Albán, and many temples and palaces were erected. Even so, the hilltop citadel retained its sacred aura and continued to be used as a burial site. As such, it was inherited by the Mixtec people, who gradually won control over the Zapotec lands in the course of the 10th century.

Although the Zapotecs were to be eclipsed as a political power, they continued to live in their ancestral lands; some 400,000 of them inhabit the state of Oaxaca to this day.

At peace The Zapotec goddess depicted on this funerary urn radiates quiet dignity. She wears the distinctive shoulder cloth known as a *quechquemitl*.

A special stadium The ritual ball game familiar in all Mesoamerican cultures was played on this court at Monte Albán. Spectators lined the grandstands along the sides.

Cities in the jungle – the Maya in their prime

The Maya built one of ancient America's most advanced and creative civilisations. Political and cultural competition between individual city-states drove them on to outstanding achievements in architecture, sciences and the arts.

The great Mayan ruler Pacal died in 683 at the venerable age of 80. He had turned the small town of Palenque, situated in the rain forest of southern Mexico in the present-day state of Chiapas, into one of the mightiest of all the Mayan cities.

During his lifetime, Pacal had a tomb prepared for himself, hidden deep under the building that archaeologists would one day call the Temple of the Inscriptions. When he eventually died, the Maya laid him to rest there with fitting honours and a rich collection of grave goods.

Almost 1300 years later, in 1952, the Mexican archaeologist Alberto Ruz Lhuillier made a sensational discovery. He had spent three years unblocking a concealed staircase, jammed with boulders and rubble, that led down from the temple into the heart of the stepped pyramid beneath it. All the hard labour eventually paid off when he found a previously unknown tomb chamber. When the massive stone slab that topped the sarcophagus was raised, he found himself looking on the remains of the long-dead ruler. Pacal's face was covered with a mask of jade mosaic that realistically reproduced his features, its inlaid eyes made of seashells and obsidian. In addition to the many precious grave goods, the tomb contained the mortal remains of six other people who appeared to have followed their ruler into death.

The rain forest backdrop

Pacal's tomb threw fantastic new light on the Mayan cult of the dead, and it also provided evidence of the fabulous wealth of the Mayan kings. Even so, there are still many gaps in our knowledge of Mayan history and culture. The mystery is the more surprising because the Mayan people survive to this day, keeping their language and something of their ancient customs and way of life alive.

Today, the Maya inhabit a broad swathe of Central America, extending from the Yucatán peninsula of southern Mexico through Belize and Guatemala into Honduras and El Salvador. During the classical period of Mayan culture, from AD 300 to 900, they had a more restricted range, centred on the Petén lowland between the Gulf of Mexico and the Caribbean. (The word *petén* means 'flat land' in Mayan.)

The Mayan world was a multitude of rival city-states in a lush jungle setting. Among the mysteries surrounding the Maya is the fact that they were able to flourish in the rain forest, an environment that is usually resistant to large-scale settlement. Yet they managed to turn features of their surroundings to their advantage. The many rivers cutting through the forest gave them a communications network and a plentiful supply of fresh water and fish. One of these rivers, the Motuga, also washed deposits of jade along in its gravel bed, and jade was the most sought-after precious stone in Mesoamerica. In addition, the jungle was home to a rich variety of wildlife that provided food: deer, rabbits and armadillos were favourites. The Maya also started breeding turkeys, which were indigenous to the Petén.

Serpent head Stylised snake heads are a common feature of the architecture of Chichén Itzá. They probably symbolised a god.

Jungle temple Chichén Itzá was a Mayan stronghold in the northern Yucatán peninsula. The Temple of the Warriors is flanked on two sides by a colonnade of several hundred pillars, many of them bearing reliefs of soldiers.

Rival city-states

The first Mayan cities grew up in the last centuries BC, when many of the city-states that rose to power in later times, such as Tikal or Uaxactún, had their origins. Much of the Maya's subsequent history was to turn on the rivalries of these statelets, which were constantly vying for supremacy over one another. As the centuries passed, different centres rose to prominence, drawing others into their sphere of influence by conquest or diplomacy, only to lose power later as a result of weak leadership or economic decline.

Pyramids and plazas

Apart from Palenque, the largest and most important urban centres were Copán, Yaxchilán, Chichén Itzá, and Tikal, together with Tikal's long-standing rival Calakmul. There were many other smaller cities, but only these were able to impose their authority for any length of time. Palenque's area of influence, for example, extended across 10,000km² (almost 4000 square miles), and by the year 600 Tikal was home to more than 40,000 people and covered an area of 60km² (23 square miles). Some of the cities were connected by roads paved with limestone, cutting straight through the jungle.

The cities were not planned; rather, they grew as necessary to meet demand. At their heart were the step pyramids with shrines on their summits, from which the smoke of sacrificial fires rose up to the gods. Broad plazas and other public buildings grew up around these ceremonial sites, along with the palaces of the ruler and leading nobles. Peasants from the adjoining countryside would join the town's citizens in the plazas to celebrate the great festivals, when priests performed sacred rituals in front of the temples that topped the pyramids.

Although the development of the cities was not planned, the layout of the centres was not haphazard, for their stone structures represented a kind of sacred geography that mirrored the Mayan cosmological and religious beliefs. For example, standing stones carved with reliefs on the great plazas symbolised the cosmic trees that were thought to connect the underworld with the heavens, while altars situated opposite these steles represented the Earth that brought forth crops to nourish the human race.

The temple pyramids themselves were regarded as sacred mountains. Entrances leading into shrines within their upper reaches would sometimes be carved to resemble the open jaws of the earth-dragon. In myth, this creature guarded the passage into the Earth's hollow innards, where the gods and the spirits of dead ancestors walked in a parallel world. Some of the step pyramids at Tikal rose up through nine successive levels, each of decreasing size, in allusion to the nine layers of the Mayan underworld, Xibalba, the 'Place of Fright'.

This architectural link to the world of the gods underpinned the Mayan hierarchy. It confirmed the power of the priests and the rituals they conducted, and also the power of the ruler, who had religious as well as secular duties.

A hierarchical society

Only the priests and nobles lived in the centre of the cities, inhabiting great stone palaces; at Tikal these were made of broken stone blocks and mortar. Most of the ordinary people lived in suburban residential areas or else on farms in the surrounding countryside.

Mayan society was hierarchical, in its general outline resembling one of the Maya's own step pyramids. The lowest level was made up of slaves, most of them prisoners of war who had escaped death

Lord of Palenque
Pacal, whose spectacular tomb was discovered in 1952, was the ruler of Palenque from 615 to 683. His name means 'Shield'.

on the sacrificial altars because of their lowly origins. Mayans could also end up in slavery, however, as a punishment for criminal behaviour or through falling into debt.

Farmers and the food supply

The free peasant farmers came next in the hierarchy, making up the bulk of Mayan society and providing the food that fed all the other classes. They were better placed than the slaves, although they could be conscripted at any time for military service or for public works. They usually lived in extended families in houses built around a central courtyard; these buildings were raised on small platforms of earth or stone to avoid flooding in the rainy season. Built of wood, they had saddle-shaped roofs made of palm leaves.

Farmers used the slash-and-burn technique, cutting down forest and burning the undergrowth to create open fields on which to grow crops. The minerals in the ash from the fires made the fields fertile for a time, but after a few years they became exhausted, for the Maya used no fertilisers. Once yields started to fall, the land was simply abandoned and a fresh patch cleared to take its place. The Maya tilled their fields with wooden picks and digging sticks. They did not have the plough, but they sometimes dug irrigation channels to water their crops.

Staple crops included maize, tobacco, tomatoes, squashes, sweet potatoes and cocoa. The Maya collected honey from wild bees' nests, kept turkeys and bred fish in specially constructed ponds. In good times farmers might enjoy a measure of prosperity in spite of the demands made by the state, which took a large portion of the crops in tax and frequently requisitioned workers for compulsory service.

The higher social strata

For the most part, craftsmen and unskilled labourers shared the same social rank as the farmers, but specialised workers, including skilled builders, stonemasons, painters, plasterers and the makers of jewellery and featherwork, occupied the next layer up in Mayan society. They worked exclusively for the aristocracy or for the state. Above them on the next social strata were priestly diviners, administrators and tax collectors, who, lived in palatial stone buildings close to the city centre.

The topmost platform of the social pyramid was the province of the high nobility, including the high priests, military commanders and, of course, the king. It was easy to distinguish the Mayan ruling class, for they wore special, multi-coloured clothing along with splendid feather headdresses and magnificent ear and arm adornments made of precious metals and stones.

Monthly symbols Each of the 13-day months in the Mayan ritual calendar had its own patron god and hieroglyphic symbol. The symbols for 15 of the months are shown above (there were 20 months in all).

■ **Mayan lands**
● **Important temples**

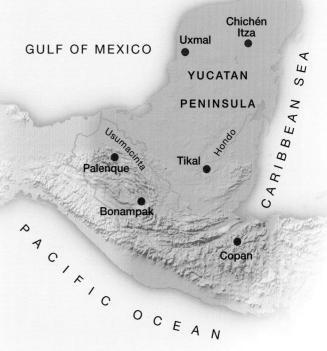

Mayan scenes of war

In 1946, an American photographer searching for Mayan remains in the Mexican state of Chiapas heard from local people of a previously unrecorded site deep in the jungle. They led him to a three-chambered building with plastered walls that were entirely covered with murals. The temple was soon given the name Bonampak, meaning 'painted walls' in the Mayan language.

The colourful murals reproduced vivid scenes from Mayan court life in about the year AD 800. The central theme was a king's presentation of his son to his people as his heir. Within that context, the murals provided a detailed picture of a successful military campaign, and of the celebrations that followed the victory.

In glowing warm colours, the artists had depicted warriors in battle dress, priests and kings in opulent state robes, all to the tune of musicians blowing trumpets and shaking rattles. There were scenes, too, of bloodletting and the sacrifice of prisoners of war. These latter images were deeply shocking to scholars at the time, for the prevailing historical opinion of the Maya was that they were a peace-loving people primarily concerned with matters of ritual and religion.

A dancing lord To celebrate military victories, Mayan lords dressed in magnificent feather costumes with elaborate headdresses and performed ceremonial dances.

Observing the stars
Astronomy was central to Mayan ritual life, and this was reflected in the design and purpose of many of their buildings. The upper windows of the Caracol or 'Snail Tower' at Chichén Itzá (background) were aligned with positions of the Sun and Venus.

Practical fabric

Mayans of all social classes wore clothes made from cotton. After harvesting, the raw cotton was spun into thread on clay distaffs, and the thread was then woven on wooden looms. Skilled weavers produced complicated patterns or dyed their materials with plant extracts to meet the demands of different customers.

The bulk of the population wore simple clothes: loincloths for men, long robes for women, and various kinds of cloak to provide warmth in cooler weather. The well-to-do wore shoulder capes and patterned cloths that trailed from the hips. Headdresses were important symbols of status and rank, and were decorated with a variety of adornments including wooden animal masks, fabrics, precious stones and the tail feathers of the quetzal bird. Leather sandals of various types completed their outfit.

God-like rulers

At the pinnacle of the social pyramid stood the ruler or *ahau*, who represented the gods on Earth. To all intents and purposes, the king ruled alone, even though he could choose to consult a state council of powerful priests and noblemen for advice. Thanks to the steles erected in Tikal and other Mayan cities, scholars know the names of many of the Mayan kings; among Tikal's rulers, for instance, were Great Jaguar Paw, Smoking Frog and Moon Zero Bird.

Secular and religious powers were united in the person of the king, and his semi-divine status was confirmed in a formal initiation ceremony that he underwent on ascending the throne. Many reliefs on steles and temple walls depict the rituals connected with the Mayan rulers. One is clearly a symbolic representation of a king's ascension to the throne; it shows him emerging from the mouth of the earth-dragon, thus comparing him with the Sun, which was thought to rise from the jaws of the Earth each day.

Court life is also illustrated in wall paintings and vase decorations. Great Jaguar Paw of Tikal, for instance, is shown sitting on a seat covered with a jaguar's pelt, while the throne of Pacal II of Palenque was fashioned in the shape of a double jaguar. The rulers' palaces were luxuriously furnished with precious vessels and decorated with tapestry wall-hangings and colourful frescoes depicting the gods in mythological scenes. Great Jaguar Paw and his leading nobles had an army of servants at their disposal, and some kings are known to have kept a court dwarf among their staff.

Festivals and warfare

After successful military campaigns or during festivals, feasts were held in the palaces to the sound of drums, rattles and flutes. Acrobats and dancers provided entertainment for the assembled nobles and priests, and various narcotic substances were consumed in addition to the food.

Official receptions for visiting dignitaries provided other opportunities for pomp and circumstance; on such occasions all participants had to conform to a strict order of rank and dress code.

Although the inscriptions that Mayan rulers left behind were mostly concerned with military campaigns and conquests, in all likelihood the kings would have relied as much on diplomacy and strategic marriage alliances to expand their power, with the result that many of the ruling houses were related to one another. The wars that the Maya did engage in were also never on the large scale found in other parts of the world. Military operations conformed to an accepted, if unstated, code, and although all men had to undergo military service, the campaigns were planned and carried out with due consideration for the peasant-soldiers' agricultural obligations, and these usually took precedence over any fighting.

A Mayan military expedition generally began with an army advancing into the territory of a rival city-state with the intention of taking as many prisoners as possible. When battles were fought, they were first announced by the blaring of musical instruments, followed by a hail of missiles. Maya warriors fought with catapults, throwing spears and stone-tipped lances, and protected themselves with small round shields and with armour made of padded cotton.

The generals were drawn from the ranks of the aristocracy, and stood out from the crowd of ordinary warriors because of their elaborate feather head-dresses and other bodily adornments. In battle the aim was to kill the enemy leader as quickly as possible; once the leader was dead, the battle was considered over and the vanquished army withdrew.

Blood and the Mayan world view

Prisoners taken in battle faced a harsh fate: slavery or death on the sacrificial altar. Only the highest-ranking prisoners, however, were thought to make suitable offerings. The concept of sacrifice was central to Mayan religion: flowers, incense, food, drink and animals were regularly offered up to the gods. Ceremonies involving human sacrifice, conducted by the splendidly robed priests, were particularly important – in fact, human sacrifice was an inescapable part of the ancient Mayan world view and considered essential to avert a cosmic catastrophe of terrible proportions.

Mayan myth held that human blood came directly from the gods and contained their vital energy, passed on to humankind in the act of creation. Sacrifices were necessary to return that life-force to the gods who had originally supplied it. Sacrificial blood was vital for their survival; without it the gods would die, and their demise would inevitably bring on the destruction of the entire universe. The soil would become infertile, the rain would cease to fall, the sun itself would no longer rise and the cosmos would be no more.

Death on the altar

The victims of human sacrifice met their death in various ways. Some were shot with arrows or beheaded, but most had their hearts cut out on sacrificial altars set on the top platform of the step-pyramids.

As the hour of death approached, an individual chosen for sacrifice was treated not with contempt but with the devotion due to the god that, it was thought, he would soon become. Magnificently adorned and to the accompaniment of scared chants, the victim was led up to the topmost level of the pyramid. There, four priests seized him by the limbs and laid

Colourful pottery Mayan potters fired their ware at relatively low temperatures of 500–700°C (950–1300°F). They used very fine clay, adding iron-oxide pigments to create yellow, red, brown and black hues. To finish off, they painted the pieces with motifs from nature, history or myth.

him on his back on the altar. Wielding a razor-sharp obsidian knife, a fifth quickly cut the man's heart out and handed it, still beating, to the high priest, who sprinkled some of the blood onto the statue of the god in whose honour the sacrifice was carried out. The victim's lifeless body was then thrown down the steps of the pyramid by the four helper priests and was removed to be cremated at a later time.

Gods of life and death

The Maya imagined their gods to be invisible, non-corporeal entities who could reveal themselves in different natural forms, among them feared animals like jaguars or snakes, but also as stars, rain, maize

Weaver at work
This clay figure shows a young Maya woman dressed in a poncho-like *huipil* and working on a loom. One end of the loom is supported by a belt around her waist; the other end is fixed to a tree stump with a bird perched on it.

and a whole multitude of other phenomena. The gods were also often depicted in human form by Mayan artists.

One of the most important divinities in the Mayan pantheon was Kinich Ahau, 'Lord Sun-Eye', a Sun god who was closely connected with the dragons of the earth and the sky. Another was Itzamna, lord of the heavens, who ruled day and night; the Maya believed that Itzamna had given them knowledge of writing, and he also presided over healing and divination. The rain god Chac was obviously of vital significance to Mayan farmers. To accomplish his many tasks he had the assistance of attendants called *chacs*, four of whom were specifically associated with the four points of the compass: north, south, east and west.

The Maya prayed to two separate maize gods, Kiawil and Yum Kaax, for the fertility of their fields and a bountiful harvest. Mayan creation myths held that the gods formed humans out of maize dough, clearly indicating the importance and prestige of the crop.

Special honour was also paid to Ah Puch, the god of Death, who was usually depicted as a skeleton. Ix-Chel stood out among the female deities as the patron of women's tasks such as weaving; she was also closely connected with the Moon.

Guardians of secret knowledge

The priests were servants of the gods, responsible for maintaining contact between the human and divine worlds. They alone knew the secrets of writing, and they were also custodians of the calendar and the sciences, particularly astronomy, in which the Maya were relatively advanced.

Unfortunately, the Mayas' sacred books were almost all destroyed after the Spanish conquest, but the few that have survived indicate that book production in the form of folded codices made of paper or deer hide was well developed. The best-known example is the *Popol Vuh* or 'Book of Council', which preserves many stories of gods and heroes, as well as a list of the rulers of the Quiché Maya who produced the book. The script in which it is written is complicated, combining representational hieroglyphs with abstract symbols.

All the Mesoamerican peoples gave scientific prominence to calendrical studies, but none held them in higher esteem or pursued them with greater sophistication than the Maya. They followed the dual system familiar in other neighbouring cultures, maintaining a solar calendar of 365 days to regulate agricultural activity and a separate 260-day ritual calendar for divination and the reckoning of lucky and unlucky dates. Most Mesoamerican cultures were content to limit their calculations to periods of 52 years – the cycle of time that it took for the two calendars to fall into sychronisation. The Maya had a third calendar, however, and this measured time in longer cycles known as the Long Count, divided into periods of 20, 400 and 8000 years.

Skilled mathematicians

Mayan priests must have been skilled mathematicians; the precision and accuracy of their work with figures was not matched until comparatively recent times. They independently discovered the concept of zero – familiar to Indian scholars in the Old World but unknown to the Romans – and used a symbol representing zero in their calculations. In addition, through their astronomical observations they determined the length of the solar year more accurately than the Julian calendar, which was in use in the West up to 1582, and they calculated the orbital period of the Moon to within four decimal places, enabling them to predict lunar eclipses. They also devoted much attention to the orbital periods of Venus, the morning and evening star, and calculated its cycle, which averages 584 days.

End of an era

Despite all the sacrifices and scholarly endeavour, the classic age of the Maya came to an abrupt end in about 900, when many of the lowland cities were rapidly abandoned. The reasons for the collapse are still not clear, but Mayan civilisation did not disappear entirely. Instead its focus moved north to the Yucatán peninsula, where Mayan cities continued to flourish for centuries to come.

BACKGROUND

The end of the classic Mayan age

The sudden demise of the Mayan lowland cities puzzles scholars to this day. Most favour the theory that several different factors came together at the end of the 9th century, causing social breakdown.

One basic problem may have been the exhaustion of the soil through prolonged intensive exploitation, leading to shrinking food supplies. Shortages may have weakened the authority of the ruling class, suggesting they had fallen out of favour with the gods and sparking revolts. The continual wars between the different city-states no doubt played a part in increasing any prevailing unrest. Some historians also think that Toltecs from the Valley of Mexico invaded the Maya lands at this time – a view that others contest.

Mayan paper and hieroglyphs
The Maya produced paper by pounding the inner bark of trees, particularly the bark of strangler figs. The fibres were mixed with starch and left to dry, after which they were painted on both sides with a fine coating of white lime. Feathers and small brushes were used as pens. This fragment is from a manuscript known today as 'The Madrid codex', which is kept in the Museo de América in Madrid.

The Moche of Peru – warriors and craftsmen

The Moche civilisation arose in the river valleys of arid northern Peru. They created innovative irrigation systems, impressive pyramids and some wonderful works of art.

Practical ornament
Crafted from gold, with inlays of turquoise and lapis lazuli, this beautiful disc once decorated and protected the ear of a Moche warrior.

More than a thousand years before the Incas, one of South America's most interesting cultures evolved in the arid northern lowlands of Peru. At first sight, the area seems an unpromising one to nurture a civilisation; most of it is coastal desert, parts of which may see no rain for a hundred years or more. However, at intervals the dry lands are cut through by rivers carrying meltwater from the Andes mountains down to the sea. It was in these valley oases that the Moche culture developed, flourishing from roughly AD 100 to 700.

The Moche depended on agriculture, so the fertile river valleys were vital. They cultivated maize, beans, squash, potatoes, sweet potatoes, peppers, cotton, and the sweet, non-toxic species of yucca. They hunted small animals and sea mammals, and the ocean supplied them with a variety of fish and iodine-rich algae. When fishing, they used reed sailing-boats and rafts of a type still seen on Lake Titicaca. The fishermen on the coast also trained cormorants to fish for them.

Masters of irrigation

The prosperity of the Moche culture was owed to a large extent to irrigation. The river valleys of northern Peru are up to 140km (90 miles) apart, and only a few of the rivers have water all year round. To increase the amount of land available for cultivation, the Moche people built canals from the rivers to carry water into the surrounding fields, and they also constructed aqueducts many miles long to bring water to areas that would otherwise have been dry.

The achievements of the Moche hydraulic engineers are all the more remarkable given the few tools that were available to them. It seems they were able to estimate by eye the distance between widely separated points in order to calculate the necessary gradient for water conduits. Their aqueducts were built with primitive tools along the tops of solid walls of earth or mud brick. They used solid walls because they did not know about arches. Part of an aqueduct 15m (50ft) high and almost 2km (1¼ miles) long survives to this day outside the village of Ascope in the Chicama Valley. The longest of all the Moche irrigation canals stretches for 110km (70 miles) and is still in use.

The Moche even developed irrigation techniques for dealing with salt problems in coastal villages, where the subterranean influx of seawater pushed back the freshwater in the water table, making the land unfit for cultivation. By removing the soil from fields lying at sea level, they were able to encourage fresh groundwater, enabling farmers to achieve a harvest even in the absence of rain.

An irrigation system as sophisticated as that built and operated by the Moche implies a marked degree of cooperation on the part of the people who depended upon it. Unfortunately, very little is known of the Moche social organisation because they did not have writing; our only evidence comes in the form of artworks, architecture and grave goods.

The little information that is known suggests that every valley of the Moche

Golden hands Made of sheet gold, these realistically fashioned hands accompanied a Moche lord into the afterlife. The fingernails and folds of the skin have been shaped with a careful eye for accuracy and detail.

federation had its own chief town; the city of Moche, in the valley of the Moche River, served as an administrative capital for the region. Moche towns were little more than large villages, made up of a few streets of modest, single-storey houses. The dry climate meant that the inhabitants spent much of their time in the court-yards of their homes, where most everyday activities took place.

Pyramid of the Sun

In marked contrast to people's homes, the Moches' public buildings could be spectacularly large. In Moche itself they built one of the largest monuments ever to be constructed in the Americas, covering an area of about 230 x 140m (750 x 450ft). The sanctuary, which the Spanish would later call the Pyramid of the Sun, consisted of several stepped platforms tapering towards the top. More than 50 million mud bricks were used in its construction.

Awaiting execution?
This unusual carved wooden figure shows a Moche prisoner-of-war, stripped naked with bound hands and feet. He may have been intended for sacrifice, in which case he would probably have been led by the rope around his neck to the place of execution. One place of sacrifice was the massive mud-brick structure known today as the Pyramid of the Moon (background). The figure was found buried beneath guano deposits on Manahi Island off the Peruvian coast; it may have been left their as an offering intended to ensure agricultural fertility.

Human sacrifice in the Pyramid of the Moon

A gruesome discovery made at the Pyramid of the Moon in the Moche Valley vividly illustrated the important role of human sacrifice in Moche culture. The bodies of more than 70 men were found with their skulls crushed or their throats cut. All had apparently been healthy at the time of their death, which they met at ages ranging from 15 to 39. At least five separate sacrificial ceremonies seem to have been involved, after which the corpses were left where they fell, to decompose.

Scholars who have dated the corpses have suggested that they may have been killed in attempts to placate the gods held responsible for the El Niño weather phenomenon, which every few years brings storms and floods to the Peruvian coast.

At one time there was probably a shrine on the Pyramid's summit, and it also served as a burial place. A slightly smaller structure built in similar style lies about 700m (2300ft) away; the Spaniards dubbed it the Pyramid of the Moon.

Almost as impressive in their own way are the noble tombs first discovered in 1987 at Sipán, a small town in the Lambayeque Valley. The burial complex consisted of two pyramids with an adjoining platform that served as a funeral site. Twelve tombs have been discovered so far, and they indicate that Moche society had a hierarchical structure. The Moche buried warriors in the northern part of the platform and priests in the southern section.

The Lord of Sipán

The most spectacular of the tombs, and the first to be unearthed, was that of the so-called Lord of Sipán. In a burial chamber measuring five metres square (16 x 16ft), the archaeologist Walter Alva discovered the coffin of the ruler and alongside it a total of 1337 separate objects made of gold, copper, turquoise and other precious substances. He also disinterred the bones of eight other individuals – three men, one woman, three girls and a child – some of whom probably accompanied the ruler to the grave as sacrificial victims. The attendant figures were laid to rest in reed boxes, but the royal coffin was made of wooden planks held together by bands of copper.

Buried treasure

The Lord of Sipán was about 40 years old at the time of his death. He was buried with his upper body covered with a cotton banner onto which small, rectangular plates of gilded copper sheeting had been sewn for decoration. He had a finely worked piece of sheet gold on his chest and wore jewellery made of gold, silver and shell beads. Most notable were his earrings, made of gold and turquoise, and depicting respectively a duck, a stag with antlers and a small human figure bearing the characteristic headgear and weapons of a Moche ruler.

A crescent-shaped headdress, made from a single piece of sheet gold, was also found in the tomb, along with the remains of feathers, identified as belonging to the Chilean flamingo; the feathers were inserted into small copper tubes that had probably once served to adorn the headdress. Necklaces of gold and silver still encircled the dead man's neck.

Both above and below the body lay hundreds of grave goods. One of the most striking was a sceptre with a long, silver handle, bearing at one end a golden box in the form of an inverted pyramid; at the other, the handle ended in a chisel-like tip, raising the possibility that it might have been used as a ceremonial knife. A fresco found in the burial chamber threw some light on its possible use: it showed a Moche lord, adorned in finery resembling that found in the tomb, striking a prisoner-of-war with an object closely resembling the sceptre.

The ritual of war

To judge from the surviving archaeological evidence, warfare played a key role in Moche society – Moche potters often decorated their works with battle scenes. Typical examples show two warriors aggressively facing up to one another, each one wearing ritual clothing that included noseplugs and feather headdresses. The aim was apparently not to kill one's opponent but rather to take him prisoner; the killing might come later, as a sacrifice to the gods.

In fact, much of what is known about the Moche comes from their ceramics, which provide a wonderfully vivid insight into a lost world. Their potters produced images of gods and demons, of dances and funeral rituals, of sick people and surgical operations. Even sex was not left out, for many vessels showed couples engaged in love-making.

What is missing from the pottery record are the everyday activities: there are no images of cooking or weaving, of working on building sites or in the fields. This has lead some scholars to speculate that Moche artists may have limited their subject-matter to activities considered to have some religious significance.

A world preserved in clay

Among the potters' most typical products were vessels that had ingenious, stirrup-shaped handles that also served as spouts. Often the pots are in the form of human figures, or heads with naturalistic features. Usually the status of the figures can be discerned from their clothing and accoutrements; high-ranking nobles are sometimes shown being carried in litters. Social rank is also mirrored in the size of the figures: in group scenes, important people are shown larger than their lesser companions.

The world so vividly depicted in the works of the Moche potters survived for more than 500 years, then disappeared abruptly around the end of the 7th century. The exact reasons for its downfall – like so much else about the Moche – are a mystery. Some scholars have suggested environmental catastrophe as the likely cause – perhaps the silting up of the irrigation works – while others point at their destructive passion for warfare. All that can be said for certain is that from about 700 onward, the Moche lands came under the sway of the expanding Huari empire and their Moche's own distinctive, indigenous culture was no more.

Buried in splendour The bones of a nobleman found at Sipán in Peru's Lambayeque Valley lie as they were discovered, covered in ceremonial armour and surrounded by all the symbols of power.

Lords of the Andes – the Tiahuanaco and Huari

These two mighty cultures of the Andes left behind no written records but many impressive buildings; together, they laid the foundations for the later Inca Empire.

One of the best-known ruined cities of South America lies at some 3800m (12,400ft) up on the Bolivian altiplano, or high plains, about 20km (12 miles) south of Lake Titicaca. This is Tiahuanaco, one-time capital of a culture that radiated across the Andes region in the first millennium AD.

Agriculture in inhospitable terrain

The treeless plain on which the city stands is cold all year round, although in summer the intense noon-day heat can cause the thermometer to rise by as much as 30°C (55°F) in a single day. The wide expanse of Lake Titicaca – South America's second largest body of fresh water, with a surface area of 8300km² (3200 square miles) – helps to modify the changes in temperature, creating a climate in which a variety of plants can be cultivated. Tiahuanaco's rulers also proved adept at reclaiming swampy terrain: by building extensive irrigation works they were able to extend the area of available cultivable land.

The Tiahuanacans grew potatoes, sweet potatoes, beans and quinoa, a spinach-like crop whose seeds resemble rice; even maize flourished in the most sheltered

A liking for bright colours
This fibre cap demonstrates the Huaris' love of bright colours. They dyed alpaca wool into many hues and wove it into garments displaying geometric patterns and stylised human and animal figures.

locations. They also harvested a variety of lupin called tarwi, whose soaked and fermented seeds were cooked as a pulse; the water in which they were soaked had the added advantage of being effective as an insect repellent.

From early on, Tiahuanacan farmers brewed a maize beer they called *aque*, which they drank out of special jugs. Some of these vessels were shaped to resemble people; others were decorated with scenes of everyday life or of religious ceremonies, leading scholars to conclude that *aque* must have played a significant part in the region's ritual life.

In the days of Tiahuanaco's greatness, the waters of Lake Titicaca extended right up to the city, so its people were able to supplement their diet with plentiful fish and waterfowl. The herds of llama and alpaca that grazed on the wide, high plains of the altiplano formed a crucial part of their economy; the alpaca provided the wool they needed to make warm clothing, while llama were bred for meat and as beasts of burden, used to transport trade goods along the mountain roads. Herds of wild guanaco and vicuña were also exploited for meat and wool.

A highland metropolis

At its peak in the 7th and 8th centuries, the city of Tiahuanaco covered an area of about 2.5km² (1 square mile) and was home to up to 40,000 people. It was the administrative centre of a kingdom whose influence extended from the Pacific coast to what is now northwestern Argentina. It was also an important religious centre and a place of pilgrimage for people from the surrounding lands. The surviving ruins of its main temple complex indicate that it contained a pyramid, a square plaza in the form of an earthen platform, and a temple set partly underground.

Temples and plazas

The largest structure was the platform mound, called the Acapana, which was aligned in an east–west direction and stood 17m (55ft) high. It rose in seven steps and had an irregular, zig-zag ground plan with sides about 200m (650ft) long.

Situated north of the mound, the semi-subterranean temple was approached via a staircase eight steps deep and 5m (16ft) wide and covered an area of about 750m² (8000sq ft); the builders dug out the ground on which it lay to a depth of some 2m (6ft 6in). Pillars reinforced the side walls, which were built of massive masonry blocks decorated with stone heads of various sizes. In the centre of the temple stood three monumental carved steles.

A second complex, known as the Kalasasaya, was laid out to the east of the temple, but almost nothing is known of its original purpose. The plaza here was rectangular in shape, measuring 130 x 120m (420 x 380ft). The city's best-known monument – a portal that the Spaniards called the Gateway of the Sun – stood on the western side of the plaza.

Hewn from a single block of fine-grained volcanic andesite, the gateway monolith was relatively small – 3.8m wide by 2.8m high (13 x 9ft) – and it sheltered a ceremonial entrance just 60cm wide and 1.4m high (2 x 4ft 6in).

Ceremonial ale
In both the Tihuanaco and Huari cultures, large jugs like this one were used to hold maize beer for consumption at religious festivals. Archaeologists have found shards of shattered jugs in huge quantities, suggesting that the vessels were probably smashed after the festive drinking sessions.

What impresses visitors today is the central carving decorating the lintel. The main figure represents the principal Tiahuanacan deity, usually referred to as the Staff-Bearing God. His robe is adorned with trophy heads, he carries a staff taller than himself in each hand, and on his head he wears a rayed headdress. From his eyes run stylised tears.

In three rows on either side of the central figure are 48 semi-abstract beings sometimes referred to as the winged messengers; those on the upper and lower rows have human faces, those in the middle have condor heads. Interpretations have been attempted, but as the Tiahuanacans had no writing the exact significance of the figures remains obscure.

The ruins of another temple, known as Puma Puncu, lie on an artificial mound about a mile southwest of the centre of Tiahuanaco. The most impressive part of the remains are the monolithic slabs that covered some of the floor – polished stone blocks cut into rectangles 7m long, 4m wide and 1.8m thick (23ft x 13 x 6ft), and weighing up to 100 tonnes each. The slabs were fitted into place without mortar, but some were fastened with bronze pegs and dowels, perhaps as a precaution against earthquakes, which are prevalent in the area. The temple's ground plan suggests that it was made up of a number of neighbouring cells, but again, as there are no written records, scholars can only guess at their exact function.

The Puma Puncu temple
This illustration reconstructs the ceremonial temple from the field of ruins known today as Puma Puncu. Pilgrims would have come from far distant regions to visit Puma Puncu and other temples in Tiahuanaco's religious centre.

The priests carried out sacrificial rituals in the central courtyard.

Outer floors of stamped clay were probably painted deep red, blue or green, while the temple walls were decorated with fabrics and woven hangings.

It is thought that the Sun Gate of Tiahuanaco once served as the west gate of Puma Puncu.

Empire of the north

The city of Huari grew up in the 3rd or 4th century near the present-day town of Ayacucho in the Ayacucho Valley, midway between the Andes and the Pacific coast of northern Peru. Huari enjoyed more temperate surroundings than Tiahuanaco, and in its heyday in the 7th century was the larger of the two with perhaps as many as 75,000 inhabitants. The distance between the cities – they lay 1250km (800 miles) apart – and the different climate ensured that each kept its individuality, but they kept in close contact and shared a similar artistic style.

The Huari culture spread outward from the 7th century onwards, eventually making its influence felt from Ocoña in southern Peru to the Chicama Valley and Cajamarca in the north. The temple of Pachacmac, south of the modern Peruvian capital of Lima, became famous for the oracular utterances of its priests, and came to exert a considerable influence over the entire Huari region.

The Andean axis

The architecture and art of Huari clearly display the cultural and religious influence of Tiahuanaco, but scholars still argue over what the exact nature of the relationship

The Kalasasaya complex
Researchers disagree over how the Kalasasaya temple plaza in Tiahuanaco would have looked in ancient times. Some of the many sculpted stone heads that decorated the plaza can be seen along the foot of the walls.

between the two cities might have been. They produced ceramics with similar motifs: beside great cats, condors and gods with rayed headdresses, the potters of both cultures often used decorations made up of geometric patterns. Both cultures produced objects in similar shapes. They both made jugs with side-handles, incense vessels with wavy rims, and flared beakers known as keros which had narrow bases and broad rims. Both cultures practiced bronze-working, a new technology in the region at the time. But only the Huari made colourful textiles out of feathers and cotton.

The weavers' art

Like the Tiahuanacans, the Huari were outstanding weavers, spinning the wool of vicuña, llama and alpaca into artistically sophisticated fabrics. Some textiles have survived in tombs in the arid desert on Peru's south coast, so the evidence of their craftsmanship has been preserved.

Such garments reached the coast through the extensive trade networks that had long linked the Andean highlands with the sea. The coastal dwellers exchanged their cotton, which they grew in the lowland river valleys, for the highlanders' alpaca wool.

Some Tiahuanacan fabrics have been preserved in the Sun temple on Coati Island in Lake Titicaca. One notable item is a colourful cloak of vicuña wool; the

Fine feathers This fabric was made with red, blue and yellow parrot feathers. It depicts three figures with raised arms and gaping mouths and eyes.

EVERDAY LIFE

Fine fabrics with feathered details

To manufacture their speciality feather fabric, Huari weavers sewed brightly coloured feathers onto a densely woven background of plain cotton. They favoured geometric patterns and designs featuring people, animals and mythical beings.

The feathers came from parrots, cranes and toucans and were in fantastic shades of green, white, yellow, blue, black-brown and orange-red. They were used to make precious sleeveless robes and head-dresses that were almost certainly just for special occasions.

The Chimu, who succeeded the Huari as rulers of northern Peru, continued to practice the craft.

---

weaving is so fine it counts 100 threads to a single centimetre. The very finest Andean wool was supplied by the chinchilla. This rodent lives at altitudes above 4000m (13,000ft), where it is protected by fur so dense that no brush or comb can penetrate it; up to 80 hairs grow from a single follicle.

Well-to-do citizens of both empires liked to dress in artistically woven shirts and poncho-like robes in beautiful colours. The fabrics served their owners not just in this life but even beyond, for they were often cut up for use as mummy bandages in which to wrap the person for burial.

The Huari also had a taste for colourful fibre hats. These were typically square and vividly decorated with geometric patterns and animal motifs that were repeated on all four sides and, if possible, matched the designs on their clothing.

The caps were fashioned from a finely woven fabric made up of symmetrical knots; open bundles of coloured thread were worked into the knots in every second row to create a pile 3–4mm deep (about a sixteenth of an inch). Small tips protruded from each of the cap's four corners. Some of the caps were oddly shaped, apparently to fit heads that had been deliberately shaped in childhood to create a flattened skull.

End of empires

Between the years 600 and 900, the Huari culture spread widely across much of Peru, then suddenly their empire collapsed, dissolving into many minor states. Tiahuanaco survived for another 300 years, but eventually it, too, fell into decay, to be replaced soon after by the emergent Inca Empire.

Totonac temple-builders of the Gulf coast

The Totonac capital of El Tajin is one of Mexico's finest ancient sites. Its most remarkable ruin is a pyramid with 365 niches – one for each day of the solar year.

When Spanish conquistadors under Hernán Cortés landed on the east coast of Mexico in 1519, the first people they met were the Totonacs, whose cities and culture greatly impressed them. The Totonacs occupied land on the Gulf coast in the present-day state of Veracruz, where their descendants still live today.

The beginnings of the Totonac culture go back to about AD 500, and it reached its peak between 600 and 900. In the early period they were subject to many influences, particularly from the great city of Teotihuacán in the Valley of Mexico, and from the Maya of the rain forest lands to the south; elements of the earlier Olmec culture had also left a mark. Later, the Totonacs developed their own distinctive style. They are thought to have been the creators of the mysterious smiling clay figures of Las Remojadas.

The temple city of El Tajin, about 200km (125 miles) northeast of modern Veracruz, was the political and religious heart of the Totonac culture. The word *tajin* means 'lightning' in the Totonac language, an indication of the city's close connection with weather gods.

El Tajin's ceremonial centre is in a narrow valley opening towards the south, and had temples, palaces and ball courts, extending over an area of about 70 hectares (170 acres). It was divided into two parts: one part lay between two streams and was overlooked by the Pyramid of the Niches; the other stood on a rise that had been levelled by terracing. The principal feature of this raised platform was one of the city's most massive building complexes. It covered nearly 3.4 hectares (8½ acres) and was probably the main seat of government. Priests also lived in the building.

Beyond the ceremonial centre, which formed the city's nucleus, the Totonacs built workshops, storage facilities and residential areas

Mysterious smiles
Ceramic figurines with enigmatic smiling faces are a feature of Totonac art that puzzles researchers to this day. Whatever their exact significance, the figures usefully depict Totonac clothing, jewellery, and head gear.

Household ware Totonac potters produced elegant goods like this bowl for everyday use.

that stretched up into the adjoining hills. The public buildings were mostly made of worked stone slabs fitted together with mortar, although great sandstone or basalt blocks up to 11m (36ft) long were also used. The blocks had to be transported from a quarry about 35km (22 miles) away.

A breakthrough in building

To top their buildings, El Tajín's architects pioneered a distinctive technique that, in some ways, anticipated modern poured concrete roofing. They crushed seashells to form a fine limestone rubble that they mixed with sand, straw, small pieces of wood and finely ground pumice stone. Meanwhile, the space that was to be roofed-over was filled to the brim with soil and stones, and a wooden frame of the

required dimensions was laid on top. The lime aggregate was packed into the frame and left to dry. The process was repeated several times to build up the thickness of the roof. By this method builders were able to cover spaces up to 75m² (800sq ft) in area with solid roofs between 30 and 90cm (1–2ft) thick.

Pyramid of the Niches

The Pyramid of the Niches is probably El Tajín's most famous building because of its unique design. The six steps of the pyramid and the shrine on the top level are dotted with 365 niches, each one empty and resembling a blank window backed by bare stone.

The position of the niches around the sides of the pyramid almost certainly had some calendrical or mythological significance that has now been lost. The number of niches decreases by three per step from bottom to top, so on each side there are

The Pyramid of the Niches
El Tajín's most magnificent monument was included on the UNESCO World Heritage List in 1992. Its base covers an area of 1225m² (13,200sq ft) and it rises to a height of about 25m (80ft). Although researchers cannot be certain of the exact significance of the niches that cover the Pyramid, their number – 365 – clearly points to a connection with the days of the year.

22 niches on the bottom step followed by 19, 16, 13, 10, and 7 respectively on those above. This adds up to 87 niches on each of the pyramid's four sides, making a total of 348, plus the 17 openings decorating the sanctuary at the top bring the overall number to 365. As this figure corresponds with the days in the solar year, it is thought that the Pyramid of the Niches may have served as a sort of ceremonial calendar in stone.

Today the pyramid is the colour of weathered stone, but in its heyday the insides of the niches were painted bright red and framed in blue. The effect must have been startling, and the contrasts of light and shade that the colour scheme created may have been intended to hint at mysteries of death and the afterlife.

All of El Tajín's buildings would have been brilliantly coloured, painted in shades of black, red, blue and yellow on a stucco ground. The choice of colours probably had a meaning that is no longer under-stood; people at the time would almost certainly have recognised the function of each building from the combination of colours that decorated it.

Religion and sacrifice

Not much is known about Totonac religion. Reports written by Spanish monks indicate that, at the time of the conquest, a trinity of gods were venerated above all others: a Sun god, a goddess associated with the sky and maize, and a third deity said to be the son of the other two. The number three may have had special significance, which could have been a factor in planning the façade of the Pyramid of the Niches.

In general, divinities associated with rain and agricultural fertility were hugely important to the Totonacs. Large numbers of statues have been found of Tlaloc, a rain god who was worshipped in many of the Mesoamerican cultures.

To the disgust of the Spanish, human sacrifice played a central part in Totonac ritual life. In addition to regular sacrifices

The smiling figurines of Las Remojadas – a picture of happiness or images of ritual drug use?

Among ancient Mexico's most curious and distinctive artworks are a series of ceramic figurines representing smiling people. They are known collectively as Las Remojadas-ware, from the name of a village not far from Veracruz where they were first found, and they are thought to have been the products of the Totonac culture.

The best-known examples represent women, and it would be nice to think that their happy faces were a natural expression of delight with life. Given that most Mesoamerican artworks had cult significance, however, another and probably more likely theory is that the images represent people selected for sacrifice. Sacrificial victims were probably given narcotic drugs to induce feelings of euphoria that made the prospect of imminent death easier to bear. An alternative view is that the individuals depicted in the figurines had already been sacrificed, and the smiles on their faces were meant to represent their joy in the afterlife where they were welcomed by the gods to whom they had been offered up.

Happy drinker This clay figure of a man holding a cup may be indicative of the large amounts of alcohol consumed by the Totonacs at their religious festivals.

that took place every week or month, children were offered up in a cult festival that was held every three years. In the course of the ceremony priests mixed the blood of the sacrificial victims with scented resin and the seeds of certain plants and distributed it among the participants. The ritual was supposed to enhance their crops and to symbolise the renewal of life.

The sacred game

A distinctive feature of El Tajín is the large number of ball-game courts found there – more than in any other Mesoamerican city. The largest is 60m (200ft) long, and splendid reliefs cover its walls. The different types of ball court found across Mesoamerica suggest that the rules may have varied from place to place. In some depictions the gods them-selves appear as players, emphasising the religious significance of the contest. The ball game was not so much a sport in the modern sense of the word as a religious ritual, with the movement of the ball symbolically representing the courses of the heavenly bodies.

A violent end This relief from El Tajin depicts the sacrifice of a ball game player (above). It is not known for sure whether it was the winners or losers who were offered up to the gods in this way. The city had six large ball courts (background).

Close to the gods

To judge from the reliefs decorating the courts, a ball game at El Tajin ended in ritual human sacrifice. One carving shows a richly caparisoned priest using a knife to dispatch a player stretched out on an altar. Another figure, wearing the clothing of a ball game player, stands behind the victim, pinioning his arms behind him. A high-ranking individual sits on a throne watching the ceremony; he holds a long, richly decorated staff that is evidently a mark of authority. A skeleton – probably representing the god of death, a favourite subject for El Tajin's artists – swoops down towards the sacrificial victim.

Another carving shows seven streams of blood gushing from the gaping neck of a ball player who has just been decapitated. The streams may represent the goddess known as Seven Snakes, showing that the sacrifice was carried out in her honour.

Festivals of life

By no means all Totonac artwork is as obsessed with death as the carvings at El Tajin. An altogether happier approach can be seen in the wall paintings decorating buildings at Las Higueras about 50km (30 miles) to the south, which provide a glimpse of ceremonial life in ancient Mexico. These murals show dancers wearing bright robes and dragging long trains behind them. Carrying flags decorated with emblems, they move to the sound of conch shells and trumpets played by musicians who accompany them in procession.

Such pictures suggest that the Totonacs celebrated their festivals with gusto. This festive side to Totonac life and culture can even be discerned in El Tajin's architecture which displays none of the heavy symmetry of other Mesoamerican ceremonial centres, even including that of the Teotihuacans.

It may be that the Totonac people, living in the verdant tropical landscape of the Gulf Coast, had a totally different mental outlook from that of most other Mexican peoples.

Objects of mystery

Much about the ancient Totonac culture remains deeply mysterious. For example, various richly decorated stone artefacts have been found that are known in Spanish as *yugos* or 'yokes', *hachas* ('axes'), and *palmas* ('palms of hands'). The names give some indication of the shapes of these objects, but are not intended as an indication of function because their actual uses remain quite unknown.

Shaped like horseshoes, the yokes are made from heavy blocks of andesite, diorite or serpentine. On average, they are about 45cm (18in) long and 30cm (1ft) wide. They are sometimes open-ended, and sometimes closed by a single bar. Occasionally craftsmen chose to decorate them with images of frogs, owls or eagles. Scholars have long racked their brains to explain the purpose of these yokes. The general consensus is that they must have played some part in the ritual ball game, but experts still disagree over what that part might have been. Some reliefs show ball-game players wearing sausage-like padding, presumably fashioned from leather and fabric, around their waists, and one theory holds that the yokes were stone replicas of these body protectors, perhaps made for ceremonial use.

With similar uncertainty, the *hachas* and *palmas* are thought to have been connected with the ball game. Perhaps they also were enduring representations of pieces of equipment that were made of softer, more perishable materials.

Carvings on the objects themselves seem to indicate that they had some cult significance. Mythological motifs frequently make an appearance and, on one, a Totonac artist depicted a man seeking to escape from a cloud of bats, which in Mesoamerican cultures symbolised death and sacrifice.

Technological innovation

Totonac creativity was not limited to the arts. Their craftsmen fashioned objects with interesting technical qualities. Among these were round mirrors made of polished pyrite, their reverse sides decorated with patterns of sinuous lines that have small human figures concealed among them. Researchers have recently pointed out that these mirrors were well adapted to catch the sun and could have been used both to flash signals over long distances and also to light fires by focusing solar rays. Conceivably, the mirrors may have been priestly tools used to impress commoners with their power; it is easy to imagine the effect they could have produced by making fires flare up, seemingly out of nothing, at their command.

An enduring heritage

The Totonacs made another important discovery, although they did not realise its significance at the time. They invented the wheel and used it on toys – specifically, clay dogs perched on small revolving axles. As far as we know, they never applied the principle of the wheel for any purpose other than play, so it was not until the Spaniards arrived that wheeled vehicles were introduced to the Americas. One reason why wheeled technology was not further applied and exploited may have been simply the lack of suitable draught animals to pull carts.

Totonac culture continued to flourish after 900, and El Tajin was occupied for another 300 years. When the Aztecs started to expand their power beyond the Valley of Mexico in the 15th century, they conquered the Totonacs and forced them to acknowledge Aztec overlordship as a vassal state of the empire. By that time the Totonacs had moved their capital to

Enigmatic objects This *palma* (left) – literally 'palm of the hand' – is made from pumice stone and decorated with a carving of a water bird. Yokes or *yugos* (below) can weigh up to 40kg (90lb); this example is made of diorite.

Cempoala, 150km (100 miles) southeast of El Tajin, where Cortés visited their ruler in 1519. Some 200,000 Totonac-speakers inhabit the modern Mexican states of Veracruz and Puebla to this day.

Abbeviations: t = top, c = centre, b = below,
l = left, r = right, T = Timeline, B = background.

BPK = Bildarchiv Preußischer Kulturbesitz
RMN = Réunion des Musées nationaux

Front cover: akg-images/Erich Lessing
Back cover (top to bottom): Kunsthistorisches
Museum, Wien; akg-images/Erich Lessing;
akg-images/Jean-Louis Nou; akg-images/
Werner Forman.

1: akg-images/Erich Lessing; 2/3: Richard
Hamilton Smith/Corbis; 4/5: Kunsthistorisches
Museum, Wien; 6: The Bridgeman Art Library;
7 Interfoto/Hermann Historica; 8/9 and T: The
Bridgeman Art Library; 9: Interfoto; 10 t: photo12;
10 b: Interfoto; 11: Interfoto/aisa; 12: The
Bridgeman Art Library; 13: Bildarchiv Monheim;
14: Interfoto/aisa; 15: Interfoto/aisa; 16: dpa;
17: Scala; 18 t: Interfoto/aisa; 18 b: Interfoto;
18/19 B: Interfoto; 19: Interfoto; 20 l: imagno; 20 r:
Scala; 21 and T: Scala; 22: Alamy; 23: Bildarchiv
Monheim; 24 t: The Bridgeman Art Library; 24 b:
Scala; 25: Scala; 26: British Library; 26/27 B:
Scala/Heritage Image; 27: John Ather Archaeological
Trust Ltd./John Atherton Bowen; 28: Interfoto/aisa;
29: Interfoto/aisa; 30 t: Scala; 30 b: Interfoto;
30/31 B: Interfoto; 31: The Bridgeman Art Library;
32: photo12; 33: Scala; 34: Interfoto/aisa; 34/35 B:
Interfoto; 35: The Bridgeman Art Library; 36: Scala;
37 t and b: Interfoto/aisa; 38 and T: Interfoto/ aisa;
39: imagno; 40 and T: Interfoto/aisa; 40/41 B:
Mauritius images; 41: BPK/RMN; 42: Interfoto/
aisa; 42/43 B: The Bridgeman Art Library;
43: BPK/RMN; 44, 44/45 B, 45, 46: Interfoto/aisa;
46/47 B: Interfoto; 47: Scala; 48 and T: Interfoto/
aisa; 49: Bildarchiv Monheim; 50, 50/51 B:
Interfoto/aisa; 51 and T: Alamy; 52: Interfoto/aisa;
53: British Museum; 54 and T: KANN; 54/55 B:
The Bridgeman Art Library; 55: Interfoto/aisa; 56 t:
The Bridgeman Art Library; 56 b: BPK/RMN;
57 and T: akg-images/Erich Lessing; 58 t: imagno;
58 b: Mauritius images; 59: Interfoto/aisa;
60: BPK/RMN; 61 t and b: Interfoto/aisa;
62: BPK/RMN; 63: Mauritius images;
64: Interfoto/aisa; 65: Interfoto; 66: The Bridgeman
Art Library; 66/67 B: Mauritius images; 67: Alamy;
68 t: akg-images/Werner Forman; 68 b: photo12;
68/69 B: Mauritius images; 69: Interfoto; 70 t and b:
Interfoto; 70/71: Interfoto/aisa; 72/73: akg-
images/Erich Lessing; 74: Interfoto/aisa; 75 and T:
fl online; 76: British Museum; 76/77 B: The
Bridgeman Art Library; 77: British Museum; 78 and
T: Imagno; 79: BPK/RMN; 80: Scala; 81: Dr Georg
Gerster; 82: Interfoto/aisa; 83 t: British Museum;
83 b: Interfoto/aisa; 84: British Museum; 85: Kay
Maeritz/LOOK; 86: Interfoto/aisa; 86/87: Interfoto;
87 and T: Alamy; 88: Interfoto; 89: Interfoto/aisa;
90: Interfoto; 90/91 B: Interfoto/aisa; 91 and T:
Interfoto; 92: Corbis; 93: Scala; 94: Corbis;
94/95 B: BW Photoagentur; 95: Interfoto;
96 t: photo12; 96 b: Version Foto; 97: Interfoto/aisa;
98: Interfoto/aisa; 99: The Bridgeman Art Library;
100 t: The Bridgeman Art Library; 100 b:
Interfoto/Hermann Historica; 100/101 B: kpa;
101 and T: Scala; 102 t: BPK/RMN; 102 b: The
Bridgeman Art Library; 103: Silvestris online;

104: BPK/RMN; 104/105 B: Silvestris online;
105: British Library; 106 t: Interfoto; 106 b:
BPK/RMN; 107: Interfoto/aisa; 108: The
Bridgeman Art Library; 109: BPK/RMN;
110 t and b, 110/111 B: Interfoto/aisa; 111 and T:
BPK/RMN; 112: The Ancient Art & Architecture
Collection Ltd.; 113: Interfoto/aisa; 114 and T:
Interfoto/aisa; 114/115 B: Corbis; 115: The Ancient
Art & Architecture Collection Ltd.; 116: Interfoto/
aisa; 117: The Bridgeman Art Library; 118:
Interfoto/aisa; 119: Scala; 120/121: Alamy; 121 and
T: Mauritius images; 122: kpa; 122/123 B: Silvestris
online; 123: BPK/RMN; 124: BPK/RMN;
125: BPK/RMN; 126: Mauritius images;
126/127 B: Interfoto/aisa; 127 t: The Bridgeman Art
Library; 127 b: photo12; 128 t: BPK; 128 b:
Imagno; 129: Interfoto/aisa; 130: BPK/RMN;
130/131: Corbis; 131: BPK; 132 l: Interfoto/aisa;
132 r: Interfoto; 133 bl: photo12; 133 tl: Interfoto;
133 bc and bl: Interfoto/aisa; 133 tr: dpa; 134 t:
British Museum; 134 b: The Ancient Art &
Architecture Collection Ltd.; 135 tl: Interfoto/aisa;
135 tr: akg-images/Werner Forman; 134/135:
Bildarchiv Monheim; 135 tc: Interfoto/aisa;
136 b: Interfoto/aisa; 136 t: photo12; 137 tl and tr:
Interfoto/aisa; 137 b: Interfoto; 138: photo12;
138 b: Interfoto; 139 t: The Ancient Art &
Architecture Collection Ltd.; 139 c: The Bridgeman
Art Library; 139 b: akg-images; 140/141: akg-
images/Jean-Louis Nou; 142 and T: The Bridgeman
Art Library; 143: CH. Eger Madrid; 144: Interfoto;
144/145 B: Corbis; 145: BPK, Münzkabinett;
146: Interfoto/aisa; 148 and T: BPK/RMN;
148/149 B: fl online; 149: photo12; 150 and T: akg-
images/Werner Forman; 151 and T: akg-images/
Werner Forman; 152/153: Interfoto/aisa;
153: BPK/RMN; 154: akg-images; 155: Alamy;
156: Werner Otto Reisefotografie; 157 t: Interfoto;
157 b: BPK/RMN; 158/159: akg-images/Werner
Forman; 160: Interfoto/aisa; 161: Interfoto/aisa;
162: akg-images/Werner Forman; 162/163 B:
Interfoto/aisa; 163: The Bridgeman Art Library;
164: The Ancient Art & Architecture Collection
Ltd.; 165 t and T: Interfoto/aisa; 165 b: The Ancient
Art & Architecture Collection Ltd.; 66/167:
Interfoto; 167: Interfoto/aisa; 168 and T: Interfoto;
169: Interfoto/aisa; 170: The Bridgeman Art Library;
170/171 B: Interfoto/aisa; 171: Interfoto/aisa;
172: akg-images/Werner Forman; 173: Scala;
174 and T: Interfoto/aisa; 175: The Bridgeman Art
Library; 176: akg-images/Werner Forman;
176/177 B: The Ancient Art & Architecture
Collection Ltd.; 177: Corbis; 178: The Bridgeman
Art Library; 179: Daniel Giannoni, Peru;
180/181: National Geographic/Greg Harlin;
181 and T: Interfoto/aisa; 182 and T: akg-
images/Werner Forman; 183: Logan Museum;
184 t: Interfoto/aisa; 184 b: Mauritius images;
185: akg-images/Werner Forman; 186: Interfoto/
aisa; 186/187 B: Interfoto/aisa; 187 l: The
Bridgeman Art Library; 187 r: Corbis;

The Illustrated History of the World:
BETWEEN CROSS AND CRESCENT was published
by The Reader's Digest Association Ltd, London.

First English edition copyright © 2005
The Reader's Digest Association Ltd
11 Westferry Circus, Canary Wharf, London E14 4HE
www.readersdigest.co.uk

Reader's Digest English Edition
Series editor: Christine Noble
Writer: Tony Allan
Translated from German by: JMS Books
Design: Jane McKenna, Heather Dunleavy
Copy editor: Jill Steed
Proofreader: Ron Pankhurst
Index: Hilary Bird
Colour proofing: Colour Systems Ltd, London
Printed and bound by: Arvato Iberia, Europe

Reader's Digest, General Books
Editorial director: Cortina Butler
Art director: Nick Clark
Prepress account manager: Penelope Grose

We are committed to the quality of our products and the
service we provide to our customers. We value your
comments, so please feel free to contact us on 08705
113366, or via our website at: www.readersdigest.co.uk

If you have any comments or suggestions about the
content of our books, you can email us at:
gbeditorial@readersdigest.co.uk

First published as *Reader's Digest Illustrierte
Weltgeschichte: ZWISCHEN KREUZ UND
HALBMOND* © 2004 Reader's Digest –
Deutschland, Schweiz, Österreich
Verlag Das Beste GmbH – Stuttgart, Zürich, Vienna

Reader's Digest, German Edition
Writers: Karin Feuerstein-Praßer, Andrea Groß-Schulte,
Marion Jung, Otto Schertler, Karin Schneider-Ferber,
Dr. Holger Sonnabend Editing and design: Media
Compact Service Colour separations: Meyle + Müller
GmbH + Co., Pforzheim.

ISBN: 0 276 42988 5
CONCEPT CODE: GR 0081/G/S
BOOK CODE: 632-003-1
ORACLE CODE: 351600010H.00.24